JUNIORPLOTS

A Book Talk Manual for Teachers and Librarians

JUNIORPLOTS

A Book Talk Manual
for Teachers
and Librarians

By John Gillespie and Diana Lembo

R. R. BOWKER COMPANY   *New York*   1967
                         London

Published by R. R. Bowker Company,
a division of Reed Publishing (USA) Inc.
Copyright © 1967 by Reed Publishing (USA) Inc.
All rights reserved
Printed and bound in the United States of America

International Standard Book Number 0-8352-0063-9
Library of Congress Catalog Card Number 67-18146

To Minnie

CONTENTS

PREFACE

THERE is an unfortunate lack of published material that can serve as a guide for those who give book talks to a young adult audience. This volume is designed to help meet this need and to aid teachers and librarians in giving reading guidance to children and young people between the ages of nine and 16.

Because most book talks are planned around a theme, a thematic approach has been used in this volume. The titles have been arranged by what the authors feel to be the most important goals of adolescent reading. A number of books and articles were consulted in order to determine these goals. The most helpful were Erik H. Erikson's *Youth: Change and Challenge* (Basic Books), Robert J. Havighurst's *Developmental Tasks and Education* (Longmans, Green), and Will French's *Behavioral Goals of General Education in High Schools* (Russell Sage). From these works and their own experience, the authors were able to isolate eight basic goals for adolescents: 1) to relate one's self to the world; 2) to achieve emotional maturity; 3) to achieve economic independence; 4) to accept one's physical self; 5) to establish good social relationships; 6) to become self-reliant; 7) to develop a constructive attitude toward life; and 8) to cultivate literary appreciation. There is obvious overlapping among the goals, and this becomes especially apparent when they are adapted for use in organizing books for book talks.

For purposes of this book the goals were restated to serve as the titles of each of the book's eight chapters : 1) Building a World View; 2) Overcoming Emotional Growing Pains; 3) Earning a Living; 4) Understanding Physical Problems; 5) Making Friends; 6) Developing Self-Reliance; 7) Evaluating Life; and 8) Appreciating Books. In each of these chapters ten books are fully discussed. They were selected in a variety of ways; the final criterion being the relationship of each title to the theme of the chapter.

To compile the preliminary lists thousands of boys and girls in grades six through ten were asked to list their favorite books. These choices were examined, evaluated, and either accepted or rejected. The interest patterns of the students were determined and the lists were compared with standard booklists in the field. As a check on the opinions of the authors other librarians were asked for suggestions. Their choices were particularly valuable in selecting the titles for chapter eight, "Appreciating Books."

In addition to the basic criteria of quality and pertinence to one of the chapter themes, consideration was given to the need to provide material for various reading levels and areas of interest within each chapter; the necessity of maintaining equal coverage for both girls and boys; and the decision not to repeat titles covered in the two excellent publications of the American Library Association, *Book Bait* and *Doors to More Mature Reading*. Finally, a special effort was made to include recent titles.

The material on each book is divided into four sections as follows:

1. *Plot Analysis.* The plot is summarized and key incidents and situations are stressed. Important characters in the book are introduced by name. Audience appeal is indicated by the inclusion of ages and grades for which the book is suitable.

2. *Thematic Material.* In addition to the goal under which the book is listed, additional or secondary themes are given. This should help the librarian or teacher to use the book in a variety of book talk situations.

3. *Book Talk Material.* Specific passages in the book that lend themselves to reading or retelling before a group are suggested.

4. *Additional Suggestions.* Other books that offer a thematic or developmental relationship to the book under discussion are listed and briefly discussed.

The detailed treatment of the main titles is not intended as a substitute for reading the books. Instead, it is intended to be used by teachers and librarians to refresh their memories about books they have read, and to suggest new uses for these titles.

This volume is neither a work of literary criticism, nor a listing of the best books for young adults. It is a representative selection of books that have value in a variety of book talk situations.

The authors have had more helpers than can be identified by name. We would like to express our appreciation to the many librarians and teachers who offered direct help, and to the thousands of boys and girls who participated through interviews and questionnaires. Special thanks should be given to Doris M. Cole, who contributed the introductory chapter on the book talk. We hope that our efforts have produced a book that will be of value to those involved with young people and their reading.

JOHN GILLESPIE
DIANA LEMBO

Data relating to publisher's suggested prices appears for each title cited in this book. Prices followed by the word "net" are suggested net prices supplied by the publisher. Prices will, of course, vary from time to time and from one book supplier to another.

THE BOOK TALK

"The book talk is a sample of a book—a little piece of pie so good that it tempts one to consume the whole concoction."   MARGARET EDWARDS

ONE of the most effective ways to interest young teens in books and in the library is the book talk. It may vary from an informal, person-to-person conversation about books to a formal presentation before an audience. Whatever the form, however, the purpose is the same—to encourage the listener to read. The book talk is more effective than any number of invitations to come to the library. It will stimulate more reading than any number of booklists handed out over a library desk. It is a personal approach to books.

Unlike a book review, the book talk is neither evaluative nor critical. Rather than reveal everything about the book, the book talk gives only an enticing sample of the book's contents. Young people are more interested in the content of a book than its literary quality. A book talk should deal mainly with content. The books discussed will be chosen with literary quality in mind, but this will not be the subject of the talk. Although it may lead to debate and discussion, the book talk is not a discussion. It falls halfway between story telling and book reviewing, being comprised of brief introductions to a variety of books, held together by some common idea or theme. Through a book talk one hopes to expand the interests of the readers in the audience, and to give the non-readers some acquaintance with the world of books. Perhaps it will even stimulate them to try one.

The book talk may be used in relation to the school curriculum, to

1

stimulate interest in an area of study. It may attempt to draw the listeners to a public library or suggest the infinite range of subjects that books represent. The long-range purpose is to bring the realization to the listener that there is something to be gained from regular reading of books, something to be gained that is useful, informative, and enjoyable.

A book talk can be given to any number of people. Your audience may be an individual or a school assembly, although the job is easier and more effective with an audience of 20 or 30, the average class size. The classroom group allows for the informality and easy give and take that is lost with larger groups.

The first step in preparing a book talk is, of course, selecting the books. Obviously the selection should be based on the interests or potential interests of the audience. Fortunately, in these days of mass communication, young people are interested in nearly everything. Don't make the mistake, however, of using a book talk to promote "slow movers" in your book stock. Never include a book unless you are genuinely enthusiastic about it yourself. Students have already rejected the "slow movers" and they are quick to spot phony enthusiasm.

Consider the number of girls and the number of boys in your audience. Remember that while the girls will read a story for boys, the boys will quickly reject a book for girls. Determine the background of the group, not so much the age-level as the reading experience. Be aware of local interests, the nature of the community. Is it a seacoast town or an industrial city? Remember seasonal activities. Obviously the time to talk about football is in the fall, baseball in the summer.

Once you have chosen the theme for the talk, you must decide how many books to cover. For junior high school students a talk should not last more than 40 minutes. A 30 minute talk with ten minutes for browsing, looking at the books, and asking questions is even better.

There are generally three types of book talks. In the first an unrelated assortment of attractive books with bright jackets is brought into the room. The librarian mentions something of interest about each, holding up the book as he talks. With such an assortment he can provide "something for everyone," and with an audience of varied experience, and interests, each can still take a book or an idea away with him after the talk.

More often the book talk is developed around a theme or subject such as "courage," or "tough decisions." It should be built into a careful detailed presentation of three or four titles with "teasers" from five to ten other books that relate to the theme of the talk. If the theme is sufficiently general it is still possible to provide something for everyone in the audience, and the speaker can subtly lead the audience from book to book, subject to subject.

A shorter, more common kind of book talk when time is limited, is a detailed discussion of one book, with brief mention of several related titles—books on the same subject, the same general theme, or written with similar plots or settings.

All of the books chosen need not be new, but some of them ought to be. You can introduce a few old favorites. Books that have been popular can be used as bait by pointing out that other young people have enjoyed them.

It is a good idea to have more books on hand than you will use. You can then change your presentation if audience reaction seems to suggest a change. The composition of the group may not be exactly as you had predicted, or you may find that a given book is not going over, and you want to pass over it for another title.

One way to decide which books to choose is to imagine yourself as a member of the audience. What would you like to hear about, how long could you sit and listen?

Once the books are selected the next step is to become thoroughly familiar with them. Like story telling, preparing for the book talk requires that you know the book "by heart." This doesn't mean line-by-line memorization. The story teller reads the story over and over until he is so familiar with it that he could tell it without the book. He can exploit the dramatic moments, the moods, each incident, as he reads. The speaker who delivers a book talk should have equal familiarity with his material. How this is achieved will depend on the individual speaker. Some authorities advise that a talk should be written out in full before delivery, a good procedure for the beginner. The danger with a written address is that the talk will become a speech, an uninterrupted monolog. Some interruptions from the audience should be welcome. The talk should be more of a conversation than a speech.

Certainly part of your preparation should involve making a set of notes about what you are going to say. While you may not use the notes while you are talking, they will give you an outline to follow, a logical progression from book to book, a natural point of transition from title to title. The talk will fail to hold interest if it is just a quick series of unrelated comments about unrelated books.

The opening of the book talk is most important. You must establish rapport with your audience at the very beginning. You can do this by a reference to some recent event, something that has happened at school, something in the local paper, a recent TV program, a current movie, or even the weather. From this beginning lead into the discussion of the first book. It must be a "sure fire" title, that is readable and interesting to all. From there you can go on to more difficult books. If the group is mixed, alternate books for boys with those for girls. Go from fiction to nonfiction. Include a variety of subjects and types of books.

Begin by recounting one exciting incident. Create interest in the book by telling about some dramatic moment, some crisis in the story—stopping at the climax, before the crisis is over or the mystery solved.

Be specific. Strive for the concrete instance, the definite fact. Tell what there is about this book that makes it different, that sets it apart.

Avoid the stock expressions such as "This is an exciting book," or "Here's a book you'll love." Let the book sell itself. The book may have been exciting to you, but a reader will be disappointed if he follows your recommendation and finds it dull. The book talk must reflect accurately the spirit and mood of the book. It would be misleading to describe *Silas Marner* as a "thriller," a mystery story involving murder, robbery, drug addiction, and desertion. Book talks must be more honest.

It is a good idea to practice with a tape recorder. This gives you a chance to hear how you sound and to check up on such important points as timing and emphasis. Some authorities suggest practicing in front of a full length mirror since how you look is as important as how you sound.

The success of the book talk will depend on the preparation. The kind of preparation and the amount of time it takes will vary with different types of books. It is almost impossible to prepare a rigid program in advance since no group is completely homogenous and the speaker must be ready to change his talk to make it appeal to everyone.

Watch your listeners as you talk—all of them. If attention wanes, bring it back by a change of tempo, by lowering or raising your voice. If you can't bring it back, abandon that book and try another.

Watch yourself, too. Grooming is important, as are diction, grammar, the general manner of the speaker. Avoid unnecessary gestures. Certainly avoid all gestures that do not point up the plot as they will only distract from it.

Use the books themselves if possible. Be sure to hold them up so that everyone can see, and give the name of the author and title clearly. If it is impossible to take the books themselves, take along 30 or 40 jackets and be prepared to talk about any one of them.

Lists of the books to be discussed can be prepared in advance. They can be distributed beforehand so that students can make notes as you talk. Often, however, especially with younger groups, it is better to give out the list after the talk. Otherwise the audience will spend its time reading the lists instead of listening to what you say.

Avoid reading aloud unless you are a very good reader, and even then do it sparingly. Reading puts a book between the reader and the listener. In book talks, as in story telling, you want to get as close to the audience as possible.

Know beforehand what the time allotment is and stay within it. It is important to stop on time—another good reason for practicing with a tape recorder. Remember that the audience will be enthusiastic only if you are enthusiastic, and that the audience will be at ease only if you are at ease. The way to acquire ease and to overcome stage fright is by careful preparation.

The person giving a book talk must decide whether he is going to allow discussion during his talk and what he is going to do about questions. The answer will depend largely upon the experience and the self-confidence of the person giving the talk. Usually it is better not to encourage discussion during the talk itself as this can very easily get out of hand. If time is allowed after the talk for browsing, the informal discussion of the books can take place at that time.

Questions must, of course, be answered, but unless they can be answered in a word to two, they, too, can be left until the end of the talk so as not to interrupt its continuity. Often, however, it is possible to take advantage of a question to make the transition from one book to another.

What sort of person is good at book talks? He must know books— many books, all kinds of books, in all kinds of fields—and he must know and like people. He must be honest and enthusiastic for the books without appearing to be overzealous.

The test of the effectiveness of the book talk is not how dramatic or how artistic it is. The test is how many people want to borrow the books afterwards. Have the books at the talk and allow them to be charged out then and there if at all possible. The time to capitalize on the interest engendered by the book talk is right afterwards, when it is at its highest point.

Any librarian or teacher will find that giving a book talk is a pleasant break in the everyday routine. It is fun to prepare. It is fun to give. Young people are the best, the most responsive audience in the world.

DORIS M. COLE

1

Building a World View

Aᴌᴛʜᴏᴜɢʜ ɴᴇᴀʀᴌʏ adult in his outlook, the young person at age 14 has not had enough direct experience to develop an accurate understanding of the cultures, diversities, and problems of life in other lands. He lacks a sense of historical time, so foreign to childhood with its immediacy of experience. He must still learn to understand the historical and current development of other nations and his own American heritage. Such basic democratic values as individual liberty, political democracy, religious and racial equality, and international cooperation must be explored, largely through indirect and vicarious experiences in the classroom and in books. The exploration and study of these concepts will help the young adult to apply intelligent analysis to national and international problems and to understand his own duties as a socially responsible citizen.

The books listed in this chapter offer a variety of experiences to the young adult involved in the process of building a world view. Some will help him to develop a sense of history, others will give insight into the struggle for freedom and liberty; and all will help develop the adolescent's understanding of his traditions and his current place in world society.

Merritt Parmelee Allen, *Johnny Reb,*
McKay, 1952, $3.95; lib. bdg. $3.59 net

Mr. Allen has written over a dozen junior novels that vividly recreate America's past. *Johnny Reb,* one of his most popular, tells of the Civil

7

War from the Southern point of view. The book appeals to boys in the sixth through ninth grades.

In 1861 Ezra Todd, the hero of the story, is about to celebrate his 17th birthday. Ezra's parents, both originally Northerners, died when he was only ten years old. Since then, he has been living in a rural South Carolina community with cruel, tyrannical Jed Sears and his son, Bert.

While out hunting, Ezra is accidentally clawed by a bear that had been wounded by Wade Hampton, a wealthy landowner who lives nearby. In spite of protests from Jed and Bert, who hate the Southern aristocracy, Ezra allows himself to be taken to the Hampton mansion, Sand Hills, for a period of recuperation. Here he meets Mrs. Hampton and her two sons, Wade and Preston. The Hampton's Negro servant, Jeems, cares for Ezra, and gradually the wound heals. Ezra becomes warmly attached to the Hamptons during his short visit. He is particularly impressed by the kindly attitude and leadership ability of the father, Wade Hampton. Talk of war is in the air. Mr. Hampton leaves Sand Hills to form his own cavalry unit.

When Ezra returns to the Sears', he smarts under their constant taunts and cruelties. Finally, in a fit of temper, he leaves them and hikes to Columbia, South Carolina, to join Colonal (later General) Wade Hampton's cavalry division.

General Hampton allows the boy to join the unit. He loans Ezra one of his horses and a trainer, Private Festival Jones.

For five days, Fess teaches Ezra the fundamentals of horsemanship. At the end of this period, Ezra is able to take his place on the parade ground with the other, more experienced, men.

Fess and Ezra become great buddies, and together they live through the horror of Bull Run. During the battle, Ezra is gripped by an overpowering fear and revulsion against the scenes of combat around him. He wants to run, but, inspired by Hampton's courage, he stays on the battlefield and helps to win a Southern victory.

The pampered young aristocrats of Hampton's legion, to Ezra's surprise, have become tough, courageous fighting men almost overnight. The horrors of camp life nearly equal those of the battlefield. Food is scarce and living conditions unbearable. Thousands die of disease and neglect.

As part of the Peninsula Campaign, Hampton's Legion takes part in the bloody battle at Seven Pines. The Rebs suffer severe losses but hold their ground. Over half of Hampton's men are casualties. "Those who lived were defying the laws of nature."

Ezra is seriously wounded and taken to an army hospital, where he meets a Yankee officer, Captain George March. The Captain turns out to be Ezra's uncle, who, in civilian life, is involved in railroad construction. He offers Ezra a job with his company after the war.

Ezra's "bowlegged angel," Fess, rescues him from the terrible conditions of the hospital. While Ezra recovers, they stay with the Williams, a friendly Quaker family. Together, they manage to rout a band of Yankee soldiers intent on raiding the Williams' farm. One member of the party is Ezra's hated enemy, Bert Sears.

Ezra's life becomes a series of bloody battles and daring raids. Lack of supplies, food and clothing seriously handicaps the Southern effort. Ezra witnesses the Southern defeat at Gettysburg and the inglorious retreat that follows. During an attack on Petersburg, General Hampton's son Preston is killed. Gradually, despair and hopelessness fill the Southern ranks.

Ezra and Fess are captured by a group of Yankee soldiers, but, through Fess' cunning, they escape with valuable information about troop movements.

The Confederate Army retreats further into South Carolina. Fess and Ezra revisit the Hampton home of Sand Hills, now deserted, except for the servant, Jeems. There they are surprised and taken captive by a party of Yankee raiders led by Bert Sears. The soldiers, now joined by Bert's father, Jed, loot the house. Bert forces Ezra upstairs, ties him to a bed, and sets fire to the house. When the raiders have gone, Jeems battles his way into the burning house and drags Ezra to safety. Later, Bert and Jed are captured and executed.

The South surrenders. Ezra, relieved but sorrowful that the end has come, plans to rejoin his uncle and help in some way to rebuild the shattered country.

Thematic Material

Johnny Reb is outstanding in the fairness with which it treats both sides in the Civil War conflict. A story of great personal heroism and sacrifice, it affirms the dignity that man can maintain, even in defeat.

Book Talk Material

This novel is filled with many episodes that convey a realistic picture of the Civil War. A few are: the first battle of Bull Run (pp. 64–68) ; Ezra exchanges gifts with a Yankee sentry (pp. 80–82) ; Ezra at the hospital (pp. 98–102) ; the Quaker's attitude towards war (pp. 121–124) and Fess and Ezra save the Williams farm (pp. 126–128) .

Additional Suggestions

Other popular novels by Mr. Allen are: *Battle Lanterns* (McKay, lib. bdg. $3.67 net) , a Revolutionary War story, and two novels that deal with the opening up of the Pacific Northwest, *Make Way for the Brave* (McKay; lib. bdg. $3.89 net) and *East of Astoria* (McKay, $3.50) .

Both *The Andrews Raid: The Great Locomotive Chase* by Samuel and Beryl Epstein (Coward, $3.95) and Earl Miers' *The Guns of Vicksburg* (Putnam, $3.00) are good Civil War stories. Phyllis Fenner's excellent collection of short stories, *Brother Against Brother* (Morrow, $3.75) and Leonard Wibberley's story of a Confederate boy after the War, *The Wound of Peter Wayne* (Farrar, Straus, $3.25) can be used as well.

More mature readers may go on to: Walter D. Edmond's *Cadmus Henry* (Dodd, $3.00) or James Street's *Captain Little Ax* (Lippincott, $4.95) .

Karin Anckarsvärd, *Springtime for Eva,*
Harcourt, 1959, $2.95

This Swedish author is known for her many young adult titles. *Springtime for Eva* is an unusual story of first love set in Stockholm. In spite of an awkward translation and the emphasis on the heroine's inner thoughts, enough of the emotional impact of the original version remains to make the book a good choice for adolescent girls. They will be interested that their Swedish counterparts share many of the same problems and feelings.

The Gullbergs, Eva, her father, her mother and two half-brothers, live in an apartment in Stockholm. Mrs. Gullberg loves her pretty blonde step-daughter and knows that Eva loves her. Yet, she worries because of Mr. Gullberg's insensitive attitude toward his daughter. She fears Eva has never recovered from the childhood emotional shock of seeing her kitten brutally beheaded by their janitor. Eva is a reserved young lady who keeps much to herself, even though she loves and respects her gentle step-mother.

Lena Janssen, Eva's classmate, has always envied Eva's beauty, her good grades, and her admirers. One day, Lena mentions that her cousin, Ingemar, and his friend, the Hagman boy from Gardholm, are coming to the city. Lena persuades Eva to date Ingemar.

The date with Ingemar is boring. Eva thinks the boys are immature. She is glad when they begin the return trip to Stockholm. The roads are slippery from the early morning moisture, and they have an accident.

When she recovers consciousness, a policeman is helping Eva from the battered car. Ingemar has a broken leg and a covered stretcher holds the body of the Hagman boy. Shocked by the senseless tragedy; Eva asks herself why?

Back home, Eva determines to forget the tragedy. She meets 20-year-old David Wahlstrom, a brilliant student who lives in the same apartment building. Eva's family likes him.

David leaves Stockholm. Eva misses him very much, but the Spring passes without a letter and she makes a date with the persistent Ingemar to go to the Sunday races at Ulriksdal. As they drive in his new SAAB, Eva thinks longingly of how David had promised to take her to these races. David is there in the crowd. He stares at her and smiles. She smiles back.

David comes to the Gullberg's and protests that he has always loved her, but, fearing rejection, had gone away. Her smile at the races convinced him that he must tell her of his love. Eva knows how deeply she feels towards David and that her deep fear of men is groundless—it is possible for her to love, after all.

Thematic Material

In this novel, a girl's troubled adolescence is well portrayed. The heroine's gradual insight into her own nature will bolster many adolescents who have similar feelings of self-doubt. The Swedish setting will help young adults understand that human emotions are the same everywhere.

Book Talk Material

Since the book is introspective rather than episodic, there are no isolated parts that are suitable for book talks. Instead, with a few descriptive sentences, suggest the heroine's conflict.

Additional Suggestions

There are several other girls' stories with foreign locales: Elsa Steinmann's *Lia and the Red Carnations* (Pantheon, $3.00) is set in Italy and Dorothy Blatter's *Cap and Candle* (Westminster, $3.25) in Turkey. Both boys and girls will enjoy *Mother and Son: The Wartime Correspondence* (Houghton, $4.25) by Isoko and Ichiro Hatano, which deals with Japan during World War II.

Harry Behn, *The Faraway Lurs,*
World, 1963, $3.00

Mr. Behn has written this tragic love story with the same delicacy and grace that are present in his poetry. In a short introduction, the author tells the background of the book. While doing research in Denmark, he became fascinated with the archeological discovery of the grave of an 18-year-old Bronze Age girl, apparently offered as a sacrifice by her tribe. He named the girl Heather, and, in this novel, he related what might have been her story. This novel will appeal to girls in the upper elementary grades who enjoy the enchantment and imagination of myths and folk tales.

The book tells of the clash between two prehistoric tribes and its tragic consequences. The forest people, a gentle, peace-loving tribe have settled in a wooded area of Denmark. This chief is Goodshade, and their religion is a form of nature worship centered about a large oak tree that grows close to their village.

The Sun People are a nomadic war-like people who roam the countryside murdering and pillaging. Great Elk, their warrior chieftan, is growing old and is fearful of losing his power. Two rival factions challenge his supremacy: one is led by the chief sun priest Troll Tamer, and the other by Eagle, who is determined to recapture his lost inheritance.

Heather, daughter of Chief Goodshade, is gathering honey in the forest when she hears the sound of the lurs, the bronze trumpets of the Sun People. The Forest People are suspicious and fearful of these unwelcome visitors who have camped near their village.

Heather meets Wolf Stone, the young, handsome son of Chief Great Elk. The two are attracted to each other. They fall in love. Heather feels guilty because she is already betrothed to Blue Wing, a young warrior of her own tribe.

Wolf Stone promises Heather that he will try to prevent a war between their two tribes. However, forces within the Sun People work against him. Troll Tamer, who loves war, would like to destroy Goodshade's village, and Great Elk wants to cut down the sacred oak of the Forest People to build an invincible ship.

The Forest People are puzzled by a prophecy from their oak god that comes through Tree Woman, Heather's mother. They are told that war can only be averted by sacrificing their most prized possession to the god.

To further his own ends, Eagle convinces Blue Wing that the Sun People will leave only if their Chief and High Priest are killed. The two conspire to commit this double murder. Blue Wing visits the Sun People, ostensibly to attend an athletic contest and display his skill with bow and arrow. While the crowd is momentarily distracted, he slays Troll Tamer. At the same time, Eagle slips a deadly poison into Great Elk's drink. Wolf Stone is proclaimed the new chieftain. He persuades the Sun People to settle in a new land where they will live peacefully, and announces that Heather Goodshade will be his bride. The rejected Blue Wing is overcome with jealousy and murders Wolf Stone. Seeking revenge, the warriors of the Sun People kill Blue Wing.

The Forest People are preparing for a strange religious ceremony when news of the carnage reaches Heather. Numb with grief, she watches her people hollow a coffin out of the tree trunk. She suddenly remembers the prophecy—they must sacrifice their most prized posses- sion to prevent war.

In ceremonial robes, the tribe advances towards her. Tree Woman hands her a potion. She drinks. "In a moment her fear was gone, swept away by the sunny stillness of the forest, the timeless voice of peace . . . she thought of Wolf Stone waiting for her in the glade only a little distance away."

Thematic Material

The central theme is stated by the author in his introduction: "Whatever makes us what we are—customs, traditions, and heritage—are much older than we realize." This novel is also a variation on the Romeo and Juliet story.

Book Talk Material

As this book would have appeal for a rather special type of reader, perhaps only a short description of the central conflict need be given. Because the plot is extremely complex, it is difficult to suggest isolated passages that would be suitable for reading aloud. However, Chapter I (p. 19–25), in which Heather sees the arrival of the Sun People, could be read aloud.

Additional Suggestions

Harry Behn's later novel, *Omen of the Birds* (World, $3.50), set in Etruscan times, or Josephina Niggli's *A Miracle for Mexico* (N.Y. Graphic, $4.95) should appeal to readers who enjoy *The Faraway Lurs*. For the less serious, suggest Joan Aiken's *The Wolves of Willoughby Chase* (Doubleday, $3.25).

Frank Bonham, *Burma Rifles: A Story of Merrill's Marauders,* Crowell, 1960, $3.50

At one point in this novel, the hero, young Jerry Harada, comes to the conclusion that, "of all the terrible things which could befall a man, war was the worst." Despite the grim picture of warfare that emerges from this story, it is popular with both junior and senior high school boys. The horror of war is tempered only by the author's admiration and compassion for the brave men who fought during World War II in the jungles of Burma.

For the Haradas, a Japanese-American family living in California, the consequences of the Pearl Harbor attack are personal and immediate. A few of their neighbors and former friends suspect all Nisei of subversive activities. Prompted by fear and ignorance, these misguided patriots visit the Harada farm and destroy the ham radio set that had been built by the Harada's 19-year-old son, Jerry. Shortly afterwards, the family is forced to sell their belongings and submit to internment in a relocation camp.

The internees are visited by a group of U.S. soldiers, led by Jerry's boyhood friend, Russ Bennett. Their mission is to recruit young Nisei to act as interpreters and translators for the U.S. Army. Jerry volunteers.

The same prejudices and suspicions that had prompted the raid on the Harada farm haunt Jerry during his army career. His training period is further complicated by his naivete and his desire to please his friends. Although he knows that taking photographs is forbidden on an army post, he builds a small pin-hole camera so that his buddies can have pictures to send home. The camera is discovered, and Jerry is severely reprimanded. Later, on a troopship bound for the Pacific, Jerry 'borrows' a sextant from the navigation room in an effort to determine their exact position. Again he is caught and only the intervention of his friend Russ saves him from a court martial.

Jerry's training period comes to an abrupt end. He is sent to eastern India to be assigned to Merrill's Marauders. The aim of their present campaign is to drive the Japanese out of Burma, and reopen the Burma Road, the lifeline to China.

Jerry volunteers for a special assignment in the combat area. He is flown to the front to interrogate a captured Japanese pilot. Jerry's cleverly-worded questions make the pilot reveal information about troop movements. While awaiting for the plane home, Jerry joins a patrol on a daring raid. In this first exposure to combat, he is wounded.

During his recuperation in New Delhi, Jerry continues to work for the Army Intelligence Service. He questions many Japanese prisoners, learning first hand about the fanatic sense of honor and fatalism that motivates many of the Japanese fighting men.

Jerry rejoins his batallion in time for one of the bloodiest battles of the campaign—the Battle of Nhpum Ga. For ten days, his surrounded unit withstands the suicidal onslaught of the Japanese. Each night, Jerry creeps close to the enemy outposts to collect information about the next day's attack. Finally, the siege is lifted and the enemy retreats.

The Marauders plan a final campaign before the monsoon season. For this action, Jerry is assigned to a small unit assigned to blow up a heavily guarded stretch of railroad track. The operation seems doomed until Jerry disguises himself as a Japanese officer and persuades the sentries to surrender.

When the driving rains arrive, the men know that the heavy fighting will stop for a while—later there will be more battles and more deaths before the final victory.

Thematic Material

To many teenages, World War II is now so remote that it can be easily glamorized. This novel authentically describes the ugly realities and is a fine tribute to the sacrifice and bravery of the American soldier. Secondary themes deal with the maturation of the hero, and the particular problems faced by members of a minority group.

Book Talk Material

Interest can be aroused by giving a short summary of the plot. Specific passages that can be read to a group are: The destruction of Jerry's radio set (pp. 25–28); Jerry's decision to make his own camera (pp. 58–61); Jerry questions his first prisoner (pp. 127–131) and engages in his first skirmish (pp. 138–141).

Additional Suggestions

Frank Bonham has written several hard-hitting junior novels that boys will enjoy—another of his titles is *War Beneath the Sea* (Crowell, $3.75) which deals with the dangers of submarine warfare.

Mature readers might continue with other works dealing with World War II, such as Richard Matheson's *The Beardless Warriors* (Little, $4.95), John Hersey's *Into the Valley: A Skirmish of the Marines* (Knopf, $3.50) or William L. White's *They Were Expendable* (Harcourt, $3.25). An adult, non-fiction account of General Frank Merrill and his men is given in *The Marauders* (Harper, $5.95; lib. bdg. $5.11 net) by Charlton Ogburn, Jr. For younger readers use Robb White's *Torpedo Run* (Doubleday, $2.95) or James Forman's *The Skies of Crete* (Farrar, Straus, $2.95).

Thomas A. Dooley, *Doctor Tom Dooley, My Story,*
Farrar, Straus, 1962, $2.95

Because of his inspiring record of service to his fellow man, the late Dr. Dooley has been called "The Splendid American." He wrote three books which tell of his work in South East Asia. They are: *Deliver Us From Evil* ($3.95), *The Edge of Tomorrow* ($3.95) and *The Night*

They Burned the Mountain ($3.95, all Farrar, Straus). This is a one-volume abridgement of these three books and is intended for youngsters from the sixth through the ninth grades.

In the fall of 1954, thousands of refugees are streaming into the coastal city of Haiphong in North Vietnam seeking transportation to South Vietnam and freedom. They are escaping from the Communist regime scheduled to assume control in May, 1955, according to the Geneva Treaty.

The U.S. Navy, helping in this rescue operation, has set up a camp where these refugees can receive shelter, food and drugs while awaiting embarkation. Lieutenant Tom Dooley, a 27-year-old medical school graduate, is placed in charge.

Dr. Dooley becomes an expert scrounger—he finds a relatively dry tract of land on the outskirts of the city suitable for the campsite; from the U.S. Army he receives 400 tents and, from the French forces, the manpower to set them up; he "borrows" supplies and drugs from the U.S. ships and sends "begging" letters back to America for more equipment and drugs.

An endless stream of refugees passes through the camp. Arriving without possessions, half-starved and disease-ridden, each has his own story of hardship and Communist brutality.

Dr. Dooley's working day lasts 16 hours. Only occasionally does he allow himself the luxury of a hot bath aboard an American ship or a visit to the orphanage of Madame Ngai.

The last day for embarkation arrives. Hundreds of thousands of refugees have passed through "Camp de la Pagode" during the ten months of its existence.

Back in the U.S. and now out of the Navy, Dr. Dooley feels that his job is only partly done. He wants to return to South East Asia to begin 'Operation Laos.' With the blessing of the Laotian government, Dr. Dooley and three of his former helpers from Viet Nam—Norman Baker, Peter Kessey and Dennis Shepherd—set up a small hospital and clinic in Vang Vieng, an isolated village in Northern Laos. At first they are greeted with hostility and fear but, with the help of their young interpreter, Chai, and such diverse blandishments as showing Walt Disney movies in the evenings, the native Laotians are won over. Soon news of the American doctor and his "miracle cures" spreads throughout the countryside, and patients pour into the jungle hospital. But Dr.

Dooley's objective is not to create an outpost that he will operate permanently. He wishes to begin something that the natives can eventually take over and continue. Therefore, after training a staff, Dooley leaves Vang Vieng and heads north to Nam Tha, a city close to the Chinese border.

To service outlying villages, Dr. Dooley and his men build a floating clinic, and journey down the Nam Tha River dispensing medicine, food and clothing.

A shortage of funds brings Dr. Dooley back to America again. Enthusiasm for his work is so great that he is able to found MEDICO, an organization devoted to establishing clinics in other underdeveloped countries.

In the fall of 1959, Dr. Dooley undergoes an operation for cancer. After a short recuperative period, he resumes his grueling schedule of attending meetings, visiting MEDICO hospitals, and fulfilling speaking engagements. His health continues to decline. On January 18, 1961, the day following his 34th birthday, he dies at Memorial Hospital in New York City.

Thematic Material

Dr. Dooley's story is one of extreme heroism, sacrifice and altruism.

In this autobiography, he includes fascinating background information on the culture, political struggles and living conditions in the countries of South East Asia.

Book Talk Material

The book is filled with warm, tender, often humorous incidents that can be used to introduce it to a group. Here are a few to choose from: Dr. Dooley's doubts about his mission in Viet Nam (pp. 2–4) ; purifying the water (pp. 11–12) ; a typical day at "Camp de la Pagode" (pp. 17–19) ; a mandarin tells how a village escaped from the Communists (pp. 27–31) ; little Lia and her "American" leg (pp. 33–34) ; overcoming the refugees' fear of Yankee drugs (pp. 45–46) ; introduction to Chai, the interpreter (pp. 69–71) ; the story of Savong (pp. 84–85) ; Dr. Dooley and the witch doctors (pp. 98–100) .

Additional Suggestions

Young readers may wish to read Dr. Dooley's three original works. An account of the last months of Dr. Dooley's life is given in *Before I Sleep,* edited by James Monahan (Farrar, Straus, $4.50). Two other adult titles of interest are *Letters from the Peace Corps,* edited by Iris Luce (McKay, $2.95), and William Walsh's *A Ship Called 'Hope'* (Dutton, $4.95).

The story of Tom Dooley brings to mind his mentor, Albert Schweitzer. Two recommended biographies of Dr. Schweitzer are Jacquelyn Berrill's *Albert Schweitzer: Man of Mercy* (Dodd, $3.50) and the older title *Albert Schweitzer, Genius of the Jungle* by Joseph Gollomb (Vanguard, $3.95).

Jean Lee Latham, *Carry on, Mr. Bowditch,*
Houghton, 1955, $3.50

Miss Latham's fictionalized biography of Nathaniel Bowditch recreates one of the most fascinating and romantic periods in our history —the age of the sailing ship. The text is supplemented by many excellent black and white drawings by John O'Hara Cosgrave III. This book won the Newbery prize in 1956, and is popular with students from the fifth through the eighth grades.

In 1779, when Nathaniel Bowditch is six years old, he and his family move to the seaport town of Salem, Massachusetts. Nat's father had been a sea captain but after his ship was sunk on Anquilla Reef, he turned to the cooper's trade.

Although Nathaniel does well at school and is anxious to continue, his father is forced by economic difficulties to take Nathaniel out of school when he is only ten. For two years, the boy helps at his father's cooperage. One night, he overhears his father say that there will soon be a change in store for him. Nathaniel dreams that he will be allowed to return to school, but instead, his father has indentured him for nine years to the firm of Ropes and Hodges, ship chandlers. His hopes of studying for a degree at Harvard seem lost forever.

As the chandler's bookkeeper, Nat learns about ships and sailing. In the evenings, he continues his education by reading voraciously and studying mathematics. He reads through the entire *Chambers's Encyclopedia,* produces his own almanac at the age of 16, and even teaches himself Latin so that he may translate Newton's *Principia.*

Through his sister, Lizza, Nat meets Elizabeth Boardman, the daughter of a Salem sea captain. Elizabeth visits him often at the chandlery, and they become close friends.

At last, the period of indenture is complete and Nat, now 21, goes to sea. He becomes clerk and second mate on a ship bound to collect a cargo of coffee at Bourbon (now called Réunion). To facilitate transactions, Nat teaches himself French. On board ship, he studies navigation, discovers errors in the tables of Moore's *Navigator,* and evolves a simple way to take lunars (measurements that determine longitude at sea.)

Home once more, Nat realizes that he loves Elizabeth and they are married shortly before he sails again on the Astrea. While in port at Alicante, Nathaniel learns from the captain of another ship that Elizabeth is dead. They had been married only six months.

Nathaniel has signed on the ship as its supercargo—the person in charge of the sale and purchase of cargo. This allows him plenty of free time to continue his work on navigation. Nat feels that many shipwrecks are caused by the use of inaccurate navigation tables. His goal is "to check every figure in every table that's published."

On a later voyage, the application of his navigational knowledge saves the Astrea in its encounter with dangerous monsoon head winds.

Nathaniel continues checking navigation tables. In one work alone, he finds 8,000 errors—enough to convince him that he should write a new book on the subject.

Back home, he begins writing. He learns that his two brothers have died in shipwrecks. Realizing that his book might prevent similar tragedies, Nathaniel drives himself even harder. Eventually his book *The Practical Navigator* is published, and Harvard College awards him an honorary Master of Arts degree. He marries one of Elizabeth's closest friends, Polly Ingersoll.

Again Nathaniel goes to sea, this time as captain and part-owner of his own vessel. On the homeward trip, the ship is engulfed in a thick, deadly fog. Using his navigational tables, Nat saves the ship.

Thematic Material

Carry On, Mr. Bowditch, is an American success story. In spite of many disadvantages, Nathaniel Bowditch was able, by his initiative and perseverance, to achieve a place of eminence in the world of mathematics. The biography is enriched by interesting information on American political life following the Revolution, plus many fascinating details about sailing ships.

Book Talk Material

After a suitable introduction, one of the following passages might be used to create interest: Nat learns of his indenture (pp. 37–42) ; Sam Smith tells him the history of the ship's log on Nat's first day at the chandlery (pp. 47–51) ; Nat's introduction to *Chambers's Encyclopaedia* (pp. 56–57) ; or Nat discovers his first error in Moore's *Navigator* (pp. 119–121) .

Additional Suggestions

Jean Lee Latham has written many interesting biographies for young people. A work similar to the Bowditch biography is *Trail Blazer of the Seas* (Houghton, $3.50) , the story of Matthew Maury, who charted wind and ocean currents, and founded a maritime academy. Others are: *Young Man in a Hurry* (Harper, $3.50; lib. bdg. $3.27 net) , the life of Cyrus Field, and *Man of the Monitor* (Harper, $3.95; lib. ed. $3.79 net) , the story of John Ericsson.

Two additional sea stories that boys enjoy are: Stephen Meader's *Guns for the Saratoga* (Harcourt, $3.50) and Armstrong Sperry's whaling adventure, *Danger to Windward* (Holt, $3.50) .

Thelma Nurenberg, *My Cousin, the Arab,*
Abelard, 1965, $3.75

This fascinating account of life in a kibbutz during the emergence of the new nation of Israel is reminiscent of Leon Uris' novel, *Exodus.* Mrs. Nurenberg conveys the tremendous emotional impact of the conflict between Arab and Jew in terms that are understandable to young people. Junior high school girls will respond to the inspiring quality of this story.

In July 1947, 17-year-old Emmi Leiter and her little brother Erni, arrive from Germany to start a new life in Palestine. Their father had died in a Nazi concentration camp and their mother is awaiting passage to join them at Kibbutz Tel Hashava. They are taken to the kibbutz by 19-year-old Avram, grandson of Noah, its founder, and Paul Heller, an American student who is spending a year there.

When they arrive at the raw, unfinished outpost of Tel Hashava, Emmi meets Noah, the white-haired *vattik* (veteran) and Ora, his *sabra* (native) granddaughter. Neither Emmi nor Erni share the sense of dedication of these people. They are divorced from the settlers' problems and secretly yearn to be back in Germany.

Noah is still friendly with Abu Sa'id, an Arab chieftain whose grandchildren, Ferial and Hassan, have grown up with Avram and Ora. Hassan and Ora are deeply in love. Although the two old men try to avoid conflict between their peoples, a quarrel develops over ownership of some hill property.

Emmi is happy to leave the kibbutz and its problems to spend a day in Haifa with Alan Dufy, a young British officer. He is attracted to the gentle Emmi and she prefers him to the rough pioneers at the outpost. When she returns to Tel Hashava, she learns that her mother has drowned while escaping from an illegal refugee ship.

There is growing tension at the kibbutz. The once friendly British officers, including Alan Dufy, harass them by frequent visits to search for illegal refugees and hidden firearms. The Arab attacks grow in intensity and Ora and Hassan know that their love is doomed because of their divided loyalties.

One day an illegal refugee arrives. Although the settlers call him Shimon, Emmi recognizes him as the famous Dr. Vogel of Nürnberg, an old friend of her father's. She becomes very attached to this wise man, but Erni resents the friendship.

During a British inspection of the kibbutz, Erni betrays Shimon to the authorities. When Emmi sees the old man dragged away by her friend Alan, she realizes the importance of the settlers' struggle and the part she must play.

In spite of Arab objections, the hill property is declared part of the kibbutz and both the Arabs and the Jews know that war is inevitable. A concentrated Arab attack begins. Because the settlers are defenseless, Paul walks to the police post and returns with the British officers. Together, they repulse the attack. After four days of fighting, there is a respite. During the battle, Emmi is impressed with Avram's courage and heroism.

In the months that follow, their attachment grows. Avram proposes to Emmi and she accepts.

Ora, now reconciled to the loss of Hassan, hopes that she and Paul will also marry and help to build the new homeland.

The title comes from an allusion to the Bible: an old Arab says, "Are we not related in Abraham? . . . Through Ishmael from Shem." It also refers to Ora's statement when she discovers an Arab trick to divert their gunfire—"Oh, how diabolically clever they were—my cousins, the Arabs."

Thematic Material

The author skillfully includes background references to the partition struggle in Palestine and the Nazi persecution of the Jews during World War II. The recurring themes of personal courage and the unselfish devotion to a cause will appeal to young people.

Book Talk Material

There are many vivid scenes: the youngsters' arrival at Tel Hashava (pp. 21–32) ; Emmi's visit to Haifa (pp. 52–60) ; Ora and Hassan at an Arab wedding (pp. 61–72) ; the settlers clearance of the hill property, (pp. 153–162) ; and the Arab attack (p. 203–213) .

Additional Suggestions

Two books about the Middle East from different points of view are Anne Mehdevi's *Persia Revisited* (Knopf, $4.95) and Yashar Kemal's *Memed, My Hawk* (Pantheon, $4.95). Robert St. John's *They Came from Everywhere* (Coward, $4.95) gives an interesting account of the different people who settled in Israel after the Partition. Also recommended is *Kamiti* (Meredith, $3.00) by Richard St. Barbe Baker, a poignant tale of a young African boy's life in a tribal village.

Ann Petry, *Tituba of Salem Village,*
Crowell, 1964, $3.75

Mrs. Petry has recreated the hysteria of the Salem Witch Trials of 1692, in an absorbing tale distinguished by its historical accuracy, readable style and brilliant characterization of an accused witch—the slave Tituba. It is a worthy successor to the author's excellent young adult title, *Harriet Tubman: Conductor on the Underground Railroad* (Crowell, $3.95) . *Tituba of Salem Village* is exciting for youngsters in grades six through nine.

Mistress Endicott suddenly announces that Tituba and her husband John, native West Indians, have been sold to repay a gambling debt and must leave Barbados. They are to go to Boston with their new master, Rev. Samuel Parris, who is seeking a church there. On the ship, Tituba becomes acquainted with her new family—Rev. Parris, a harsh-spoken man; his sickly wife, his five-year-old daughter, Betsey; and his wife's orphan niece, Abigail Williams. Tituba is suspicious of this master who makes a big show of his religiosity.

Tituba lovingly tends the frail wife and the children. Betsey responds, but Abigail, jealous of the younger child, is troublesome. Looking at the cold, grey Boston harbor, Tituba is afraid of the future.

John is hired out immediately to a local tavern. While working he witnesses the hanging of a "witch." Upset by the incident he tells Tituba that the "witch" was only a deranged old woman.

Tituba tends the sickly mistress and the girls in their miserable, cold little house. In order to save money, the minister gets Tituba a job with Samuel Conklin, a kind neighbor. While Tituba is working the mischievous Abigail neglects her aunt's care. When she punishes the child, Tituba realizes she has made an enemy.

In the spring, Rev. Parris accepts a congregation in Salem Village. He is promised firewood, pay, provisions, and a deed to the parsonage. The family has to move again. John, homesick and discouraged, asks Tituba why she didn't foresee their misfortune in the cards she read for Mistress Endicott's pleasure. Abigail overhears this conversation and is intrigued.

At the end of a long day's ride, the group arrives at a dilapidated farm. One day, a haggard, unkempt woman and her child appear at the door begging for food. Her name is Goody Good. The minister chases them away.

Soon, John is hired out to the local tavern again. Lonely and fearful with John away, Tituba, over the minister's objections, insists on keeping a cat. Things begin to look brighter when the house starts to fill with provisions brought by the families' indentured girls—Mercy Lewis, Mary Warne, and Elizabeth Hubbard. Neighboring servants visit often and listen to Tituba's West Indian folktales. During these pleasant sessions, Tituba notices that Betsey falls into occasional trance-like states and she suspects that Betsey is an epileptic.

Tituba discovers that Abigail is deliberately trying to induce trance-like states in Betsey. When Tituba's skill at telling fortunes becomes known, everyone wants a reading.

When Mercy Lewis pretends to have a "fit" to cover some mis-
behavior and is treated more kindly by her owners, all the indentured
girls start to have "fits." Eventually, Abigail imitates them. Tituba
notices, however, that all the girls are healthy after their "fits" except
Betsey, whose condition continues to worsen.

Goody Sibley decides to bake a "witch cake" to find out who is
afflicting these poor girls. When Tituba, Goody Good and Grammer
Osburne, an elderly neighbor, simultaneously enter the house during
the ritual, Abigail screams triumphantly, "Tituba is the witch."

Rev. Parris beats Tituba into confessing and turns her over to the
townspeople for trial. Goody Good and Grammer Osburne are also
charged with witchcraft. At the trial, the women stoutly deny the
charges, but they are convicted anyway. Only Tituba, legally confessed,
cannot be hanged. Grammer Osburne dies and Goody Good is hanged
that summer in Boston. A year later, all imprisoned "witches" are
pardoned by the Royal Governor. Tituba is the last to leave because
Rev. Parris will not pay her jail charges. Finally, Samuel Conklin
secures her release and buys both her and John.

Thematic Material

Because of her love for her sickly charges, the heroine struggles
against the greed and craven attitude of her master. Her courage
dramatizes one person's selflessness. The author's careful historical research will add immeasurably to young people's understanding of both
the Puritan outlook and Negro history in the Bay Colony.

Book Talk Material

A few exciting book talk incidents are: Tituba discovers a stowaway
(pp. 15–19) ; they arrive in Salem Village (pp. 56–57) ; Witch Glover is
hanged (pp. 61–62) ; Goody Good arrives (pp. 73–76) ; a description of
Salem Village (pp. 82–85) ; the "witch cake" (pp. 178–183) ; the Trial
begins (pp. 220–235).

Additional Suggestions

For more on witchcraft, suggest Elizabeth Speare's *The Witch of
Blackbird Pond* (Houghton, $3.25), G. Palmer's and N. Lloyd's *A Brew
of Witchcraft* (Roy Pub., $3.95), and for the more mature reader,
Arthur Miller's play, *The Crucible* (Viking, $3.50). *Time of Trial*

(World, $3.75) by Hester Burton gives a clear account of a struggle for freedom of speech. An interesting fictionalized retelling of the Molly Pitcher legend is given in *A Hatful of Gold* (Westminster, $3.50) by Marjory Hall. Youngsters will like the story of the founding of the Jamestown Colony in Jean Lee Latham's *This Dear-Bought Land* (Harper, $3.95; lib. bdg. $3.79 net) and the story of a friendship between an Indian boy and an African slave in Betty Baker's *Walk the World's Rim* (Holt, $2.95; lib. bdg. $2.92 net).

William O. Steele, *The Year of the Bloody Sevens,*
Harcourt, 1963, $3.25

Mr. Steele is well-known for his vivid accounts of life along the American Wilderness Trails. This novel is an exciting realistic story about an 11-year-old boy who journeys from Virginia to Kentucky through dangerous Indian territory to reach his father. Youngsters in grades four through seven like this adventure story.

The Bond family have lived for three years in a cabin on the edge of the Wilderness Trail in Virginia. When his father leaves to help Benjamin Logan build a fort in Kentucky, 11-year-old Kelsey is left in charge. Kelsey's mother dies during his father's absence and he is cared for by neighbors until his father sends for him.

Kel joins Henry Worth's family, who are driving a herd of cows to Kentucky. Because of the cows' slow pace, Kel figures it will take months to reach his father. He is also sure that the Worths will turn back because of the presence of hostile Indians. While on the Trail, Kel drives off a wounded bear who kills the Worth's prize cow. This incident convinces him that the Worths will be unable to endure the hardships of the trip. He is determined to travel on with or without them. Luckily, two woodsmen appear on the Trail and agree to take him along.

Ben Horne, with his weird notions about food, continually drinks water from streams to "oil his joints" and Hoke Carr has fits of bad temper and lunges at branches with his hatchet. Yet, Kel knows that they will travel fast and tries to overlook their strange habits. The two men make frequent side trips along the Trail. On one of their excursions, they find fresh Indian tracks. To avoid danger, they leave the Trail and travel through the woods.

Not far from their destination, Ben Horne discovers that he has left a piece of equipment at the last stop. Kel offers to go back for it while the men scout the Trail ahead. On his way back, Kel hears shots. He realizes that Ben and Hoke are being attacked by Indians. Although he knows that he should go to help them, his courage fails. When the Indians have left, Kel forces himself to return. Both men are dead. When he discovers that the Indians left their belongings behind, he knows they will return and find him. Kel stumbles into the nearest hiding place—a canebrake.

For a day and a night, he wanders in this jungle-like growth. Finally, half-dead from exhaustion and starvation, he stumbles into a clearing, finds a trapped deer, and survives on its meat.

When he returns to the Trail, he sees a blaze mark on a tree—the sign that white men are around. Encouraged by this, Kel continues his journey. Finally, he sees Fort Logan in the distance. Fearful of being discovered by the Indians, he decides to wait until night before approaching it. For protection, he wedges himself inside a hollow sycamore tree.

His hiding place is discovered by Indians, who post a guard to wait for Kel to drop down. When evening comes, Kel is thirsty and exhausted. When he sees a man coming from the Fort, Kel shouts a warning. In the confusion, Kel drops from the tree, hits the Indian with a stout branch and makes his escape. He heads for the Fort knowing he must get inside quickly or be captured by the Indian. Desperately he circles the Fort looking for the gate. When he reaches it, no one responds to his knocking. He tries to call out, but no sound comes from his parched throat. With his knife, he cuts his arm, wets his swollen lips with his own blood and calls feebly for help. The men in the Fort pull him inside.

Kel recovers quickly but he feels the gnawing shame of not helping the woodsmen and confesses his cowardice to his father. Mr. Bond assures Kel that there isn't any man who "hasn't done something in his life that he wished he hadn't," and reminds Kel of his bravery in saving a man's life outside the Fort.

Thematic Material

This is a story of personal courage—Kel's fears about his cowardice are explicitly shown and soundly resolved. The author has reconstructed an interesting period of history in terms that are understandable to young people.

Book Talk Material

A short introduction to the book could include any of the following situations: Kel's sink hole encounter with the wounded bear (pp. 39–47); Kel's fears about helping the two woodsmen (pp. 87–99); Kel's nightmarish adventure in the canebrake (pp. 100–121); Kel's frightening day in the sycamore tree (pp. 158–165); Kel's desperate attempt to get inside the Fort (pp. 168–175).

Additional Suggestions

For boys and girls who want to read more about Indians, recommend *Moccasin Trail* (Coward, $3.75) by Eloise McGraw, *White Falcon* (Knopf, $3.00; lib. bdg. $3.19 net) by Elliot Arnold and *Captives of the Senecas* (Meredith, $3.50) by John Brick. Together, these titles give a balanced presentation of this historical period. Suggest Rebecca Caudill's *Tree of Freedom* (Viking, $3.50; lib. bdg. $3.37 net) for girls.

Leonard Wibberley, *Kevin O'Connor and The Light Brigade,*
Farrar, Straus, 1957, $2.75

Spun around an imaginary Irish legend, this tale of adventure is written in the light, airy style and historical setting with which we associate the author. Because of his interest in Cecil Woodham-Smith's famous book about the Crimean War, *The Reason Why* (Dutton pap. $1.55), Mr. Wibberley wrote this story for young adults. Although some junior high school girls will enjoy this work, it will appeal chiefly to boys.

In 1853, 17-year-old tenant farmer Kevin O'Connor, a descendant of kings, digs the fall crop of potatoes on his farm eight miles from Galway and worries about reports of another famine. His worst fears are confirmed by Tom of the Three Fingers, a tinker from Dublin, who says that the crops are poor all over Ireland. Although there had been nine O'Connors before the famine of 1846, only Kevin and his elderly mother survive. They welcome their old friend Tom to share what little they have.

Tom recounts the romantic legend of the large black opal, the "Foggy

Dew," which had been brought to Ireland by the Spanish Armada. It had fallen into the possession of Fergus O'Connor, an ancestor of Kevin's. The O'Connors had prospered until Phelim O'Connor, a dreadful man, had inherited it. Both he and the "Foggy Dew" had disappeared. Tom thinks that Kevin may find the opal because he is the seventh son of a seventh son. Tom claims that Kevin could find the gem, although not before he suffers great hardships.

As a tenant farmer, Kevin must pay a yearly rental to his English landlord, Lord Wedcomb. Kevin has managed to earn the money each year by farming, fishing and helping the Galway farrier, Mr. Forster. This year, however, he still lacks four shillings. His only opportunity to earn the money is to win it by lasting four minutes in the ring at the Galway Fair with the strongman, Modor.

With his blacksmith friend, Dan Blainey, Kevin goes to the Fair. Although he has cagily planned to stay away from Modor for the four minutes, Kevin finds that he cannot ignore the jeering crowd. When a young lord on horseback imperiously shouts "the man is a coward. . ." Kevin turns to look; Modor promptly tosses him out of the ring. Kevin, close to tears, tells the gentleman that he has cost him his yearly rent and asks him to dismount and fight. The lord arrogantly rides away.

No one will loan Kevin the money. He learns from Mr. Henshaw, the land agent, that the new lord wants all the tenants put off his property. In a fury, Kevin rushes to confront the new lord, Lord Wedcomb, only to find that he is the young man who called him a coward. Swallowing his pride, Kevin begs for leniency. Lord Wedcomb retorts that he is going to "use the ground to raise some decent beasts, like cattle and horses."

Although Kevin tries to lead a group of neighboring tenants in a revolt, only a few respond. When Tim O'Phelan is shot by the militia, the pitiful group scatters in confusion. Kevin escapes to Spaniard's Hill where Kathleen Neal, the dark-haired daughter of a fisherman, leads him to a cave. After hiding out for a week, he is taken by Mr. Neal to a French ship that will transport him to Dublin. Neal gives him some money and a message for Tom of the Three Fingers.

Kevin realizes that these men are part of a secret rebel organization and that he has been chosen by Tom to kill Lord Webcomb. Kevin resists but agrees when Tom threatens to turn him over to the police. At the last moment, however, he realizes that Tom intends for him to be caught and he runs for his life.

Kevin joins the Tenth Hussars, a British regiment, only to discover that the regiment is commanded by Lord Wedcomb. When he is finally recognized by Lord Wedcomb, he makes Kevin's life so unbearable that Kevin decides to desert.

Before he can leave, his regiment is ordered to Moscow to fight the Russians. After an arduous journey, they disembark in Bulgaria. Cholera breaks out. Kevin nurses his fellow-soldier Peter back to health. While they are on patrol one day, Kevin saves the life of Lady Barbara who has accompanied her brother Lord Wedcomb to the War.

The ineffectual management of the war is common gossip among the soldiers. At their new headquarters in the Crimea, the Tenth Hussars join with other regiments to form the Light Brigade. At the famous and ill-starred Charge at Balaclava, Kevin sees his regiment cut down by the guns of the Turks and the Russians. While trying to rescue Lord Wedcomb, Kevin falls from his horse and loses consciousness.

He awakens to find that he and Peter are prisoners on Count Vinarsky's Crimean estate. The Count is so impressed by the fantastic Charge that he treats them as guests. Kevin tells the Count his life story. To Kevin's amazement, the Count produces the black opal. Phelim O'Connor, who had journeyed to Russia, had placed the "Foggy Dew" in the Vinarskys' keeping before his death. The Count gives Kevin the black opal and helps him return home to Ireland.

With his new wealth, Kevin buys 20 acres of land and marries the beautiful Kathleen. To show her gratitude for Kevin's heroism, Lady Barbara persuades her brother to allow the tenants to buy their land. The "Foggy Dew" has brought good fortune to the O'Connors once again.

Thematic Material

In addition to portraying the resiliency of youth, the novel also contains the themes of man's inhumanity to man and the stupidities of war. Young adults may gain a more personal view of this period of history by reading this story.

Book Talk Material

A review of the English occupation of Ireland and the Crimean War will serve to introduce this tale. The legend of the "Foggy Dew" will intrigue the romantics in the audience (pp. 12–19). Boys will be interested in Kevin's fight with Modor (pp. 24–32) ; his stand against the militia as they destroy his home (pp. 46–53) ; and, his part in the battle at Balaclava (pp. 141–151) .

Additional Suggestions

A story about a young British ensign at the Battle of Carunna, *Greencoats Against Napoleon* (Vanguard, $3.50) by Showell Styles, may be recommended to the same audience. *Victory at Valmy* (Vanguard, $3.50) by Geoffrey Trease will also interest these readers. For those young adults who wish to pursue Irish history, a good title is *The Hound of Ulster* (Dutton, $3.50; lib. bdg. $3.46 net) by Rosemary Sutcliff. It tells the story of Cuchulain, a hero of ancient Ireland. For more on English history, suggest *Meg Roper* (Roy Pub. $3.50) by Jean Plaidy, a story about the Reformation. More mature young adults may want to read *The Cossacks* (Walck, $4.00) by B. Bartos-Hoppner.

2

Overcoming Emotional Growing Pains

ADOLESCENCE can be a period of intense emotional activity, increased anxiety, outbursts of rebellion and hostility, and confused attitudes about love and affection.

In part, achieving emotional maturity is the result of learning the socially accepted outlets for emotions and attaining freedom from the irrational fears of childhood. The capacity to give and receive affection comes with maturity.

Each of the books in the following chapter illustrates some aspect of emotional maturation. In some, decisions must be made in which the long-term result prevails over the immediate gratification of desires. Some explore the resolution of childhood fears. Others show love and affection as necessities for a happy life. Several show how defeat and disappointment, as well as success, can be dealt with objectively and without great emotional distress.

Enid Bagnold, *National Velvet*
Morrow, 1949, $3.00

This story about a girl, her horse and a famous race in England was an immediate success when it was published in the United States in 1939. Part of its charm lies in its use of the English idiom. The family solidarity, the details of horsemanship and the unique courage of the main character combine to make this a satisfying novel. Along with *Smoky, the Cowhorse* (Scribner $2.95; lib. bdg. $2.97 net), by Will James, it remains a perennial favorite especially with girls in intermediate grades and junior high school.

Velvet Brown, a puny, rather fragile-looking child, lives with her family—four sisters and a four-year-old brother—in a small village on the seacoast of England. Mr. Brown and his helper, Mi Taylor, run the local butcher shop.

Velvet relies on her mother for love and understanding for she is very much like her in determination and courage, although very much unlike her in physical appearance. Mrs. Brown, an athletic, muscular woman, was once a famous Channel swimmer.

At one time, all the girls had been interested in horses and racing. However, Miss Ada, their only horse, is old and no longer useful. Velvet still tends her with loving care but her sisters have developed other interests. Velvet, maintaining the Browns' tradition of good horsemanship, enters the local horse show even though she has little hope of winning.

One day while in the center of town, Velvet sees a runaway piebald careening through the village streets. He is a magnificent animal and she wishes she could race him. When the piebald's owner, weary of the horse's rebelliousness, decides to sell him in a lottery, Velvet persuades each of her sisters to purchase a ticket with their hard-earned shillings. In her imagination, Velvet is already seated on the piebald as they fly over the stone fences and ditches at the Grand National, England's most famous race. Even though she knows that girls are not allowed to ride in the Grand National, Velvet knows that she can win.

While delivering a meat order, Velvet meets Mr. Cellini, the elderly owner of a stable of fine horses. Mr. Cellini is impressed by her knowledge and love of horses. A few days later, Velvet learns that Mr. Cellini has died and has left her five beautiful horses. At the same time, her ticket wins the piebald.

Now, with the proud, muscular piebald grazing on a high field, Velvet not only can enter horses in the local horse shows, but she can concentrate on entering the piebald in the Grand National. All her sisters except Edwina, enter the local show, but only Velvet wins.

Mi Taylor is so impressed with Velvet's horsemanship and courage that he joins in her secret plan to disguise herself as a boy and ride in the Grand National. Although there are many complications—the high entry fee, the special riding habit, and the overnight lodging in London —Mi manages to overcome these difficulties. He also resolves the problem of Velvet's disguise by giving her a haircut and masquerading her as a Russian-speaking jockey.

With Mi's whispered advice in her ears, "Think of yer Ma!" Velvet and the piebald start in a field of 20 horses. Mi rushes to the most treacherous jump to wait for Velvet to clear the hurdle, but the crowd is so thick that he cannot see the race. Before he can return to the finish line, the race is over and Velvet has won.

After the race Velvet is taken to the infirmary for an examination. The doctor discovers that she is a girl. When the news reaches the judges, Velvet is disqualified but, to Mi Taylor and her parents, she is still the winner. Velvet becomes a celebrity. Mrs. Brown remembers her own experience after the Channel swim and advises Velvet not to be swept up in the short-lived adulation of the public. Because of the common-sense attitude of her mother, Velvet is able to avoid the sensation-seeking crowds. Later, after some of the publicity has subsided, Velvet begins to enjoy some of the pleasure associated with being National Velvet.

Thematic Material

This sentimental story combines two elements, family love and personal courage. Young girls who love horses will readily identify with Velvet and her struggle to fulfill her dreams. The close relationship between the mother and daughter is well drawn.

Book Talk Material

After giving a brief introduction to the book, one could ask the question, "What would you do?" This may stimulate readers to find the answer in the book. An exciting incident for reading aloud is the description of Velvet's victory in the local horse show (pp. 152–157). A humorous episode—Edwina primping for her boyfriend—is fun to paraphrase (pp. 116–119).

Additional Suggestions

Dark Horse of Woodfield (Houghton, $2.75) by Florence Hightower is a humorous tale that will appeal to the same audience. These readers will also like the warm family spirit in Frank B. Gilbreth, Jr. and Ernestine G. Carey's *Cheaper by the Dozen* (Crowell, $4.50) and Kathryn Forbes' *Mama's Bank Account* (Harcourt, $2.50; text ed. $1.75). Boys may be encouraged to read *Smoky, the Cowhorse* (Scribner, $2.95; lib. bdg. $2.97 net) by Will James as well as the newer title, *Wild Horses of Rainrock* (McKay, $3.95) by William Rush.

William E. Barrett, *The Lilies of the Field,*
Doubleday, 1961, $2.95

This poignant story of a modern-day miracle is a disarmingly simple commentary on the age-old problem of prejudice. The realistic characters, the idealistic moral, and the economical, yet strong prose style combine to give a special quality to this book. Though originally written for an adult audience, this book has particular appeal for a junior high school audience.

Since 24-year-old Homer Smith was separated from the Army at Fort Lewis in Tacoma, Washington, he has been traveling through the West in his station wagon, savoring his freedom. To this Negro from South Carolina, liberty has special significance. He enjoys seeing the countryside and learning that the word "South," as he knows it, is only an adjective out here in the Southwest. He also enjoys the freedom of working when and where he wishes. That is, he does until he pulls his station wagon up at a run-down farm that to his eye seems to need a hired hand.

The three nuns working in the fields scarcely glance up as Homer tells the squat woman at the house that he wants a job. Mother Maria Marthe nods her head, muttering, "Ja," and leads "Schmidt" to the roof. Homer feels vaguely uncomfortable about the way the boss lady says something that sounds very much like, "God is good, he has sent me a strong man." When the lunch bell rings, Homer is further discomforted by the meager lunch of cheese, bread, and milk.

The roof repairs finished, Homer stays for supper and is welcomed by the five women dressed in their religious garb. While vague premonitions tug at his Baptist heart and hunger pangs assail his still-empty stomach, the Sisters bring him a cot and washbucket. He hasn't the heart to leave these hard-working nuns who speak little English. The next day, while thinking there will probably be no pay for his work, the "old mother" calls sharply to him to follow her to the debris-laden foundation of a nearby burned house. Mother Maria Marthe fixes him with her businesslike stare and commands him: "You will build a chapel here." Thoroughly irritated by her dictatorial manner, he promises only to clean out the debris. After supper that evening when Homer asks for his pay, he and Mother Maria Marthe converse by quoting from the Bible. Mother Maria exhorts Homer to cast his lot with them. For all his experience Homer has never been given the responsibility of undertaking and completing a project of any significance.

Despite his many misgivings about the situation, Homer stays. On Sunday he drives the Sisters into the small town of Piedras and eats his first filling meal of the week at the diner while the Sisters attend Mass. The priest personally thanks him for helping these poor East German refugee nuns who are trying to establish a farm for the Spanish orphans of the area. Homer mutters that the "old mother" better get over the idea that God has given him to her.

His feelings crystallize when Mr. Livingstone, a contractor and executor of the nuns' property, tells Homer that the project that Mother Maria Marthe has outlined to him won't work: Homer knows that what Mr. Livingstone means is that it won't work because he is a Negro. He resolves to stay and build the chapel. He gets a job two days a week as a machine operator for Mr. Livingstone. The rest of the time he works on the chapel. In the evenings he provides guitar music, song, and despite his South Carolina accent, gives English lessons to the Sisters.

People begin to bring bricks when they see the chapel's progress; even Mr. Livingstone sends a truck load. But Homer becomes restless. One night after weeks of hard work, he goes to the city for ten days of freedom. Once his money is gone, he finds work on a demolition job. Here he sees some extra bath tubs—he remembers the nuns and their bucket.

He returns to the farm with a bathtub for the Sisters and two colorful glass windows for the chapel. Without a recriminating word, Mother Maria Marthe and the others greet him warmly. Soon everyone wants to help him with the chapel; Homer, far from being appreciative, becomes annoyed because he wants this church to be his private creation.

Finally, the church is finished. Several days before the first Mass is to be celebrated, Homer enters the little church and sits quietly. Then, he silently packs his station wagon and starts East. He is through wandering and is ready to return home.

Not many years later, the chapel—named after St. Benedict the Moor—becomes a famous tourist attraction. It is considered a beautiful example of "primitive" architecture. Inside hangs a picture of a large, dark-skinned man drawn from memory by Sister Albertine. Everyone who knew him speaks of him. Mother Maria Marthe says he was a "man of greatness. . . ."

The book's title comes from the Bible verse which Mother Maria

Marthe tells Homer to read (Matthew 6:28, 29): "And why take ye thought for raiment? Consider the lilies of the field, how they grow; they toil not, neither do they spin: And yet I say unto you, That even Solomon in all his glory was not arrayed like one of these."

Thematic Material

Homer's accomplishment of a heroic deed (further symbolized by the allusion to the classical first name), fits into the young adult's concepts of self-acceptance and the problems of facing a situation realistically. The theme of racial and religious tolerance is an inherent part of the story. The author convincingly shows the hero's inner struggle to control his emotions and to channel them into constructive thought and behavior. It has appeal to young persons who experience the same inner tensions.

Book Talk Material

This story does not lend itself to episodic-type book talks. The reading or paraphrasing of Chapter Seven (pp. 89–92) will make a fine introduction to the book through the use of the author's flashback technique. The situation in which Homer and Mother Maria exchange messages by using Bible quotations could also be read (pp. 32–34).

Additional Suggestions

There are several titles that will appeal to the readers who enjoy this book. They are: *Jamie* (Little, $4.75) by Jack Bennett, the story of a young South African boy forced into maturity by the tragic death of his father; *The Little World of Don Camillo* (Farrar, Straus $3.00) by Giovanni Guareschi, a novel about a beloved Italian priest; and *The Legend of the Cid* (Bobbs, $3.50) by Robert Goldston, the story of the famous 11th-Century Spaniard and his legendary feats of battle. Young girls will also like Margaret Joyce Baker's *Castaway Christmas* (Farrar, Straus, $2.95). For more mature readers an excellent title is *A Bell for Adano* (Knopf, $3.95) by John Hersey.

Walter Farley, *The Black Stallion Mystery,*
Random, 1957, $2.95; lib. bdg. $3.09 net

Although the books in the "Black Stallion" series have little character development and slight plots, they fulfill the young reader's demand for fast-paced, suspenseful action. This accounts for their continuing popularity. *The Black Stallion Mystery* is satisfying by itself, even though it is obviously written as part of a series. Boys and girls in grades four through seven go on to read more in the series.

The day after "the Black" has won the Brooklyn Handicap Race at Aqueduct Race Track, Alec Ramsay, owner-rider of the famous horse, Black Stallion, and his trainer, Henry Dailey, visit a Long Island horse farm to examine three yearlings from Spain. When they see the year-lings, they are positive that these horses and "the Black" have the same sire because of the tell-tale conformation. They are perplexed because they were told by the Arabian sheikh who willed "the Black" to Alec that the sire, Ziyadah, was dead.

Curious to learn the truth, Alec and Henry and "the Black" fly to Don Gonzalez' bull farm in Spain where the yearlings are registered under the sire's name—El Dorado. Alec is concerned when he meets the young, temperamental Don Gonzalez who is consumed by "afición"—a passion for bullfighting. Alec asks to see El Dorado, but Don Gonzalez tells him to be patient. Alec's curiosity leads him to the pasture that night to find El Dorado. As he crosses the field, an enraged bull attacks him. Using his shirt as a matador uses a cape, Alex backs himself to the pasture wall and escapes.

The next morning, bruised and sore, Alec is very angry about his predicament. When he finally sees El Dorado mounted by Don Gon-zalez, he knows that the horse is neither sire to "the Black" nor the three yearlings.

Alec and Henry confront Don Gonzalez who admits that El Dorado is not the sire of the yearlings. He promises to take them to the real owner. The Spaniard betrays them once more, however, and leaves them in a desolate remote mountainous country. As the two men with "the Black" struggle up a dirt road, they glimpse far above them a mysterious horse that seems to glow in the dark.

When they arrive at the top of the plateau, they find a magnificent horse farm with Bedouin tents surrounding a luxurious mansion. Alec is not surprised that his host is Abl-al-Rahmin and his wife, Tabari, an old childhood friend. It is Tabari's father who had willed the horse to him before the sheikh was accidentally killed by "the Black." Both Henry and Alec are comforted to know that Tabari's husband has brought them there because he believes that the ghost horse is the very much alive Ziyadah. Abl-al-Rahmin wants to capture the horse with "the Black's" help. Alec agrees to try and together they set out in the moonlight to catch the ghost horse. The hunt is called off, however, when "the Black" falls into a trap and injures a leg. Henry tells Alec that he thinks the trap was meant for Alec and that they should leave at once.

One night as Alec is reading the old sheikh's books, he smells the strong odor of horse liniment coming from a chimney in the mansion. He follows it to a subterranean secret stall where he finds Ziyadah along with a glittering sequined halter. Alec traces the secret passage to its end—Tabari's bedroom. Hidden in the closet, he watches as she passes him dressed in her riding clothes. He follows her back through the passageway to the pasture gate where, mounted on Ziyadah, she waits for him to follow her. He cannot understand why Tabari wants him to follow, but he saddles "the Black" and follows her lead. During a nightmarish race, Tabari draws a pistol and attempts to kill "the Black"but her shot is wild and kills Ziyadah instead. This terrible act brings Tabari to her senses; heartbroken she flings herself upon the dead horse. Alec pities her, even though he cannot understand her corroding desire for revenge against a horse that accidentally killed her father. He leaves Tabari to tell her husband the truth about Ziyadah and the ruse she devised to get "the Black" to their horse farm. Alec feels sorry for her, but as Henry says, "her husband loves her, so he'll help her."

During the plane ride back to Spain, Alec is intrigued by the mention of a mysterious red horse, Flame, in a Spanish newspaper. His curiosity suggests the next adventure in the series.

Horsemen and Walter Farley fans know that a black Arabian horse is rare. Indeed, Arabian sheikhs seek them for their personal use; this adds particular significance to the title.

Thematic Material

Although all of Mr. Farley's characters are stereotypes, Alec does show emotional development in his final understanding of the unhappy Tabari. The examination of Alec's fears and doubts as he unravels the mystery is important. The love and understanding between a young man and his horse is effectively shown.

Book Talk Material

A brief introduction to the plot is all that is necessary. Alec's unexpected and rugged bullfight in Don Gonzalez's pasture is an exciting incident for retelling (pp. 39–45).

Additional Suggestions

Pagan the Black (Pantheon, $3.00; lib. bdg. $3.19 net) by Dorothy Benedict and *Drinkers of the Wind* (Farrar, Straus, $3.50) by Carl Raswan are both good titles for young readers who can't get enough of horse stories. Eilís Dillon's fine Gaelic stories, *The Lost Island* (Funk, $2.75), *Island of Horses* (Funk, $3.25), and *The Singing Cave* (Funk, $3.25) combine mystery, animals, and good writing. They make suitable reading for the young person who is ready for a more mature story. Older girls may be tempted to try Mabel Allan's *Catrin in Wales* (Vanguard, $3.00), an excellent mystery story.

Harold Keith, *Rifles for Watie*,
Crowell, 1957, $4.50

Rifles for Watie (pronounced way-tee) received the Newbery Medal in 1958. The novel conveys the individual courage, divided loyalties, and human tragedy of the American Civil War. This novel appeals more to boys than girls of the junior high school age.

In the spring of 1861, violence erupts on the Kansas-Missouri border. The farmers on the Kansas side are terrorized by frequent raiding parties of pro-slavery Missouri bushwhackers. On the farm of Edith and Emory Bussey, one of these raids creates a turning point in the life of their 16-year-old son Jeff. He and two of his friends, John Chadwick and Dave Gardner, decide to volunteer for service in the Union Army. All three walk to Fort Leavenworth and join the Kansas Volunteers.

Jeff's first year in the army is something of an anti-climax. It consists of army drills, tiring marches and a few foraging operations. He is well-liked and makes many friends, including Noah Babbitt, a tramp printer from Illinois, and Jimmy Lear, a 14-year-old drummer boy. Jeff also makes an enemy—Captain Asa Clardy, a sadistic army officer who delights in persecuting the boy.

While occupying the rebel town of Tahlequah, Jeff meets the Washbourne family and is impressed with their kindness and quiet dignity. He is particularly attracted to Lucy, the youngest daughter. Lucy's father and her brother, Lee, are both serving in General Stand Watie's Confederate Cherokee Cavalry unit. In conversations with the Washbournes and other Southerners, Jeff realizes that the issues involved in the war are not as well defined as he once thought—there is good and bad on both sides.

At last, Jeff sees combat action. He and Noah distinguish themselves at the Battle of Prairie Grove by manning a deserted cannon and helping to repel the enemy charge. Much to Jeff's amazement, each is awarded the Congressional Medal of Honor.

The inhumanity and savagery of war become apparent to Jeff when he witnesses the execution of a Confederate spy caught behind Northern lines. When the soldier's personal belongings are collected, Jeff discovers that the boy was Lee Washbourne, Lucy's brother.

Because of his fine combat record, Jeff is chosen to act as a spy behind enemy lines. While in Confederate territory, he is captured by a group of Watie's men. To hide his real identity, he volunteers to serve in the Southern army. Just when Jeff has collected information about Southern troop movements, he is stricken with an attack of malaria and is unable to return to his unit at Fort Gibson. Instead, he gives the information to a runaway slave, Leemon Jones, who manages to cross the battle lines and complete Jeff's mission.

During his illness, Jeff stays with the Jackmans, a kindly Southern family who nurse him back to health. While at the Jackmans, Jeff learns that Watie's men are receiving smuggled rifles from Fort Gibson. The identity of the Union officer who is selling them to the South is unknown. Jeff is determined to remain until he finds out the name of the traitor.

After his recovery, the boy rejoins Watie's unit and is welcomed back by the men. When he thinks of the warmth and kindness shown him by his supposed enemies, Jeff feels shame and guilt about the nature of his mission. At one point, he contemplates remaining with his friends in the South. However, an incident occurs which takes the decision out of Jeff's hands.

While engaging in a scouting expedition, the boy witnesses the delivery of a shipment of smuggled rifles. The Northern traitor is his hated enemy, Captain Clardy. Clardy recognizes the boy. To escape a Southern firing squad, Jeff is forced to flee to the North. For days, he endures incredible hardships and many narrow escapes. Finally he stumbles into a Union encampment and is greeted by his friend Noah.

When the war ends, Jeff and his two friends, John Chadwick and Dave Gardner, march back to their homes together. The three men are very different from the young boys who had left four years earlier.

Jeff has many thoughts about the future. He plans one day to return to the South and find Lucy Washbourne. Together, he hopes, they will find happiness and a chance to help reunite the divided country.

Thematic Material

The ugliness and tragedy of war are well presented. In his own actions, Jeff shows individual heroism and great integrity. The central conflict of the novel arises out of Jeff's discovery that people and causes are often a mixture of both good and evil.

Book Talk Material

Some of the incidents that can be used to arouse interest are: The bushwhacker's raid on the Bussey farm (pp. 9–13) ; Jeff and his friends leave their homes to enlist (pp. 15–19) ; Jeff works in a field hospital (pp. 69–72) ; Jeff repays a kindness and returns the "spoils of war" (pp. 77–87) ; the Battle of Prairie Grove (pp. 127–134) and the death of Jimmy Lear (pp. 143–146) .

Additional Suggestions

Other novels for this age group with the Civil War as a background are: Peter Burchard's *North by Night* (Coward, $3.95) , Lee McGiffin's *The Horse Hunters* (Dutton, $3.25) and Frances Browin's *Looking for Orlando* (Criterion, $3.50) . More mature readers will enjoy Hal Borland's *The Amulet* (Lippincott, $3.50) . The hero of *April Morning* (Crown, $3.50) by Howard Fast, set during the American Revolution, faces problems similar to those of Jeff Bussey. An additional suggestion would be Harold Keith's more recent novel, *Komantcia* (Crowell, $4.50) .

Stephen Meader, *Who Rides in the Dark?*,
Harcourt, 1937, $3.50

Stephen Meader's adventure stories for boys show a fascinating variety of settings—from Colonial America in *River of the Wolves* to the Korean War in *Sabre Pilot* (both Harcourt, $3.50) . In *Who Rides in the Dark?*, eventful and exciting action is combined with authentic details of rural New Hampshire life in the mid-1820's. Boys—and some girls—from grades six through eight enjoy this fast-moving story.

One stormy October night, Silas Penny, a team driver who hauls into Boston, picks up orphaned, 15-year-old Dan Drew on a lonely road in New Hampshire. Silas dissuades the boy from heading West to seek his fortune and instead finds him a job as stable boy at the "Fox and Grapes," an inn and way station in Deptford. Although his employers, Skilly Bassett and his wife, are somewhat gruff and distant, Dan soon makes friends with other townspeople—Ben Tucker, the blacksmith, the Crandell family and Ethan Hayes, a boy of Dan's age. Even the taciturn Indian, Gunticus, promises to make a pair of snowshoes for Dan.

Deptford is far from the peaceful spot Dan had imagined. The countryside is terrorized by the Stingers, a gang of hijackers, led by Captain Hairtrigger. One evening, Dan foils an attempt by Hairtrigger to rob the tavern. Although the highwayman escapes, Skilly Bassett is somewhat grateful that he "ain't lost a shillin'."

Winter sets in and something happens which makes the townspeople momentarily forget the Stingers. An abandoned carriage is found in the snow. It contains the body of a young woman and a half-frozen three-year-old child. The Crandells adopt the little girl, Delores, and nurse her back to health.

Shortly afterwards, a mysterious stranger, Dr. Barlow, comes to stay at the inn. Slowly he gains the confidence of the people of Deptford, but Dan's suspicions are aroused when the doctor shows an unusual interest in Delores.

On the pretext of making a sick-call, the doctor visits the Crandells and kidnaps the little girl. A thorough search is made, but Barlow has disappeared as mysteriously as he arrived. Dan uncovers a slim shred of evidence and traces the escape route to a farm owned by the village recluse, Newt Nixon.

Meanwhile the robberies are becoming more frequent and daring. The villagers, in desperation, organize a vigilante committee.

When a stagecoach containing silver bullion is robbed, Dan is sent out to alert the vigilantes. As he approaches Newt Nixon's farm, he accidentally stumbles on the underground hideout of the Stingers; but before he can retreat, the gang takes him prisoner. Dan discovers that Delores is also a captive of the robbers.

When all hope of rescue seems to have vanished, a vigilante group arrives. With the help of Gunticus, they traced Dan to the Nixon farm. All but Hairtrigger are captured.

An all-night pursuit follows. When the highwayman is cornered at last, his horse loses footing, and both horse and rider plunge to their deaths in a rocky chasm.

Before his death, Hairtrigger talks—he had been a doctor. Because of a scandal, he had turned to crime to support his family. When he learned that his wife had died on a journey to visit him, the highwayman had come to the "Fox and Grapes" disguised as Dr. Barlow in an attempt to find his only child, Delores.

Dan and Gunticus share the reward for capturing the Stingers, but an even greater reward comes to Dan. Silas Penny and his wife buy a small farm and adopt Dan. In Silas' words, "I'd like a good stout boy to help around the place and be kind of a son to us." Dan has a home at last.

Thematic Material

Who Rides in the Dark? is a suspenseful adventure story. It contains incidental material on life in early 18th-century America as well. The themes of Dan's courage, growing sense of responsibility and search for identity could also be used.

Book Talk Material

A short summary of the plot to the arrival of Dr. Barlow should be sufficient to tempt readers. The dust jacket, which pictures a highwayman silhouetted against a full moon, can be used to arouse interest. Episodes that might be read to a class are: Dan foils the tavern robbery (pp. 13–16) and his first encounter with Newt's wife, "Big Liz" Nixon (pp. 67–69). The description of a "harvest hum" (pp. 47–52) and a Thanksgiving celebration (pp. 86–90) are excellent examples of Americana.

Additional Suggestions

Other historical novels by Stephen Meader, such as *The Buckboard Stranger* (Harcourt, $3.50) and *Jonathan Goes West* (Harcourt, $3.50) are recommended. The adventure stories of Howard Pease and Armstrong Sperry have appeal and such titles as Esther Forbes' *Johnny Tremain* (Houghton, $3.75), Alonzo Gibbs' *The Least Likely One* (Lothrop, $3.50) or Conrad Richter's *The Light in the Forest* (Knopf, $4.95; lib. bdg. $3.99 net) can also be used.

Sterling North, *Rascal: A Memoir of a Better Era*,
Dutton, 1963, $3.95

Sterling North has written a number of fine historical works for both the Landmark and North Star series. He is probably better known for his novels that recreate life in rural America during the early 1900's. Both *Rascal* and *So Dear to My Heart* (Avon. pap. $0.60), an earlier novel, have this background. Both contain material based on actual experiences of the author. *Rascal*, a 1964 Newbery Award Runner-up, takes place during a year of Sterling North's boyhood—from May, 1918 to April, 1919. Boys and girls from grade six on up are captivated by this delightful book.

At first glance anyone would think that young Sterling's status is ideal. He is only 11 yet almost completely free of parental control. He is allowed to engage in activities that an average boy would be denied— such as, building an 18 foot canoe in the living room, or keeping a veritable menagerie of pets (skunks, woodchucks, several cats, Poe-the-Crow and a lovable St. Bernard named Wowser). There are wonderful swimming and fishing holes close to his home in Brailsford Junction, Wisconsin and, a quiet, gentle atmosphere that is associated with small town life of that time.

But Sterling's life is not always as pleasant as it appears. He is often lonely. His father's permissiveness sometimes approaches indifference, for he is often away on business trips and the boy is left to fend for himself. The boy misses his family, particularly his mother who died four years earlier. His sisters, Theo and Jessica, live away from home and can visit only occasionally. His brother, Herschel, is in the American army fighting in France.

Because both Sterling and his father do not want to hire a housekeeper, the boy has many responsibilities. He does the shopping, cooking and most of the household chores.

A new interest appears for Sterling when he captures a racoon that he names Rascal. He and Rascal become close friends and they soon go everywhere together. When Mr. North takes Sterling on a camping trip to Lake Superior, Rascal comes along as one of the family. At the Irish Picnic and Horse Fair, the two defeat Sterling's rival, Sammy Stillman, in a pie eating contest and witness a thrilling race in which Mike Conway's horse Donnybrook defeats the Rev. Thurman's Model T.

Spanish influenza strikes Brailsford Junction, and Sterling is sent out of town to visit Uncle Fred, Aunt Lillie, and their family. They are hard-working tobacco farmers who are burdened with an enormous number of chores; but, they too, welcome Rascal as part of the family.

Bringing up a racoon, particularly one who is as intelligent and mischievous as Rascal, does present difficulties for Sterling. For example, Rascal is attracted to bright shiny objects, and this eventually accounts for the disappearance of Theo's engagement ring. Rascal is also attracted to the neighbors' sweet corn patches. Warnings are issued and shotguns are loaded. Sterling, in desperation, is forced to build a cage for Rascal and keep him locked up. To complicate matters, Rascal's visit to Sterling's nature-study class ends in disaster: the animal is teased unmercifully by Sammy Stillman and, in self defense, bites him. As a result, a rabies scare hits town. Through the combined influence of Theo and Jessica, father hires a housekeeper who, to say the least, is unsympathetic to having a racoon in the family.

Under these pressures, and realizing that Rascal needs and deserves his freedom Sterling comes to a decision. One night he takes Rascal in the canoe to the far bank of a creek. They wait. Soon they hear the soft crooning call of a female racoon. At first Rascal hesitates, but then runs to join his future mate. The novel ends, "I paddled swiftly and desperately away from the place where we had parted."

Thematic Material

Self-reliance and growth toward maturity are important themes in this novel. A boy's kinship with nature is presented with affection and deep feeling. The historical aspects of the book can also be used.

Book Talk Material

Rascal is filled with wonderful incidents that are ideal for reading during a book talk. A few are: Sterling and his friend Oscar Sunderland capture Rascal (pp. 18–23) ; Sterling has skunk trouble (pp. 29–30) ;

Rascal learns to eat at the table (pp. 32–34); the family searches for Theo's ring (pp. 50–52); the pie eating contest (pp. 126–128); Sterling brings Rascal to school (pp. 138–141).

Additional Suggestions

Other animal stories with similar themes are: Jim Kjelgaard's *The Black Fawn* (Dodd, $3.25), Joy Adamson's *Born Free: A Lioness of Two Worlds* (Pantheon, $4.95), and Joseph Lippincott's *The Wahoo Bobcat* (Lippincott, $4.75). More mature readers may wish to try Gerald Durrell's *The Overloaded Ark* (Viking, $4.95) or Gavin Maxwell's *The Ring of Bright Water* (Dutton, $5.95).

Scott O'Dell, *Island of the Blue Dolphins,*
Houghton, 1960, $3.00

The rare quality of this Newbery Award book lies in Mr. O'Dell's ability to depict the majesty of the heroine's lonely struggle. Based on authentic records, it is the unusual story of an Indian girl isolated for 18 years on an island far off the coast of California. The story is well written and the main character is vividly presented. Girls in grades five through eight are fond of this inspiring story. A young girl's picture on the jacket serves to discourage many boys who would otherwise enjoy the book.

Unable to cope with unrelenting raids by the Aleuts, the natives of the Island of the Blue Dolphins (San Nicholas) decide to leave their home. Although Karana is glad to go, she is troubled. She sees her older sister, Ulape, board the rescue vessel, but not her little brother, Ramo. The motherless 12-year-old girl has seen her father, the chief, slain by the Aleuts, and cannot bear to leave without all of her remaining family. When she sees Ramo running down the cliff path toward the shore, Karana unhesitatingly jumps off the departing ship and swims to shore. She plans to scold Ramo, but she is so happy to be reunited with him that she only bemoans the loss of her yucca fiber skirt.

The ship has left without them and she unhappily surveys the deserted island village now overrun by many wild dogs led by a large, yellow-eyed runaway from the Aleut ship.

One day, Karana lets Ramo retrieve a hidden canoe located beyond the wild dogs' cave. When he does not return, Karana searches and finds his body. He has been killed by the dogs. Karana is overwhelmed by her latest loss and vows revenge.

She struggles daily with the small problems of living and tries to honor her tribe's taboo against females using weapons. Because she needs protection from the menacing dogs, Karana overcomes her superstitions and makes a spear from a tree root.

Time passes slowly. Karana tries to leave the island in the canoe, but it leaks so badly that she returns. Because she is escorted back to the island by a herd of blue dolphins (an omen of good luck to the Indians), Karana renews her resolve to endure. She builds a new home enclosed by a whale rib fence, but the dogs become bolder every day. Karana devotes herself to fashioning a special sea-elephant tooth spear to kill the yellow-eyed pack leader. In the ensuing fight, Karana wounds the large dog, but he escapes. Three days later, she finds him lying wounded in the grass. She carries him home.

Rontu, or Fox Eyes, as Karana names him, becomes a faithful friend helping to dispel her loneliness. The girl and her dog make a happy pair; Karana repairs the leaking canoe and makes a special hooked spear to catch the delicious devilfish (octopus). Only once does Rontu disappear. Karana finds him defending himself against the two dogs who have become the leaders of the pack. After his victory, Rontu never leaves her side again.

Although Karana hides from the dreaded Aleut ship that returns again, she is discovered by a girl from the ship. Karana realizes that the girl, Turtok, is lonely too. Though they do not speak the same language, they become friends. Karana is saddened by Turtok's departure and touched by her parting gift of a black bead necklace.

Time passes more slowly. Karana misses Turtok. She befriends a group of sea otters and her animal family grows. She values her animal friends more than ever.

One day Rontu dies. Karana realizes the years are passing, and that she is no longer a young girl. She thinks more and more of Turtok and her sister, Ulape. But her lonely life continues, bearable only because she has found a replacement for Rontu, his son whom she calls Rontu-Aru.

She has almost given up hope of rescue when a sailing ship arrives. She hears a man's call from the ship. Karana dresses carefully in her tribal raiment, but when she reaches the beach with Rontu-Aru and the birds, the ship has sailed. She hears the man's call nights after in her dreams.

Two years later, another ship appears. Hurriedly, she follows the path to the sound of voices. This time she is not too late.

The title is taken from Karana's descripton of the origin of the island: "Whether someone did stand there on the low hills in the days when the earth was new and, because of its shape, called it the Island of the Blue Dolphins, I do not know. Many dolphins live in our seas and it may be from them that the name came."

Thematic Material

The heroine's control of her emotions and her realistic appraisal of the situation are stressed by the author. The motivations of the Indian girl are examined in greater depth than is usually accorded the fictional Indian. Young adults will admire and respect Karana's fortitude. Her transformation from her early instincts of fear and revenge to her acceptance of love for all living things is well presented. The author's knowledge of the marine life gives added interest.

Book Talk Material

There are several exciting episodes that can be used in book talks: the fight between the Aleut crew and the Islanders (pp. 22–23); the dogfight between Rontu and the two usurpers (pp. 108–111); the attempted capture of the devilfish by Karana and Rontu (pp. 118–120). Interest can also be aroused by a brief outline of the story highlighting Karana's desire for revenge against the dogs followed by the tender description of the rescue of Rontu (pp. 92–98).

Additional Suggestions

The same type of fortitude is described in Elizabeth Coatsworth's *Here I Stay* (Coward, $3.95). Other recommended tales of survival are: *Fire-hunter* (Holiday, $3.25) by Jim Kjelgaard, a story of resourcefulness in a prehistoric setting and *Ten Leagues to Boston Town* (Macrae Smith, $3.25) by Dorothy Butters, the story of 16-year-old Debbie and her brother, orphaned during the American Revolution. Elizabeth Borton de Treviño's *Nacar, the White Deer* (Farrar, Straus, $2.95) will appeal to young girls and boys who enjoy the animal friendships in *Island of the*

Blue Dolphins. Ivan Southall's *Hills End* (St. Martins, $3.75), the story of seven children fending for themselves after a flood, can be used with both boys and girls as an additional selection. More sensitive readers may be tempted to try Ann Nolan Clark's *Santiago* (Viking, $3.25; lib. bdg. $3.19 net), a Newbery Award winner.

James Street, *Good-bye, My Lady,*
            Lippincott, 1954, $4.95

Mr. Street's literary reputation was made with a series of historical novels, some of which deal with the American Civil War. In *Good-bye, My Lady,* he moves to the present and produces a simple and moving narrative that is a special favorite of boys and girls from the upper elementary grades through high school.

Uncle Jesse Jackson, a Mississippi redneck, lives with his orphaned 14-year-old nephew, Skeeter, in a cabin on the edge of the swamp. Jesse is illiterate, somewhat inclined to be lazy, but is well-meaning and honest in his love for the boy. Together they manage by selling cord wood and alligator hides to the local storekeeper, Cash Evans. Their only other friends are the Watsons, a Negro family whose son, Gates, has distinguished himself by attending college. Although Jesse's needs are few and his resources limited, he dreams that one day he'll pay Cash for the buzz saw he bought on credit, and maybe even buy himself a set of false teeth (he calls them Roebuckers), as well as a .20 gauge shotgun for the boy.

For several nights, Skeeter's sleep has been disturbed by a strange sound that comes from the swamp—a haunting laugh unlike anything he has ever heard. When they investigate, Skeeter and Jesse find a strange dog-like animal that escapes before he can be captured. Finally Skeeter, by using boiled meat as bait, is able to catch the strange animal. The animal appears to be a dog yet it laughs and cries like a human being instead of barking. It also cleans itself as a cat would.

The boy adopts the dog and names it Lady. He begins to train Lady for bird hunting. At first the task is hard because Lady kills wantonly, everything from water rats to one of Watsons' chickens. Gradually, the boy's patience and understanding produce results. On a bet, Lady is pitted against Cash Evans' prized Irish setter, Millard Fillmore, and wins the ownership of the buzz saw for Jesse.

News of Lady's accomplishments spreads. People come from miles around to see the strange animal that can laugh and cry, and yet out-hunt any dog in the area.

One day, a salesman brings Cash a classified advertisement from a sportsman's magazine. It reads: "Lost—a Basenji female in the vicinity of Pascogoula swamp in Mississippi . . . Liberal reward for recovery. Old Brook Kennels. Old Lyme, Connecticut." Skeeter is shown the advertisement which refers to Lady. He must now decide whether to keep the dog that he loves and feels is his own, or return Lady to her rightful owner. Heartbroken, Skeeter decides to return the dog.

The man from the kennels, Mr. Grover, arrives and Skeeter bravely delivers the dog to him. With the $100 reward money he buys Uncle Jesse his set of Roebuckers and the .20 gauge shotgun for himself. To help take Lady's place, Cash gives Skeeter his Irish setter.

Jesse is proud of Skeeter and the manly courage that he has shown. In front of everyone at the general store, Jesse allows Skeeter to drink a cup of black coffee—the first privilege of his new adult status.

Thematic Material

The elements of personal courage and sacrifice are more movingly depicted here than in the conventional animal story. The book also has value as a regional American novel that gives many details of life in the Mississippi swamplands.

Book Talk Material

The author's simple but colorful prose style makes passages from the novel ideal for reading aloud: Skeeter's first encounter with Lady (pp. 11–18) ; the drawing up of a grocery list (pp. 38–40) ; the capture of Lady (pp. 87–90) or how Skeeter cures Lady of killing water rats (pp. 130–141) .

Additional Suggestions

Another fine novel by James Street (written with Don Tracy) is *Pride of Possession* (Lippincott, $3.95) , the story of a boy's desire for revenge after a wild boar has killed his father. Robert Ruark's *Old Man and the Boy* (Holt, $4.95) deals with a tender friendship between a young Southern boy and his grandfather. Other titles are: Hal Borland's *The Dog Who Came to Stay* (Lippincott, $4.95) and Jean George's *Gull Number 737* (Crowell, $3.50) .

Ester Wier, *The Loner,*
McKay, 1963, $3.75; lib. bdg. $3.44 net

Ester Wier has written few books in the juvenile field. Her other juvenile title is a fine novel with an Australian setting, *The Rumpty-doolers* (Vanguard $3.95). *The Loner,* a runner-up for the Newbery Award, is a slim, quickly read book which nevertheless leaves a lasting impression on its readers. It is enjoyed by young people in the upper elementary and junior high school grades.

Boy—no one ever called him anything else unless they were angry with him—can scarcely remember his mother and father. He does know that they were migrant workers without security or a permanent home. Boy is now about 14, although no one really knows his age. He has been on his own for several years—hitching rides, begging food and moving with the workers from camp to camp.

In one camp, he is adopted by a young girl, Raidy, and her family. The boy and girl form a close friendship but this ends tragically when Raidy is killed in a harvesting accident in Idaho. Embittered and alone once more, the boy strikes out on his own.

In the Montana hill country he is found near death from exhaustion and starvation by Boss, a gargantuan woman who lives alone in a trailer and tends her large flock of sheep. Boss, too, is "a loner." Her only son, Ben, was killed two years ago by a grizzly. Since this accident, she has lived alone with her sheep and two collies, Jup and Juno. Her only visitors are Tex, the camp tender who brings her supplies, and Angie, Ben's widow, who teaches school in the neighboring town.

Boss pities the poor boy and nurses him back to health. Together they decide to name him David, from the Bible. David feels that he will never be as fine a shepherd as his biblical counterpart. He mistakenly feels that Boss resents him and continually compares him with her dead son. Actually, Boss feels a growing affection for the boy but in her gruff way is unable to communicate this feeling. It is only when David runs away and Boss abandons her flock to find him that he realized she really cares for him.

He still seems unable to prove his worth. On one occasion, he gives the wrong command to the sheep dog, Jup, and nearly drives the flock over a steep precipice. Later, he volunteers to rescue Cluny, the lost maverick of the flock. David accidentally falls down a deserted mine shaft and the rescue must be effected without him.

The only bright spots in his life are the visits of Angie and Tex. Angie begins to teach him how to read and write, and Tex helps him to understand Boss. He tells David how keenly Boss still feels about Ben's death and the fanatical hatred she harbors towards the bear that attacked him. Without telling Boss, Tex teaches David how to shoot, knowing the grizzly has been seen in the area lately.

David begins to live up to his name. He helps Boss rescue part of the flock trapped in a snowstorm and, with Angie's aid, saves Tex when he is accidentally caught in one of Boss' bear traps. Later, while Boss is ill, he tends the entire flock.

One day, he sets out to recover Cluny who has wandered away again. While following her trail in the woods, David sees fresh bear tracks. He rushes back to the cabin, grabs the shotgun and returns to the woods. There David confronts the grizzly and, with a single shot, kills it.

In the spring, Boss moves her flock from the grazing grounds back to her ranch and finds a new herder to take over the wagon. She decides to stay at the ranch so that David can go to school. The two have found a home and, as David says, "Home is a special word to a loner."

Thematic Material

The major theme, apart from David's growth toward maturity, is the interdependence of mankind. Everyone, whether he will admit it or not, wants and needs the love and understanding of his fellow men.

Book Talk Material

There are several episodes in the book that can be used in a book talk: Tex explains to David what a loner is (pp. 33–36) ; David picks his name (pp. 46–48) and David's adventure in the mine shaft (pp. 95–99) .

Additional Suggestions

Anthony Fon Eisen's *Bond of the Fire* (World, $3.95) tells of the adventures of a Cro Magnon boy named Ash. In Paul Annixter's *Swiftwater* (Hill & Wang, $2.75) , the young hero accepts a man's responsibilities when his father is unable to care for his traplines. Other titles are James R. Ullman's *Banner in the Sky* (Lippincott, $3.95) and Ralph Moody's *Man of the Family* (Norton, $4.50; lib. bdg. $4.36 net).

Maia Wojciechowska, *Shadow of a Bull,*
Atheneum, 1964, $3.50; lib. bdg. $3.41 net

In this somber tale, the author captures the rhythm of the Spanish people and the personal conflict of a young boy. Miss Wojciechowska's style reflects the austere grandeur of the Andalusian countryside. It is reminiscent of Hemingway, both in the knowledge of bullfighting and in the deceptively spare construction. This story won the 1965 Newbery Award. Introspective readers in grades six through eight will find the story significant and rewarding. A glossary of Spanish words and bull-fighting terms is included.

Manolo Olivar, the son of the revered dead matador, Juan Olivar, dreads his 12th birthday. On that day everyone in the town of Arch-angel expects him to fight his first bull and follow in his father's footsteps. Nine-year-old Manolo is a coward. He cannot even bring himself to jump off a hay wagon with the other boys or ride a bicycle.

One day, after jumping back in fright from an approaching auto-mobile, Manolo cowers while six village men chide him. They remind him that his long nose—a sign of bravery—is just like his father's. They also remind him that he'd better not jump away from the bull. These six *aficionados* (devotees of the bullfighting art) begin to instruct him. They take him to Cordova and Seville for the Sunday bullfights and on Thursdays they go to the local arena. When Manolo sees his first bullfight, he wants to leap out and rescue the bull, not kill him. Manolo is momentarily swept up in the hysteria of the crowd when the matador dedicates the bull to him, but at the "moment of truth" (the kill), the old terror returns.

He knows that a gypsy fortune teller said that his father would be a great torero. Manolo also knows that no fortune teller came to celebrate his birth. He permits himself to hope that his mother will not let him fight, but overhears her tell a neighbor, "It is his fate." He goes to the local museum to see his father's *traje de luces* (the "suit of lights" or ceremonial costume) and the mounted head of Patatero (his father's killer); he goes to look at his father's statue in the park, but nowhere is there an answer to his overwhelming fear. Knowing that his poor Andalusian people suffer all the plagues of mankind, Manolo realizes that for a few moments in the bull arena they watch Death being cheated and find comfort for their dreary lives. This knowledge does not allay his own fear.

Manolo is certain that the elderly Count de la Casa will have a bull ready for him to fight on his 12th birthday, just as he did for his father. So Manolo starts practicing with his grandfather's cape and *muleta*. He becomes very proficient at the *veronicas, medias* and other bullfighting passes. He begins to gain confidence until the men remind him that the kill is all-important. Discouraged, Manolo finds out from his classmate, Jaime Garcia, that he should practice running backwards to strengthen his leg muscles and should squeeze a ball to develop his sword hand in the same way Jaime's brother Juan does. Although he practices faithfully, his feeling of success is short-lived. When Count de la Casa visits Archangel on Manolo's 10th birthday, he decides that the boy will fight a three-year-old bull at the annual Spring *tienta*. Manolo is desperate: now even the extra year has been taken away from him.

Manolo learns that Jaime's brother has been caping bulls in the pastures at night for practice and decides to visit him. During the visit, Juan's crippled father tells him that he watched Manolo's father fight his first bull at the *tienta*. Manolo feels very sorry for both Mr. Garcia, who wanted only to be a bullfighter, and his son, Juan, who has the same *afición*. He promises to ask the Count to let Juan come to the *tienta*.

He and Juan go to the local arena one night to practice with the bull that the 18-year-old El Magnifico will fight the following day. Manolo is humble before Juan's confidence and dexterity in the moonlit ring. Suddenly, the bull topples Juan. Without hesitating, Manolo rushes in and successfully distracts the bull. While Juan leads the bull back to the stall, Manolo's fear returns. Manolo cannot understand Juan's aplomb, although Juan explains that it doesn't take much to be brave if you have *afición*. He offers Juan his honored place at the coming *tienta*. Though tempted, Juan refuses because he does not want to deprive Manolo of this glorious privilege.

Stricken with fear and guilt, Manolo goes with his tutors to visit El Magnifico who has been seriously gored by the enraged bull. When the local doctor arrives, he commands Manolo to help him treat the wound.

He listens attentively as the doctor laments: the "tragedy is that boys like him (El Magnifico) know of nothing else they want to do."

Manolo finds that he wants to help the doctor and learn to be like him. Before Manolo only knew he was afraid to fight his bull, but now he knows that there is some other work he really wants to do. Still, he has to face the ordeal of the *tienta*. He wonders if his father had been afraid, too. When Manolo asks his mother about his father, she tells him that his father was a man of honor and principle who "would never do anything he really did not want to . . ." Manolo comes to a decision.

After a prayer to the patron saint of bullfighting, Manolo leaves for his "moment of truth."

Manolo generally makes a good showing in the bull ring but realizes that he cannot finish. He tells the Count he can do no better and that Juan Garcia should take over to carry on the tradition for Archangel. As Juan takes his place in the ring, Manolo goes to the stands and sits with his new friend, the doctor. He no longer lives under the shadow of the bull.

Thematic Material

Many adolescents live in the shadow of real or imaginary fears. Resolving them is a large task. The realization that one cannot run away from an emotional crisis is one of the most difficult situations a young adult faces. Both of these points are well expressed and resolved in this story.

The Spanish setting and customs and the bullfighting background bring an added dimension of interest.

Book Talk Material

Manolo's first introduction to a bullfight in the local arena sets the theme of the book (pp. 29–42). Another excellent episode for a book talk is the moonlight scene the night Juan and Manolo cape El Magnifico's bull (pp. 83–95). Similarly, a brief introduction to the plot will create interest.

Additional Suggestions

Two other books that the same introspective readers will like are: Mari Sandoz's *The Horsecatcher* (Westminster, $3.25) and Karen Anckarsvärd's *Doctor's Boy* (Harcourt, $3.25): the hero in the former wants to tame wild horses, not collect scalps; in the latter, to be a doctor. *Old Mali and the Boy* (Little, $3.95) , by D. R. Sherman, is set in India and deals with a young boy's responsibility for a hunting accident. It will appeal to older boys and girls. Older girls will also enjoy Sally Watson's *Witch of the Glens* (Viking, $3.50) about a gypsy lass who is accused of witchcraft. For more mature readers suggest *A Separate Peace* (Macmillan, $3.95) , by John Knowles.

3

Earning a Living

THE ABILITY to earn a living is a great concern to boys —and increasingly to girls—between the ages of 14 and 20. Economic independence is a symbol of adulthood in our culture. The young person must intelligently choose an occupation which is suited to his abilities and which can provide him with a satisfactory way of life. For most jobs there must be some preparation. The training period tends to grow longer as our society becomes more complex and occupations more specialized. The transition from complete economic dependence in childhood to adult economic independence is often difficult and is complicated in this society by considerations of status and position.

The books in this chapter deal with the achievement of economic independence. Some of them identify the duties of the individual as a member of the basic economic unit, the family.

Elizabeth Allen, *The Loser,*
Dutton, 1963, $3.00

This novel is an expansion of a short story that originally appeared in the magazine *Seventeen*. The author stresses the need for young people to examine adult values in a responsible manner so that they may become constructive members of society. Junior and senior high school girls enjoy the story.

Lovely Deitz (Deirdre) Ames has been a winner all her life—beauty queen, star student, member of the best school clique, and a member of the "Jeunes Filles" (a social group from Hoover High). Her fat, poetry-writing younger sister, Lee (Leelah) is not as fortunate.

As Deitz and her mother watch Lee at the Little Theatre tryouts, they notice an unusual-looking boy sitting near them. In this Southwestern town, the "in" crowd wears ivy-league clothes. No one is carelessly dressed like this fellow. Although one of the boys in the back row snickers, "There's a loser," Deitz observes that it doesn't seem to bother this stranger. Deitz and the young man strike up a conversation. His astute criticism of the amateur lighting and scenery impresses her. She is so intrigued by this sophisticated fellow that she scarcely notices when Lee doesn't get the part.

As Deitz drives the family home, Mrs. Ames tells her that the young man is Denny Hawks, who dropped out of Harvard his first year. Mrs. Ames was not able to graduate from college because of financial difficulties. She admonishes her daughters to, "always take advantage of your opportunities." However, she knows that Lee works hard only in the courses she likes and that Deitz refuses to take Honors English because she will have to work harder. She has even decided to attend college for only one year.

Although their father, Dr. Ames, has a successful practice, life has not always been easy. The family has made many sacrifices to finance Dr. Ames' return to medical school to become a specialist. Deitz even took a summer job at a children's camp to help out. Now that they are settled in a comfortable home and Deitz has gotten back into the clique at Hoover High, she is bored. Even her dates with Scot, the "Boy of the Year," are dull; his snobbish attitude has become irritating.

Dietz is thrilled when the off-beat Denny waits for her after school and takes her to The Vine, a college hangout. On the way, he tells her he hand-tooled his jalopy, in spite of his parents' insistence that he drive a foreign sports car. As they drink *espresso*, Denny philosophizes about art and literature and condemns suburban domesticity and middle class values. Disturbed, Deitz realizes that her family fits Denny's description of surburbia.

Despite Scot's opinion that, "He's a hood," Deitz starts to date Denny regularly. They spend a lot of time together during lunch hour, after school and evenings at The Vine. Deitz learns that Denny's parents are trying to force him to wear the right clothes, drive a sports car, play golf at the Country Club, and attend a prestige college. However, he resists and spends his time reading at the library and working out at a gym. He praises Lee's poetry and asks for a copy of one of her poems.

Deitz begins to question the values of some of her frivolous activities. She decides that Denny knows the real values in life.

Denny continues to expound his arrogant attitudes toward conventional standards. One evening as they discuss Deitz' parents, Denny applauds Dr. Ames' decision to return to school so that he could have a more lucrative practice. When Deitz insists that her father went back to school so that he could be a better doctor, Denny laughs and says that he must be stupid. Shaken by his change in attitude, Deitz abruptly tells him that perhaps he's the stupid one. She is sure that she has lost him when he silently drives her home.

To her amazement, Denny appears for their regular lunch date, and persuades her to skip school for the afternoon. Although her mother forbids her to use the car for a week because of this escapade, she gets permission to drive Lee to a local poetry reading contest in which Lee has entered a poem. Denny, who has also submitted a poem, accompanies them. When Lee recognizes Denny's First Prize poem as the one she gave him, she abruptly leaves the hall.

Lee's dramatic departure, an encounter with Mrs. Hawks who tells her that Denny flunked out of college, her mother's statement that he lies, and her father's observation that his soft hands never built a car, combine to shake Deitz' faith in Denny. She goes to The Vine once more with him hoping to resolve her doubts. During the evening, someone congratulates Dietz on her forthcoming job at the summer camp. When Denny ridicules her for working at a kids' camp for such poor pay, Deitz finally realizes that she really doesn't believe in the things he says. She asks to go home.

On the way, Scot bullies Denny into a drag race. Both boys are caught by the police. When his father refuses to help him this time, Denny escapes from the police.

Deitz realizes that everyone must accept his own responsibilities. She notices that her sister is slimmer, and neater and more popular. Deitz decides to make an effort too, and enrolls for the Honors English course. Although things continue to brighten for Deitz, she is upset when she learns that Denny is under psychiatric care in New Mexico. Then she realizes that, although Denny has been a loser, he now will have a chance to win.

Thematic Material

This perceptive story deals directly with the problem of conformity, the difficulty of accepting many of society's codes of behavior and still retaining individuality.

Book Talk Material

The story can be outlined briefly to arouse interest. Suggest Denny's allure, and tell how Dietz succumbs to his pseudo-sophistication (pp. 9–11). A description of the couple's conversation will also be effective (pp. 50–54).

Additional Suggestions

For girls who are interested in poetry, suggest Miriam Gurko's story about Edna St. Vincent Millay, *Restless Spirit* (Crowell, $3.50). Junior high school girls enjoy the following titles about girls who make decisions: Molly Cone's *Real Dream* (Houghton, $2.75), Elizabeth Ogilvie's *Ceiling of Amber* (McGraw, $3.50) and Elizabeth Friermood's *That Jones Girl* (Doubleday, $3.50).

Bob Allison & Frank E. Hill, *The Kid Who Batted 1.000*,
Doubleday, 1961, $3.50

This amusing baseball story is a favorite with boys. Its continued popularity also suggests that the combination of a simple plot, sustained action and easy style is effective in engaging the young sports story enthusiast. Although the characters are stereotypes, the author attempts to show some development in the young hero. Junior high school boys enjoy this wildly improbable tale.

Popoff Pendergast, the Chicks' manager, is desperate. Last year at this time his team was at the top of the American League; this year it is falling apart. Last year's sensational rookie hitter, Longball Wilde, isn't hitting; neither are Pescara, the shortstop, nor Bomber Scoggins, the first baseman. To make it worse, Popoff's best pitcher, Pretzels Litzenberg, has a bad arm.

When the Chicks' owner, Zeke Chickering, demands that Popoff fire his good friend Pretzels and hire two new men, Popoff refuses. Mr. Chickering, warns Popoff that he has two weeks to get the team going or both he and Pretzels are through. Popoff tells Pretzels the bad news. Even though Pretzels tries to joke about it, he knows that Popoff is serious when he suggests that he'd better find a couple of players. He agrees to become a scout.

After two unfruitful weeks scouting the minor leagues, Pretzels lands in Floraville, Oklahoma, a small railroad junction. As he rushes to catch a train to Ten Strike to scout another player, he collides with a young fellow. Pretzels misses the train, but he talks with 17-year-old Dave King and his girlfriend, Luella Mayfield. At Dave's suggestion, the harassed Pretzels hires the only taxi in town to take him to Ten Strike. Pretzels thinks about the boy's level blue-eyed stare as his open taxi passes a large farm a few miles from Floraville. Suddenly, a baseball knocks him unconscious.

When Pretzels awakens, he is staring at those same blue eyes from a bedroom at the King farm. Dave apologizes for hitting him with the baseball. After a doctor's examination and a good sleep, Pretzels feels well enough to take a walk around the King farm. He is curious when he sees Dave grab a bat and fend off some stones that Luella throws at him in mock anger. Dave never misses. He explains that he can hit anything pitched to him, balls or stones. Dave, however, is more interested in showing Pretzels his Plymouth Rock chickens which he hopes some day to raise on a large farm. He and Luella already own a few; all named after characters in Longfellow's poem, "The Courtship of Miles Standish." They plan to enter Dave's most promising thoroughbred, "Govenor Bradford", in the local fair. However, Dave's favorite is the rooster "Hobomuk" because of his intelligence and personality. He will, for example, perch on Dave's bat.

Dave has many talents. In addition to his batting prowess, he cures Pretzels' bad arm by applying his homemade salve, "Chickeroo." There is only one flaw: Dave hits only foul balls. Pretzels goes to Seminole City to scout a noted, but overestimated bush league hitter. However, he returns to the King farm determined to chance a wild plan he has devised to use both Dave's foul balls and the "Chickeroo" salve to

EARNING A LIVING · 63

rescue the Chicks. Dave can't understand why the Chicks want to sign someone who can only hit foul balls.

With "Hobomuk" in tow, they arrive at Sportsman Park in St. Louis to meet the team. Pretzels pitches a winning game and four pitchers fail to strike out young Dave. This convinces Popoff and Zeke to give Pretzels' plan a trial. Although Pretzels starts Dave as a pinch-hitter, his unusual facility for hitting foul balls and getting walks rapidly becomes known. The newspapers applaud "Mister Foul Ball" and the rooster who crows "Cock-a-doodle-doo" whenever the Chicks cross home plate. By the time the team lands in Fenway Park in Boston, Dave is upset by the notoriety. He tells Pretzels that he has to learn how to hit properly. Pretzels worries because if this happens, his strategy will be ruined.

He tries desperately to protect Dave from publicity and finally writes Luella to come.

Meanwhile one of Dave's hits comes so close to the foul line that Zeke Chickering benches him in favor of Longball Wilde. Pretzels tries to cheer Dave by explaining how every ball player dreams of getting to first base every time he's up at bat. Neither this nor the newspaper's box score on Dave's perfect 1.000 batting average, change Dave's intention to hit fair balls. When Clendennin Cabot, the publisher of the local "Clarion," spearheads the "League of Sportsmen in Baseball" movement against the misuse of the walk, Pretzels knows how Dave will react and decides to allow Dave to take batting practice.

Meanwhile the team continues to win as they make their final westward swing of the season. By the time they get back to St. Louis, things become even more difficult for Pretzels: "Hobomuk" is stolen and Zeke Chickering tells Dave he will fine him $1,000 if he continues to practice hitting. "Hobomuk" is rescued, but Dave refuses to stop practicing. Pretzels now realizes that Dave, anxious to be rid of the nickname "Foul Ball Dave", is determined to hit. Pretzels only hopes that Luella can dissuade him. When Luella and Mrs. King finally meet the team in Washington, D.C., Luella explains to the exasperated manager that Dave simply has to hit to prove to himself that he can.

Bomber Scoggins teaches Dave how to hit one kind of pitch. With his keen eye and coordination, Dave learns quickly. When that special pitch comes toward Dave, Pretzels has given him permission to hit it. A month later, in the World Series, Dave hits. He makes a home run that wins the game.

Everyone is delighted until they learn that Dave and "Hobomuk" are returning to Floraville to start a chicken farm. No enticement will keep Dave on the team. It is a sad parting for Pretzels.

Thematic Material

The story is primarily humorous entertainment. However, it does suggest that a glamorous vocation may not always be a sensible goal for a young person. The young hero's determination to work out his life for himself reinforces the young adult's desire to work out his own destiny.

Book Talk Material

Just the idea that a 17-year-old boy hits "at least a piece of every pitch" but never makes a real hit will intrigue prospective boy readers. A brisk retelling of Pretzels' misadventures in Floraville will introduce the story effectively (pp. 11-22). The scene in which the rooster "Hobomuk" begins his baseball career will amuse any audience (pp. 77-81).

Additional Suggestions

Douglass Wallop's *The Year the Yankee Lost the Pennant* (Norton, $3.95) is a good additional title. *Backstop Ace* (Westminster, $3.25) and *Relief Pitcher* (Westminster, $3.25) by Dick Friendlich are also good titles for the same readers. Duane Decker's popular baseball story, *Grand-slam Kid* (Morrow, $3.50) will interest the young adult. Some baseball readers may be tempted to explore the sport of football with Bob Well's hillbilly family in *Five Yard Fuller* (Putnam, $3.50). For those readers who enjoy a humorous story, not necessarily about sports, suggest *The Pushcart War* (Scott, $3.95) by Jean Merrill.

John F. Carson, *The 23rd Street Crusaders,*
Farrar, Straus, 1958, $3.00

John F. Carson's sports novels have become very popular with young readers. They combine fast-moving plots with plenty of play-by-play descriptions. The *23rd Street Crusaders* tells of one man's efforts to salvage a group of boys on the verge of serious delinquency. Boys from the sixth through the eighth grades enjoy this sports novel.

The seven boys had been placed on a one-year probation by Judge Meredith. It was difficult for them to think of themselves as juvenile delinquents. It's true that they had been in a few scrapes but the latest one had been more serious than the boys had realized. They had roughed up Mr. Hayes, the owner of their drugstore-hangout, because he had ordered them out of his store. Now each boy had a police record, and was required to report monthly to the probation officer, Harold Burke.

The boys enjoy playing basketball. All seven try out for their high school team only to find that Coach Utley has already chosen his team from last year's regulars.

They continue to meet after school and shoot baskets at the outdoor West Side Park. A middle-aged stranger watches them intently during these practices. One day, he introduces himself and offers to be their coach. His name is Ed Sorrell. At first the gang refuses—the chief opposition coming from hot-headed Hank Shane. But when Sorrell shows an uncanny knowledge of the sport, the moderates of the group— Joey Gibbs, Tony Sisco, and Danny Shapiro—come around. Soon, all seven accept Ed's offer. Their first problem is to find an indoor place to practice. Ed negotiates with Rev. Gilson of the 23rd Street Church to use his basement gym. As payment, the boys perform janitorial duties. Ed imposes a strict training program on them, but Hank rebels. His hostility towards Ed leads to an ugly fist-fight. Although Ed wins, he handles the aftermath so tactfully that Hank decides to remain with the team and accept Sorrell as his coach.

Joey Gibbs is particularly curious about Ed's past. He learns that Sorrell had a son who had died of polio in a reform school.

Hank chooses the West Side Pirates as a name for the team. Soon members of the church begin to show interest. Frank Gaylord, a member of the Church Board, contributes some basketballs, and the Church Sewing Guild volunteers to make uniforms and warm-up jackets. The ladies of the sewing circle decide that 'Pirates' is too fierce a name for a church group. When the uniforms arrive, the word "Crusaders" is emblazoned on each jacket. The "Pirates" have been transformed into the 23rd Street Crusaders.

Although the boys win their first games, a new crisis threatens to break up the team. At the scene of an attempted robbery, three of the boys find part of a shirt that is identical to one often worn by Hank.

The boy later proves his innocence, but not before suspicion and false accusations have almost destroyed the team's spirit.

Ed brings the team back together and the boys resume their winning streak. Meanwhile, Joey continues his detective work by questioning Johnny Davis, a sports reporter, who knows something of Ed's past. Joey discovers that Ed was the basketball coach at Brayton University. He was made so distraught by his son's death that he left his wife, Martha and moved to the city of Stanton to sort out his thoughts.

The Crusaders win against their own high school team, the Stanton Lions. As a result, when Coach Utley resigns, the Crusaders become the school's official basketball team.

Through his sports column, Davis spreads the news of Sorrell's success with the Crusaders. Martha Sorrell learns her husband's whereabouts and comes to town hoping for a reconciliation. She brings with her a contract from Brayton University that will allow Ed to resume his former position.

Without explanation, Ed leaves town suddenly. The Crusaders are afraid he has returned to Brayton. On the night of their first game as the high school team, the boys are coachless and dispirited. But, during the third quarter, Ed reappears and leads them to victory. He has had many days of thinking, and has at last decided to return to Stanton and accept the position left vacant by Coach Utley. He and Martha will start a new life. As Ed Sorrell says, "There's something about being a Crusader that gets to be a part of you."

Thematic Material

The author shows that young people can overcome certain environmental handicaps if given proper guidance by someone who cares. In this case, a group of potential hoodlums is transformed into a disciplined, fair-minded team. The qualities of good sportsmanship and integrity are stressed.

Book Talk Material

This book can be effectively introduced by giving a short plot summary. Incidents of particular interest are: the boy's day in court (pp. 4–9) ; Sorrell strikes a bargain with Rev. Gilson (pp. 31–35) and the arrival of the new uniforms (pp. 55–57) .

Additional Suggestions

A somewhat similar theme is found in the author's *Floorburns* (Farrar, Straus, $3.00). Other popular sports novels by John F. Carson are: *The Coach Nobody Liked* (Farrar, Straus, $2.95) and *Hotshot* (Farrar, Straus, $2.95). His only excursion into science fiction, *The Boys Who Vanished* (Meredith, $3.50), is also good. William Heuman is another writer of entertaining basketball stories. One of his better books is *City High Five* (Dodd, $3.25).

Tom E. Clarke, *The Big Road,*
Lothrop, 1951, $3.50

An area of American history that has remained relatively unexplored in junior novels is the Depression of the 30's. Perhaps authors feel that the subject is too depressing for young adults. This novel does not spare readers any of the grim details of life during this period, but it conveys hope for a better future. *The Big Road* makes excellent reading for boys in grades eight through ten.

In 1933, the stump farmers on the Olympic Peninsula in Washington State are hard hit by the Depression and 17-year-old Vic Martin is overwhelmed by his family's poverty. His home situation is also far from ideal. Vic bears countless cruelties from a heartless stepfather; and his mother, though sympathetic, is powerless to help him.

When, in an act of charity, his mother gives away the lumber that Vic had painstakingly collected to build a boat, the boy feels completely betrayed. One morning, he wakens before the rest of the family, packs his few meager belongings, and hitches a ride to Seattle to join the Navy.

In Seattle, he finds that the Services are not accepting enlistees. To save hotel-money, Vic goes to an all-night movie theater. When he awakens in the morning, he finds that he has been robbed and that his few possessions have been stolen.

Unable to find work, Vic decides to ride the rails back to his hometown. On the freight train, he meets three hobos—a middle-aged bald man named Curley, and two teenagers, Billy and Blackie. The three initiate Vic into the world of the hobo. They stay in a hobo jungle and teach him the proper techniques of begging for food and money.

Vic soon learns the peculiar code of honor that governs the hobo's life. Unable to face the humiliation of returning home, he accompanies the three as they head east into the interior of Washington State.

When the train stops at Skykomish, Blackie leaves the group "to hit a couple of doors." He returns as the train is pulling out of the station. While trying to board it, he is swept under the wheels and killed. Although the others take Blackie's death philosophically, Vic is so shaken by the tragedy that he decides to leave the group.

At the next stop, Ephrata, Vic is picked up by the town marshal who gives him a bed for the night in the local jail. In the morning, the marshal finds him a job on a farm owned by Mr. and Mrs. Albrecht.

Conditions on the Albrecht farm are much worse than Vic had experienced at home. Mr. Albrecht is even worse than his stepfather, and Mrs. Albrecht is unable to control him. Vic is fired from the job when he refuses to help butcher some wild horses that Mr. Albrecht has cruelly shot. He leaves the farm, unpaid for his two months' work.

Again he hits the rails. Vic is persuaded by a hobo named Heavy to join him and head for California. Once more, Vic's life is an endless round of begging for food, visiting soup kitchens, and living in hobo jungles.

Around the campfire in the jungle at Rosedale, the boy hears an old hobo sing a song, "The Black Sheep." It begins: "Don't be angry with me, Dad, or drive me from your door; I know that I've been wayward, but I won't be anymore." Overcome by loneliness and despair, Vic realizes the hopelessness of his situation. He hops the next freight and returns home.

Thematic Material

The author has written from personal experience about a period in our history that many would prefer to ignore. Vic's decision to return home and face reality illustrates the boy's growth toward emotional maturity.

Book Talk Material

A few incidents that could be used are: Vic is robbed in the theater (pp. 50–54) ; Vic hops his first freight (pp. 57–60) ; he tries his hand at begging (pp. 67–73) and Blackie's death (pp. 114–121) . The glossary of hobo terms and expressions (pp. 251–252) might also be used to arouse interest.

Additional Suggestions

Two other recommended books by Tom E. Clarke are: *Puddle Jumper* (Lothrop, $3.50) and *Alaska Challenge* (Lothrop, $3.50). In addition, use Peter Dawlish's *The Boy Jacko* (Watts, $3.50), the story of a boy's struggle to claim his inheritance, and the excellent collection of short stories edited by Albert Tibbets, *A Boy and His Dad* (Little, $3.95). More mature readers might try E. R. Braithwaite's *To Sir, With Love* (Prentice-Hall, $3.95), or William Canaway's *Find the Boy* (Viking, $4.00).

Doris Gates, *Blue Willow,*
Viking, 1940, $3.50; lib. bdg. $3.37 net

Since its appearance in 1940, *Blue Willow* has been one of the best and most-loved stories for young girls. It is a special favorite with girls from the fourth through the seventh grades.

Janie Larkin would be the last person to admit that she is lonely. In her proud and independent way, she tries to give the impression of self-sufficiency, but inwardly she feels the lack of many things that other ten-year-olds have. Since the time that her father was forced to abandon his farm in the Dust Bowl, the Larkins—father, stepmother and Janie— have lived the nomadic life of migratory workers. Janie misses the stability of a permanent home and the warmth of lasting friendships. She has no dolls or toys, but she does have one possession which she prizes above everything else. It is a plate with blue willow trees painted on it that had belonged to her mother.

Mr. Larkin and his family come to the San Joaquin Valley to work on the cotton harvest. They move into an abandoned clapboard shack a few miles from the work camps. They meet their neighbors from across the road, a Mexican family named Romero. Janie becomes friends with their ten-year-old daughter, Lupe.

The Romeros take Janie with them to the County Fair. It is a magical day for the little girl. She inspects all the animals, spends time reading in the library booth and, courtesy of Lupe, even has a ride on the merry-go-round. With the nickel that her mother gave her to spend, Janie decides to buy something that she can share with everybody—a package of chewing gum.

The Larkins receive Bounce Reyburn, the foreman for Mr. Anderson, the owner of the land where the Larkins are staying. In a surly, unpleasant way, he demands rent for the miserable shack. Rather than face the problems of moving on, Mr. Larkin pays the man.

One day, when there is no work in the cotton fields, the family goes fishing in a nearby stream. They catch several catfish and enjoy a wonderful fishfry. Janie wanders off, leaving her parents dozing under a tree. She sees a beautiful farm and meets its owner, Mr. Anderson. Although she says nothing, Janie realizes that this must be their landlord. Far from being the gruff, uncharitable person she had expected, Mr. Anderson appears to be very kind. He gives Janie a dozen fresh eggs to take home to her folks.

Janie's good fortune continues. She enrolls in the Camp Miller School, where her teacher, Miss Peterson, takes a personal interest in her. Also, her father wins seventy-five dollars, the second prize in the Wasco County Cotton Picking Contest. With this money, the Larkins spend a glorious day in town. They buy four second-hand tires for the car and a beautiful winter coat for Janie. As a special treat they have dinner in a restaurant. If her father could only find steady work so that their family wouldn't have to move on, Janie would be the happiest girl in the world.

But trouble develops. Mrs. Larkin becomes dangerously ill with pneumonia. She is unwilling to call a doctor because of the expense. Janie is so alarmed that she walks into town to see the Romeros' doctor. She explains the situation to Dr. Pierce and offers him her blue willow plate if he will come to see her mother. He doesn't take the plate, but he does care for Mrs. Larkin until the crisis is passed.

Harvesting is over, and the Larkins have to move again. Although they have very little money, they hope to stay a few days longer so that Mrs. Larkin can completely recover.

Bounce Reyburn reappears and demands more rent. Because they are leaving soon, Mr. Larkin refuses to pay. An ugly quarrel develops. Janie gives Bounce her blue willow plate as partial payment.

A few days pass. There is so little money left that Mr. Larkin says they must move immediately. Janie, afraid that she will never see her plate again, visits the Andersons and requests one last look. Mr. Anderson knows nothing about the blue willow plate. He is also completely unaware that Bounce has been collecting rent from the Larkins. The dishonest foreman has been pocketing the money. Mr. Anderson fires Bounce and asks Mr. Larkin to take his place. Janie is overjoyed.

Mr. Larkin builds an adobe cottage complete with running water and a fireplace. When the Larkins move in, they put Janie's blue willow plate in a special place of honor on the mantlepiece.

Thematic Material

Children often take for granted many of the simple things that Janie longed for. Through identification with the heroine, young people can develop understanding and sympathy for those less fortunate than themselves. In spite of their poverty, the Larkins represent a strong family unit built on love, mutual respect, and the ability to sacrifice for the sake of others.

Book Talk Material

After a brief introduction to the plot, one could read one of the following passages: Janie meets Lupe (pp. 16–20) ; she shows Lupe her willow plate (pp. 22–25) ; Janie at the fair (pp. 55–61) ; the fishing trip (pp. 69–72) ; Janie awaits her new school teacher (pp. 87–90) .

Additional Suggestions

Two other recommended novels by Doris Gates are: *Cat and Mrs. Cary* (Viking, $3.50; lib. bdg. $3.37 net) and *Sensible Kate* (Viking, $3.50; lib. bdg. $2.96 net). Additional titles, though slightly more difficult, are: Thomas Fall's *My Bird Is Romeo* (Dial, $3.25), Eleanor Farjeon's *The Glass Slipper* (Viking, $3.00) and Neta Frazier's *One Long Picnic* (McKay, lib. bdg. $3.59 net) .

Mina Lewiton, *Elizabeth and the Young Stranger,*
McKay, 1961, $3.25; lib. bdg. $2.96 net

Mrs. Lewiton is noted for her skillful presentation of social themes. Her sensitive and tactful approach is the hallmark of her style. This title explores prejudice in a small community. Junior high school girls will sympathize with the heroine's plight.

Elizabeth Innis, a senior at the Camden Hollow High School, has hopes of attending college and becoming a doctor. Her widowed father, Drew Innis, an attorney, seems unaware of his daughter's aspirations as he leaves many of the practical problems to their housekeeper, Constance. Constance has old fashioned ideas about education and doesn't think Elizabeth should go to college. Elizabeth resents her narrow and petty attitudes, even though she must obey her.

Elizabeth and her boy friend, John Bye, go to the Camden Hollow Carnival, and are joined by Eunice Bigley, a classmate. Everyone feels sorry for Eunice because her father disgraces the family by getting drunk and stealing. Eunice mentions that a new family from Denmark has moved to town and that their son, Andre, will be in their class.

The following Monday, Andre Hofner enters school. Although he tries to participate in class activities, the students make fun of his foreign accent. When Elizabeth retells the incident at home, Constance is unsympathetic, and reveals suspicious attitudes towards "foreigners."

Andre proves his ability by writing a superior composition for the new English teacher, Miss Van Alen. Elizabeth feels an increasing respect for this young man who wants to be a doctor.

When Andre unexpectedly comes to borrow a book from Elizabeth, she consents to go for a walk with him. Andre tells her how lonely he is and of his family's hardships in Europe during World War II. They meet often, but Elizabeth has not summoned the courage to tell her father.

One afternoon, a meddlesome neighbor, Lois Case, reports to Constance that Elizabeth is seeing a great deal of Andre. Lois also intimates that Andre is responsible for the theft of her missing garden tools. When Constance tells this to Mr. Innis, he is furious and won't listen to Elizabeth's explanations. He threatens to prosecute Andre on charges of theft, if Elizabeth doesn't stop seeing him. Numbed by her father's injustice, Elizabeth gives in.

One night, Elizabeth meets Miss Van Alen who tells her that Eunice's father was responsible for the disappearance of Lois Case's garden tools. Elizabeth begs Miss Van Alen to come home with her and explain this to her father.

Miss Van Alen not only clears Andre's name, but also persuades Mr.

Innis to recommend Eunice for a summer job. Mr. Innis tells Elizabeth that she will attend college in the fall.

At a party, it is announced that Andre has won a scholarship to Harvard. At last Elizabeth can introduce Andre to her father.

Thematic Material

Irrational prejudice is well illustrated here. This story stresses the theme that everyone should be judged according to his individual worth.

Book Talk Material

The central theme of the novel is revealed in Andre's first reception in class (pp. 26–28). The scene in which Elizabeth meets the Hofners reinforces the theme (pp. 79–85).

Additional Suggestions

Girls will enjoy Helen Doss' *Family Nobody Wanted* (Little, $4.95), and Lore Segal's *Other People's Houses* (Harcourt, $5.95). Both boys and girls will like Emily Neville's *Berries Goodman* (Harper, $3.50; lib. bdg. $3.27 net), the story of two suburban boys who encounter prejudice. More mature young people will enjoy reading Dick Gregory's *nigger: An autobiography* (Dutton, $4.95).

K. M. Peyton, Pseud., *The Maplin Bird*,
World, 1965, $3.75

Kathleen and Michael Peyton's knowledge of the sea, command of historical detail, and lively style combine to make this a fine novel for young adults. As in their earlier book, *Sea Fever* (originally published in England as *Wind Fall*), the added element of a well-sustained mystery increases the interest for young readers. Girls in grades six through nine like this story.

Although 16-year-old Toby Garland and his younger sister Emily work very hard for their uncle, Gideon Boot, they are mistreated. Their parents died in a cholera epidemic that ravaged England in 1850 and, since that time, their life has been nothing but work and punishment in the Boots' Bardwell home. The youngsters remember better times in their sea-side cottage and aboard their father's fishing smack, My Alice. After a brutal beating, Toby tells Emily that they must leave. He plans to float My Alice off the mud flats on the highest Spring tide and sail down the river to Southend, where he hopes to get help from a friend of his father's. Toby overhears the Boots plotting to steal his smack. He decides to leave that night. Emily hurriedly gathers her few belongings and the two escape aboard My Alice.

The following morning they approach the quiet port of Southend, famous for its mile-wide mud flats, the Maplins. When Toby discovers that his father's friend is dead, Emily tries without success to find a job in Southend. Toby meets a rough young fisherman, Dick, whose family hires him to work on their fishing smack.

One night, My Alice comes to the rescue of a trading ketch that has run aground during a storm. The mate explains that while his boat was foundering it had been boarded and robbed by a local pirate, the "South End Shark." Toby and Emily see in the distance the silhouette of the pirate's black-hulled yacht. They help rescue the occupants of the grounded boat. During this rescue, the villagers line the shore. One of them—Mrs. Seymour, a wealthy landowner—brings the survivors to her big house on the hill. When Mrs. Seymour hears Emily's story she hires her as a housemaid.

Emily soon adjusts to her new environment. She meets Mrs. Seymour's two children—her daughter Selina, who is bored with life and her son Adam, a handsome but somewhat mysterious young man. Emily notices that Adam has a model of a black-hulled ship, The Maplin Bird, in his room.

One evening, when a customs man calls at the Seymour home, Emily helps Adam to avoid him. The following morning, she finds a charred piece of The Maplin Bird in the smoldering fireplace.

A month later, Emily spends an enjoyable day with Toby and Dick. Dick tells her that The Maplin Bird is a smuggler's yacht that has been running brandy from France. As Emily walks back, Adam rides alongside and escorts her to the gatehouse. Emily is fascinated by the romantic Adam; she is elated to think that she alone knows he's the "South End Shark."

A few nights later, Adam returns after one of his escapades. The following morning, Emily watches a revenue cutter tow The Maplin

Bird up the river. Unknown to her, Adam has arranged for Toby to free The Maplin Bird from the cutter. Toby almost succeeds, but two shots from the cutter sink the yacht.

The customs men collect enough evidence to identify Adam as the smuggler. Emily helps him to escape once more. Before he leaves he asks her to forgive him. Emily thinks he has gone forever.

Toby, who has broken his leg trying to free The Maplin Bird, is brought home to the Seymours' to recuperate and Selina, at last, finds something worth while to do—she nurses Toby back to health.

Adam returns home once more. He persuades Toby to take him to safety in France in My Alice. Confused by her infatuation for Adam and concern for Toby, Emily decides to accompany them. After a grueling attempt to cross the Channel in a storm, My Alice, taking water dangerously, scurries into Ramsgate on the Kent coast, closely pursued by a revenue cutter. The authorities arrest Adam. Toby and Emily watch sadly as Adam sails away with his jailers.

They return to Mrs. Seymour for help. Mrs. Seymour rehires Emily as a day worker and gives the youngsters a cottage of their own. Emily realizes what a lovesick, muddle-headed girl she has been. She now feels confident about the future.

Thematic Material

Family relationships and social conditions of the period are examined through the development of the main characters. The book will give young people an excellent picture of an adolescent's struggle for economic independence. In addition, the difference between romantic infatuation and genuine love is stressed in the plot.

Book Talk Material

After a brief introduction, read the section in which Emily and Toby come to the rescue of the trading ketch (pp. 58–59). Young adults will sympathize with Emily's job hunting (pp. 48–51), as well as Selina's desire to do something useful (pp. 108–109).

Additional Suggestions

Readers who like the fine brother and sister relationship in this story will enjoy Paul-Jacques Bonzon's *The Orphans of Simitra* (Criterion,

$3.50) , the story of a young boy's search for his sister. Boys will also like K. M. Peyton's *Sea Fever* (World, $3.50) , Farley Mowat's *The Black Joke* (Little, $3.75) and Richard Armstrong's *Cold Hazard* (Houghton, $3.00) ; each title is an excellent sea adventure. Rachel Varble's *Three Against London* (Doubleday, $2.95) is the story of three young people who seek their independence in 17th-century London. It has appeal for girls who like historical fiction.

Louisa A. Shotwell, *Roosevelt Grady,*
World, 1963, $2.95; lib. bdg. $2.88 net

Louisa Shotwell has created a touching and realistic picture of a Negro family's struggle to escape from the life of the migrant worker, and establish themselves in a permanent home. This book is popular with students from grades four through seven.

Nine-year-old Roosevelt Grady and his mother share a secret. Their secret is their hope that one day the Gradys will have a home of their own. Four years ago, they had been forced off their little farm in Georgia and since then the family has roamed the county as part of Cap Jackson's crew of migrant workers. The family has grown to six: Mamma, Papa, Roosevelt, the baby Princess Anne, five-year-old Matthew, who has a lame foot and, seven-year-old Delois, whom everyone calls Sister.

At one camp, Quimby's Quarters, Roosevelt has a wonderful new experience—he is given a bed of his own. It is a hammock that his parents find in the attic in which they are living. Also, Roosevelt encounters Manowar, a young orphan slightly older than himself, who works in another crew. Manowar is a cheerful boy who is extremely popular with the other children. At first, Roosevelt is jealous of Manowar's popularity but, gradually, they become close friends.

A few weeks later their paths cross again at another camp called Willowbrook. Manowar and Roosevelt attend a special three-week school session arranged for the children of migrant workers.

Roosevelt confides in Manowar his secret longing that his family will someday be able to settle down. Manowar tells Roosevelt about a little town close by called North Galilee where, at Eliot's Bus Camp, families live in converted buses for only $3.50 a week. To Roosevelt, this sounds like a perfect home. Together, the boys write a letter to the mayor of North Galilee requesting year round work for Mr. Grady.

Although the reply is not encouraging, the Gradys, quite by chance, do go to North Galilee with Cap Jackson's crew to pick pears. They move into one of Mr. Eliot's converted buses. While there Mr. Grady is able to find a position in the local fertilizer plant. The job will last at least through the winter. This means that the family will now be able to have Matthew's foot treated, and Roosevelt will be able for the first time, to attend a regular school. Roosevelt's happiness is complete when Manowar is adopted by the Gradys.

The family celebrates by going to see the Labor Day parade. Only Mrs. Grady stays behind. She has a pleasant and important task to complete—the making of window curtains for the Grady's new home.

Thematic Material

Roosevelt Grady illuminates a social problem in American life that is often forgotten—the lot of the impoverished migrant worker. Although the Gradys have few material possessions, the family displays an inner strength built on bonds of love and integrity, which help them to endure and finally to overcome their problems.

Book Talk Material

This short novel is filled with incidents that would be excellent for use in a book talk. Some are: Mamma tells the children about home in Georgia (pp. 26–31) ; Roosevelt's bed at Quimby's Quarters (pp. 37–39) ; Manowar tells a "whopper" (pp. 47–52) ; the Gradys talk about the Promised Land (pp. 64–67) and Matthew meets a neighbor, Mrs. Clay (pp. 79–82) .

Additional Suggestions

Girls who enjoy *Roosevelt Grady* should also like Lois Lenski's *Cotton in My Sack* (Lippincott, lib. bdg. $4.29 net) and *Prairie School* (Lippincott, lib. bdg. $4.29 net) . G. Faulkner and J. Becker's *Melindy's Medal* (Messner, $2.95) or Jean Little's *Mine for Keeps* (Little, $3.95) might also be suggested. With boys, use Jesse Jackson's *Call Me Charley* (Harper, $2.95; lib. bdg. $2.92 net) or *Charley Starts from Scratch* (Harper, lib. bdg. $2.92 net) .

James L. Summers, *Senior Dropout,*

Westminster, 1965, $3.50

Mr. Summers has added another fine title to his long list of popular young adult books. This novel combines clarity of expression, well drawn characters and a timely subject. Boys and girls in junior and senior high school will enjoy this story.

As he leaves San Luis Obispo by bus to join his father and new stepmother in Milwaukee, 17-year-old Lon Renton remembers his mother's tragic death two years ago, and his father's decision to enter him in Grayrock Military Academy.

At first, Lon was lonely under the strict regime of the Commandant, Captain Dart, but gradually he learned to hide his feelings. He has decided that there are only two ways to survive—to be stupid or pretend to obey. At the Academy, he had become successful in following the latter course, but now he is apprehensive about fitting into his father's new life.

Mrs. Thelma Renton (just the kindergarten teacher-type he had imagined) meets Lon at the Milwaukee bus depot. She tries to be friendly and understanding but Lon, conditioned to be aloof and distant, doesn't respond to her kindness.

Matters do not improve when Mr. Renton comes home. Lon feels divorced from his father who now seems much older and no longer the golden man of his memories. His father seems more concerned with Thelma's adjustment to the new situation than Lon's.

At Thelma's urging, Lon goes sightseeing in her car. During this trip he meets Hermine Mannheim, a pretty girl who lives nearby. They are attracted to each other immediately. On their first date, Hermine tells Lon about her old-fashioned, "very German" family. Before she leaves, she says that she loves him. For the first time since his mother died, Lon believes completely what someone has told him.

When he returns home, his father is annoyed that Lon has used Thelma's car and forbids him to drive it again. Lon is dumbfounded; he realizes that his father completely misunderstands Thelma's attitude toward him.

Lon and Hermine continue to date; he confesses that he loves her, too. Once school starts, Lon joins the neighborhood crowd—the "Greenfields", as the boys call themselves. They agree that Lon is lucky to have the bright and beautiful Hermine for a steady. Lon does not do well at school. He has lost interest and wants his freedom.

Lon, feeling uncomfortable at home, spends much of his time at the Mannheims'. His father accuses him of never bringing his friends home, but Thelma defends him. For once, Lon feels that Thelma understands him. However, when he discovers books about adolescent behavior in her bedroom, he knows that Thelma thinks of him as a disturbed young boy.

Things go from bad to worse. Lon becomes even more dependent on Hermine's affection and respect. He decides to drop out of school and get a job in order to marry her. When he tells her of his plans, she hesitantly accepts his proposal.

Lon starts job-hunting over Christmas vacation, but encounters so much opposition from Thelma and his father that he moves out and rents a dingy room. He finally gets a junior time-keeper job in a furniture factory and quickly learns the dull and uninspiring job routine. Hermine tries to persuade Lon to return home, but he refuses.

Gradually, Lon begins to realize that his present job will lead nowhere and that he has misunderstood the intentions of those around him. He goes home, knowing that his attitude has changed and that things will be better.

Thematic Material

The conflict between generations is well developed through the hero's rebellious yet emotionally dependent nature. The need that young adults feel for economic independence is well explored. Mr. Summers, a native of Milwaukee, describes the city effectively.

Book Talk Material

Lon's introduction to Captain Dart and Grayrock will set the theme (pp. 9–15). A description of his adjustment to military academy life can also be used (pp. 15–17). Lon's first meeting with Hermine will interest the girls (pp. 40–48). Other passages to read or paraphrase: Lon tells his parents about dropping out of school (pp. 120–123); his search for a job (pp. 136+); he leaves home (pp. 143–149).

Additional Suggestions

Jeannette Eyerly's *Drop-Out* (Lippincott, $3.25), in which a sensible attitude prevents an unfortunate early marriage, will appeal to girls.

Other titles by Mr. Summers, *Trouble on the Run* (Westminster, $3.25) and *The Trouble with Being in Love* (Westminster, $3.25) are recommended. For the more mature reader, *West Side Story* (Random, $3.95) by Leonard Bernstein and others and *Durango Street* (Dutton, $3.75) by Frank Bonham deal with contemporary problems of minority groups.

Lee Wyndham, *Candy Stripers,*
Messner, 1958, $2.95

Miss Wyndam has written several career novels, primarily about glamorous occupations like modeling and ballet dancing. In *Candy Stripers,* she has combined a frothy girl's story with interesting details about the duties of junior hospital aides, called Candy Stripers. Girls in the seventh and eighth grades enjoy this novel. It can be particularly valuable with reluctant readers in this age group.

Fifteen-year-old Bonnie Schuyler is not looking forward to the summer. She will be spending it at home, in Hamilton, New Jersey, because her father has rented their summer cottage at the shore. Her boy friend, Rock Caldwell, is leaving town to be a camp counselor, and her best friend, Anne Moore, has moved away.

Bonnie has almost resigned herself to a dull, dismal summer when her friend, Nancy Wheeler, suggests an alternative—to join the junior volunteer aides at Hamilton Medical Center. To escape boredom, Bonnie becomes a Candy Striper.

In general, the trainees are a pleasant group: Pixie Chase, who lives up to her nickname; shy, quiet Carol Kent; slow but well-meaning Denise "Dense" Chapman; and dedicated Ginny Lou Elkin. Ony Mavis Watts, who looks at the program as a glorified man-hunt, is unpleasant.

At first, the glamor of the situation interests Bonnie. She is impressed with her dedicated teachers, Mrs. Brent and Mrs. Collins. Each evening, Bonnie's family, particularly her 12-year-old sister Laura, eagerly await the retelling of the day's experiences at the hospital.

When she begins floor work, Bonnie discovers that being a Candy Striper involves tiring and sometimes monotonous chores. Lacking the dedication of her co-workers, she becomes somewhat discouraged and depressed. Then she meets David Adams, a young, handsome lab worker who is spending his college vacation working at the hospital. David seems to go out of his way to be kind to her. Believing that David is genuinely attracted to her, Bonnie falls in love with him.

One day, while on duty, Bonnie tries to break up a pillow fight between Mavis and her friend, Paula Palmer. They are discovered by Miss Winters, the stern fourth floor supervisor. Before explanations can be given, all three are dismissed. Only now does Bonnie realize how much her life at the hospital means to her.

Laura pieces together the facts behind the dismissal and attempts to correct the injustice. She visits the hospital and tells her story to Mrs. Collins. An investigation is started and Bonnie is reinstated.

A series of explosions destroy a local chemical plant, and emergency cases stream into Hamilton Medical Center. Bonnie proves her worth by unselfish and untiring work with the injured. Even Miss Winters admits that she was wrong in her first appraisal of Bonnie.

Although she is now happily adjusted to her work, Bonnie faces a crushing disappointment. While out driving with David, she blurts out her feelings towards him. In a kindly manner, David explains that he is fond of her as he would be towards a younger sister.

At the end of the summer, Bonnie attends the capping ceremony for the senior Candy Stripers. Once more, she is impressed with their dedication and sense of purpose. When she remembers all of her own experiences at the hospital, she realizes how much she has learned in these last two months. Although she is still uncertain of her eventual career, Bonnie knows that for now she wants to remain a Candy Striper.

Thematic Material

Candy Stripers manages to avoid a major pitfall in the "career" novel—the occupational material is not contradicted by the plot. Bonnie's duties remain basically those that would be entrusted to a Candy Striper. The novel is of value as an introduction to a service vocation.

Book Talk Material

A short plot summary will create interest in reading this novel. It is usually unnecessary to read or retell specific incidents in the story. However, one could use: Bonnie's first encounter with Miss Winters (pp. 69–72) or the pillow fight incident (pp. 103–105) .

Additional Suggestions

It is not difficult to find additional fiction and non-fiction about nursing that would be suitable for this age group. Here are three suggestions: Eloise Engle's *Dawn Mission* (Day, $3.50), Sheila Russell's *A Lamp Is Heavy* (Lippincott, $5.00), and Lois Hobart's *Elaine Forrest, Visiting Nurse* (Messner, $2.95).

4

Understanding Physical Problems

An INDIVIDUAL'S greatest physical growth occurs
during the first six months after birth and in the period of adolescence.
The advent of puberty produces many problems. Young people are
preoccupied with their physical characteristics. Girls are particularly
concerned with attractiveness, while boys are more conscious of prowess
and athletic ability.

The adolescent must learn to take pride in his physical self, his size,
weight, and other features. He must understand and accept his
strengths and limitations.

Young people must also develop sympathy and understanding for
those around them who have special physical problems. Physical differences, whatever their cause, should be accepted, and young people
should seek knowledge of how physical handicaps can be overcome.

In the following chapter books have been included to illustrate how
young people face conflicts related to physical maturation. Some involve
the common problems of adolescent growth, while others deal with
more serious themes such as adjustment to severe physical handicaps.

Robert Burch, *Skinny*,
Viking, 1964, $3.00; lib. bdg. $2.96 net

This portrait of a young boy who calmly accepts the adversities of his
life is reminiscent of another moving book, *The Yearling* (Scribner,
$4.50; text ed. $4.20). The author has written a regional story of great
simplicity about a young boy's search for a home. Boys and girls in
grades five through eight like this unaffected story.

Ever since his pa died, 11-year-old Skinny—he'd never been called anything else—has been helping Miss Bessie run her hotel in a small Georgia town. He likes to help around the hotel, doing dishes, patching the roof and welcoming new arrivals. Occasionally, he is embarrassed when someone questions him and finds out that he can't read. He explains that he never got beyond the first grade because his mother died a long time ago and, when his father didn't feel well, he had to work on the farm. Mr. Grice, the Sunday School Superintendent, says Skinny's father drank; Skinny says it isn't so. Now he is too big to go back with all those little people. Besides, he has a lot of fun helping Peachy the cook and Roman, the good-natured handyman who tells him stories about what it is like on the Georgia Chain Gang. Miss Bessie wants to adopt Skinny but the County Board won't let her unless she is married.

For excitement, Skinny goes to the annual watermelon-cutting. The pleasure of the games with his friends and the anticipation of his favorite food are cut short when he learns from Mr. Grice that his lost dog is back at the farm. He hikes out to the ramshackle farm house. R.F.D.—named after the service that delivered him—isn't there, but Skinny keeps an all-night vigil. When morning comes, he sights R.F.D. and coaxes him to come home.

The boy and his dog arrive back at the hotel in time to welcome a new guest—the best-dressed gentleman Skinny has ever seen. Skinny's hopes are soon soaring because Mr. Frank J. Rabbit, or Daddy Rabbit as he prefers to be called seems to like Miss Bessie. Skinny hopes they get married so that he won't have to go to the orphanage.

Meanwhile, the jovial Daddy Rabbit invites Skinny and Miss Bessie to the carnival at Vickstown. While a power failure strands the couple at the top of the Ferris wheel, Skinny strikes up a conversation with the owner's son, Calvin. Skinny learns that Calvin has been to school and can write. When Calvin suggests that they run away, Skinny tells him that he doesn't want to now, but if he ever does, he'll let him know.

Skinny keeps hoping that Miss Bessie will marry Daddy Rabbit, but by the time the carnival works its way to their town, nothing has happened. Skinny goes to the carnival once more and agrees to run away with Calvin. They decide to meet that night down at the railroad yard. Skinny shows up, but Calvin doesn't. Skinny is delighted that the plan has failed, because the very next day Miss Bessie tells him that she and Daddy Rabbit plan to be married and to adopt him.

Roman tells Peachy that he doubts that such a wandering man can settle down. He proves right. The sight of all his friends leaving for a new construction job is too much for Daddy Rabbit and he leaves, too. He does return briefly, but Miss Bessie reluctantly sets him free because she knows he would be miserable settled down.

During this time, Calvin comes to explain his absence at the railroad yard. Skinny proudly shows him around the hotel. Before he leaves, Calvin asks Miss Bessie to choose him, if she ever needs another boy. But, with Daddy Rabbit's final departure, even Skinny can't stay anymore.

Miss Bessie takes Skinny downtown to get some new clothes, even though he protests he doesn't need any. When he returns to the hotel, he finds that a young man from the orphanage, Parker Ross, has come for him. Parker turns out to be a friendly fellow, who even suggests that R.F.D. come along as their house mascot. Though tempted, he tells Parker that he wants to leave his dog with Miss Bessie, because he knows she'll be lonely.

A few months later, Miss Bessie, Peachy and Roman receive a letter from Skinny written by one of his friends. It is signed simply, "Goodby, Skinny." He has found a home.

Thematic Material

Skinny's success at cheerfully accepting his scrawny physique enables him to face the many hard facts of his life more confidently. Most boys and girls will feel empathy with his courageous view of life. Young adults will also get a good picture of the rural South of the 1930's.

Book Talk Material

The opening pages in which Skinny acts as the hotel manager will make a humorous introduction. The chapter in which Skinny sets out to recapture R.F.D. will fascinate younger readers. Start with the poem at the beginning of the chapter and conclude with the private watermelon feast (pp. 29–40) .

Additional Suggestions

Previous titles by the author, *Tyler, Wilkin and Skee* (Viking, $3.00; lib. bdg. $2.96 net) and *A Funny Place to Live* (Viking, $3.00) , can be suggested to younger readers. Stephen Cole's book, *Pitcher and I* (Farrar, Straus, $2.95) is a fine additional choice. It is the story of runt-sized, jug-eared Pitcher who shows his classmates that it takes more than physical assets to make a man. The story of the sturdy orphan girl, *I, Keturah* (Day, $.95) by Ruth Wolff, is recommended especially for girls. More mature young adults will enjoy *The Names and Faces of Heroes* by Reynolds Price (Atheneum, $3.95).

Beverly Butler, *Light a Single Candle,*
Dodd, 1962, $3.25

Miss Butler is usually associated with teen-age historical novels such as *Song of the Voyageur* (Dodd, $3.50) and *Feather in the Wind* (Dodd, $3.50). *Light a Single Candle,* however, has a contemporary setting. In this novel, the author writes from her own experience about a girl's painful adjustment to blindness. This novel appeals to girls of junior high school age.

Cathy Wheeler's 14th birthday begins perfectly—she receives a box of pastel chalks as a present and goes on a wonderful bike-hike with her friend, Pete Sheridan. Now, if her appointment with Dr. Kruger would bring encouraging news, the day would be ideal.

Cathy has been wearing glasses since the age of five, but in spite of increasingly strong lenses, her eyesight is deteriorating.

Dr. Kruger's news is heartbreaking to Cathy. She has glaucoma, a condition that wll eventually produce blindness. There is a slim hope that an operation may save her remaining sight.

Cathy undergoes the operation. Though now completely blind, she has the hope that her sight may eventually return. When Cathy returns home, her mothers and father help her to adjust. Even her pesty eight-year-old brother, Mark, is considerate. At first she makes quick progress. She learns Braille and begins to enjoy her Talking Books.

Miss Creel, a stern, severe teacher from the State School for the Blind, visits the Wheelers and suggests that Cathy should come with her to the state institution at Burton, 100 miles away. The Wheelers refuse, but Cathy, feeling that her friends have rejected her, gives in to self pity and consents to go with Miss Creel.

Her year at Burton is horrible. The teachers are unsympathetic and the students, in general, are petty and unpleasant. Her only friend is Daisy Brown, an outcast from the group because she has been accused of stealing.

At the end of the school year, Cathy leaves Burton. She decides to buy a guide dog and re-enter her regular school in the fall. After a month's orientation course using a mechanical training dog, Cathy graduates to working with her own dog, a lovable German shepherd named Trudy. In time, Trudy becomes Cathy's seeing eye.

When the school term begins, Cathy leaves Trudy at home, and instead, accepts an offer of aid from a school chum, Joan Norton. At first Cathy welcomes Joan's constant attention, but after some weeks she realizes that Joan is using her to boost her own ego. Gradually, through the help of another friend, Mary Beth Robertson, and the attention paid her by the editor of the school newspaper, Steve Hubert, Cathy gains enough confidence to take Trudy to school. Tactfully she begins to assert her independence.

At the close of the first semester, her grades are so good that her English teacher, Miss Vincent, recommends that she join the staff of the school newspaper. Cathy's period of trial is over—she now knows that she is still able to make friends and play a useful part in school activities.

On one of her visits to Dr. Kruger, Cathy learns that she probably will never regain her sight. The news does not create the crisis that it would have 18 months before, because Cathy has learned that it is "better to light a single candle than to sit and curse the dark."

Thematic Material

Two types of courage are present in this book—the courage to accept a handicap and the courage to fight back. Particularly interesting are the many authentic details that concern problems facing a blind person.

Book Talk Material

A brief introduction to the story should be enough to create interest. Passages which could be used are: Cathy's visit to Dr. Kruger on her birthday (pp. 16–21) and her first attempt to read Braille (pp. 51–54).

Additional Suggestions

Other books that deal with blindness are: Elizabeth Yates' *The Lighted Heart* (Dutton, $4.50) and Borghild Dahl's *Finding my Way* (Dutton, $3.00) and *I Wanted to See* (Macmillan, $4.95). Biographies of Helen Keller are also popular with this age group. There are many, ranging from junior biographies, such as Lorena Hickok's *The Touch of Magic* (Dodd, $3.50) and Helen Waite's *Valiant Companions* (Macrae Smith, $2.95) to Miss Keller's own works, *The Story of My Life* (Doubleday, $4.95) and *Teacher* (Doubleday, $4.50) .

C. H. Frick, *Five Against the Odds*,
Harcourt, 1955, $2.95

Although Mr. Frick is not as prolific as many other sport story writers, he has built an enthusiastic following with only a handful of novels. Though far from being great contributions to young adult literature, they are above average in content and treatment. The inclusion in each of fast, exciting sports action has helped to increase their popularity. Junior high boys, and some sixth graders, whether sports enthusiasts or not, find *Five Against the Odds* an entertaining novel.

Suffering the effects of a crippling polio attack is a major tragedy in anyone's life. To 17-year-old Tim Moore, whose major interest is playing basketball, the results seem even more heartbreaking. For years his entire family—Grampa, Grandma, twin brother Jim and younger brother Denny—have encouraged this interest. With his two brothers, Tim had even hoped to lead the high school team to the state championship and thereby gain sports scholarships for himself and his brother Jim. The fulfillment of these dreams now seems shattered. To Tim, reality consists of the hospital bed on which he now lies.

Tim's recovery in the hospital is encouraging. During his five-month stay, he learns to walk with the use of crutches and a brace. Tim feels that his condition is not as serious as that of the other patients. All of them are mature men—like his friend Mac—to whom loss of mobility has also meant loss of livelihood and disruption of family life.

It is when he comes home, that Tim feels the enormity of his handicap. His initial self-pity turns to bitterness and finally to a desire to isolate himself. He not only refuses to attend basketball games, but even leaves the room if basketball is mentioned.

Unknown to Tim, his complete withdrawal has far-reaching effects. Lacking the advice and support of their former leader, the basketball team suffers a disastrous losing streak. Hostility toward the team and its coach develops inside the school. Signs mysteriously appear in the hallways demanding the ouster of the Moore brothers from the team.

An overheard remark made by Coach Van Winkle makes Tim realize that he might be partly responsible for the team's present condition. At first tentatively, and later with greater confidence, he attends games and practices. Soon he begins advising, cajoling, and even prodding his teammates to help them regain their lost spirit. His techniques work and gradually Catonga High reverses the losing trend.

Other events also help Tim come out of his shell. He develops an interest in architectural drawing, and submits plans to a "Home of the Year" contest, in the hope of winning the first prize, a college scholarship. Also, through some deft amateur sleuthing, he clears the name of a teammate's father, Mr. Dusenberry, who had been falsely accused of setting fire to his used-car lot.

As the team continues to win victories, the hostility of the crowd gradually disappears. Soon both Tim and the basketball team regain the support of the school. In the midst of this, Tim's emotional comeback receives two blows—his architectural drawings are returned without a prize, and his brother Jim is awarded the scholarship that, just one year before, Tim had been certain of receiving.

Tim continues to work unsparingly with the team. Miraculously, Catonga High does win the Indiana State Championship. Tim's satisfaction is complete when Mr. Dusenberry, now able to collect his insurance money, gives Tim a reward of $3,000 to finance his college education.

In a sense, both the Moore family and the Catonga High basketball team have been five against the odds. Both have deserved their victories.

Thematic Material

Mr. Frick has not attempted to write a profound novel. Yet, the themes of adjusting to a handicap, working with others, and facing up to crushing disappointments, make this novel particularly valuable.

Book Talk Material

This novel is very popular. Word-of-mouth usually assures its circulation. In a book talk, one of the following episodes could be read: Tim's first steps in the hospital (pp. 22–24); his homecoming (pp. 34–37); his first day back at school (pp. 43–46).

Additional Suggestions

Other sports novels that involve overcoming physical handicaps are: William Cox's *Five Were Chosen* (Dodd, $3.25) again about basketball, and Maria Kirchgessner's *High Challenge* (Harcourt, $3.50). The latter concerns a boy who is unable to become a pilot because of a physical disability. Biographies can also be used: Roy Campanella's *It's Good To Be Alive* (Little, $5.00) and Gene Schoor's less-adult *Roy Campanella: Man of Courage* (Putnam, $3.50). Paul Brickhill's *Reach for the Sky* (Norton, $4.95; lib. bdg. $4.73 net) is another excellent nonfiction title.

Marie Killilea, *Karen,*
Prentice-Hall, 1966, $4.95

Some indication of the fantastic popularity of *Karen* is given by the author in its sequel, *With Love from Karen* (Prentice-Hall, $4.95). In the preface to this work, Mrs. Killilea states that she has received over 27,000 inquiries about Karen and her family. It has already become a modern classic of human endurance and the power of love. *Karen* will capture the hearts of young girls from the sixth grade up.

In *Karen*, Mrs. Killilea has combined three narratives. It is primarily the story of her child, Karen, who has cerebral palsy, but it is also the story of the remarkable Killilea family and their struggle to organize a Cerebral Palsy Association.

When Marie and Jim Killilea realize that their baby has cerebral palsy, they begin a series of pilgrimages to doctors around the country seeking advice and help. In each case the verdict is the same—nothing can be done. A chance encounter with Dr. B., a Southern physician gives the family hope—the one element missing in their lives. He prescribes a strict program of physiotherapy but, because of financial problems, the Killileas find that this is impossible. However, they learn many of the therapeutic techniques and begin Karen's training at home. The difficulties at times seem insurmountable but there is always the charm, courage, and almost superhuman endurance of little Karen to renew their energy.

Progress is slow and painstaking but gradually Karen advances from walking with parallel bars to the use of "skis" and, finally, at the age of 10, to her first joyful steps with crutches.

When she is five, Karen is able to attend kindergarten, but as she grows older, teachers find it impossible to carry her about. Mrs. Killilea reluctantly has to withdraw her from school. However, Karen is fortunate, in having excellent home teachers, like Mary Robards, whose patience and understanding help her progress. At the end of the book, 11-year-old Karen is able to print her first words.

The other members of the Killilea family are Karen's older sister Marie, who suffers attacks of rheumatic fever and tuberculosis; Rory, Karen's mischievous but thoroughly delightful younger brother; and Gloria, who comes to the Killileas as a baby sitter when only 12 and later becomes part of their family. As the author says, "She adopted us." Lastly, we meet Marie and Jim's wonderful friends and neighbors, and the Killileas' innumerable pets, including a roguish Irish setter named Shanty.

Throughout the book, Mrs. Killilea tells about her crusade to enlighten the American public about the facts concerning cerebral palsy, and to help the thousands who have cerebral palsy find a place of dignity and usefulness in society. At first she begins by organizing a group in their suburban community of Rye, N.Y. Later, through visits, speaking engagements, and countless letters, she organizes new groups and makes contact with other existing associations. On July 15, 1948, the results of their work take shape in the creation of the United Cerebral Palsy Association.

The book, though, belongs essentially to the little pigtailed heroine, Karen, and her epic of courage and triumph. Every reader will want to cheer her final words, "I can walk. I can talk. I can read, I can write, Mom Pom, I can do anything."

Thematic Material

The qualities of patience, love, courage, self-sacrifice, and endurance are all present in this book. It is a moving tribute to the human spirit.

Book Talk Material

Because of its episodic nature, *Karen* is filled with many wonderful sections that are ideal for reading aloud. In time you will find your own favorites, but here are a few to start with: the Killileas gather weeping willow limbs to cure their sick rabbits (pp. 60–63) ; Karen finds a protector (pp. 67–68) ; Karen's first day in school (pp. 110–114) ; Karen learns not to be afraid of water (pp. 87–92) ; a train trip to Washington,

D. C. (pp. 115–117) ; going to the beach (pp. 145–148) ; and Karen's first use of crutches (pp. 215–219) .

Additional Suggestions

Readers will certainly want to continue Karen's story in *With Love from Karen* (Prentice-Hall, $4.95) . Young readers will also enjoy the story of the young Indian girl, Maya, in Aimée Sommerfelt's *The Road to Agra* (Criterion, $3.50) . Other books that deal with similar conflicts are: Elsie Barber's *The Trembling Years* (Macmillan, $4.95) , June Opie's *Over My Dead Body* (Dutton, $4.95) and Lorraine Beim's *Triumph Clear* (Harcourt, $3.25) .

Kim Yong Ik, *Blue in the Seed,*
Little, 1964, $3.95

This is an unusual story made memorable by the graceful, lean prose of the author. It is the story of a young boy's search for identity in an exotic Korean setting. The result is a sensitive story for young people. Both boys and girls in intermediate and early junior high grades will enjoy this book.

Although Chun Bok knows that all the people on Cheju Island have dark eyes, he does not know why he and his widowed mother have blue ones. He asks her often if her mother had blue eyes too. Omanee, his mother, answers that if he studies hard at school on the mainland of Korea, everyone will see that his blue eyes have brought him luck. Bok, as he is called, doesn't want to go to school, but he doesn't mind leaving behind him all his tormentors who scornfully call him "Fish Eyes." Nor does he mind leaving behind his querulous grandmother, who plagues her daughter-in-law with the same taunts of "Fish Eyes." As long as Omanee and his fine ox come along, Bok is happy to leave.

As soon as they are settled in their small house on the mainland, Omanee leads Bok to the schoolhouse and agrees to give the teacher seventy *won* for Bok's desk and chair before *Tano Day* (a Korean holiday) . Bok is overcome with shyness in front of these new dark-eyed classmates. He keeps to himself and averts his head when anyone tries to speak to him. Although the children are kind, Bok cannot respond.

One day, the school monitor, a girl named Jung Lan, shares her lunch with him and encourages him to enter the games. Unfortunately, one of Bok's straw sandals flies off as he tries to kick the ball, and Pal Min, one of the boys, shouts, "Bird Eyes" at him. Smarting at the dreaded, yet expected name, Bok tries to prove that he is better and bolder than any of them. He drinks five portions of sweet water, four more than anyone else, in response to Pal Min's dare, "How much can you drink, Bird Eyes?"

Bok refuses to go back to school. Instead he goes to the village where the elders promise to teach him. Two days before the holiday Jung Lan brings Bok three pieces of silver that the children have saved so that he may buy tennis shoes like theirs. Bok realizes that they are trying to tell him that they are sorry for calling him names.

He sets out to buy the shoes. On his way he overhears the elders talking about his blue eyes; he stops to listen. He learns that long ago on Cheju Island a blue-eyed sailor arrived and made a home. Bok hears one of the men tell how miserable he had been as a youngster because one of his eyes was larger than the other. He had bought a pair of glasses to hide this deformity. Bok goes out and buys himself a pair of glasses with the three pieces of silver.

The next day, with the glasses and the seventy *won* for the desk in his pocket, he goes to school. As he approaches, he puts on the glasses but at the last moment he loses courage and runs away. In the distance he hears the children's shouts. Completely discouraged, Bok gets his ox, and joins the crowds on their way to the *Tano Day* festival. He decides to spend the seventy *won* on iron shoes for the ox. Having frivolously spent his friends' gift and his mother's money to indulge his self-pity, Bok doesn't know what to do. He finally takes the ox to bathe him in the sea, but his classmates are there and run after him. Pal Min catches him and pulls off his glasses. Bok fights back. When the struggle is over, the school yard is devastated and the ox is gone.

After searching over the mountainside for his ox, Bok spends the night in a Buddhist monastery. The monk tells him that he will lose nothing if only he will see the world with his inner eyes. Bok ponders over this: what can it mean? When he closes his eyes, he can see only the blue eyes of his mother smiling at him.

Finally, he comes to the festival arena in the town, where an ox fight is in progress. Bok recognizes the winner, but has a hard time convincing the judge that the animal belongs to him and not to the fat man who is claiming the prize. His classmates and the shoeman verify his story and he is allowed to lead his victorious ox away. He takes him back home, even though the ox is entitled to fight again for the big prize.

While wading through a rice paddy on the way home, Bok is bitten by a poisonous snake. His classmates, sharing his victorious march home, take care of his wound and carry him home. His mother and teacher are so happy to see him that they arrange to help him repay his debts honorably. As he rests in the comforting circle of his friends and loving mother, he looks into his mothers's smiling blue eyes. The monk's words cross his mind for he knows that inside he is smiling, too.

The title comes from the answer to Bok's question to his mother, "Did your mother's mother have blue eyes?" "I do not know . . . It is blue in the seed and that is all I know."

Thematic Material

It is a difficult task for a young person to accept his appearance, especially when a distinguishing physical characteristic sets him apart from his peers. This unique story explores a universal problem as it affects an Asian youngster. Although the foreign setting shows some of the cultural differences in the acceptable behavior of children, the author also emphasizes codes of personal courage and honor that are similar to both cultures.

Book Talk Material

A brief condensation of the plot will interest most readers. The children's fight (from the point at which Bok loses his ox until his meeting with the monk) will serve as good material for a dramatic reading (pp. 63–75) .

Additional Suggestions

Younger readers will also enjoy the author's earlier book, *The Happy Days* (Little, $3.95) ; more mature readers, Sivasankara Pillai's *Chemmeen* (Harper, $5.00) . Betty Cavanna's story about a young Japanese girl who goes to live with her grandmother in Kansas, *Jenny Kimura* (Morrow, $3.50; lib. bdg. $3.32 net) ; and Lois Duncan's story of an American Indian girl's struggles, *Season of the Two-heart* (Dodd, $3.25) are good additional selections.

Joan Phipson, *Birkin*,
Harcourt, 1966, $3.50

The Boundary Riders (Harcourt, $3.00) was Miss Phipson's first juvenile title published in this country. She has also written two successful novels about the Barker family, *The Family Conspiracy* and *Threat to the Barkers* (both Harcourt, $3.50 each). As in her previous books, *Birkin* takes place in a rural Australian setting. It is particularly suitable for both boys and girls in grades five through seven.

Birkin is the name given to a motherless black calf after it is adopted by two 16-year-old boys, Allen Willis and Bob Jackson. All of the younger boys and girls in the little settlement of Coolabin are fascinated by the care and feeding of Birkin. As the boys' interest wanes, three of the younger children take over the responsibility of the calf. Each of the three is something of a social misfit. Francie Newman a 13-year-old, is shy and withdrawn, and Angus Buchanan, a recent arrival from Scotland, has different manners and speech habits and has not been accepted by the group. Lastly, Tony Bell is a sullen, grumpy 12-year-old boy whose problems arise from a bad limp. Tony never speaks of his handicap, but instead remains aloof and distant from the rest of the gang.

In taking charge of Birkin's welfare, several accidents occur that severely test their strength and courage. One day, while Francie is leading the young steer to pasture, a low flying plane frightens Birkin and he runs into a culvert dragging Francie behind him. She is knocked unconscious, but, upon recovery, adamantly refuses to give up her responsibilities towards Birkin. Several weeks later, during a severe rainstorm, Birkin leaves his paddock and wanders into the highway. He is struck by a passing automobile and badly injured. Tony finds him and nurses him until help arrives. As a result of this thorough soaking and exposure, Tony becomes ill and is hospitalized. But after his release he too resumes his responsibility.

A third adventure inadvertently turns Tony and Birkin into the town's heroes. While trying to cross a swollen river, on the outskirts of town, Birkin is swept downstream by the current. Tony follows in a makeshift boat. When he finally reaches Burkin, they are miles from town and must spend the night in the woods. The next day, while leading Birkin back home, the two happen on the wreckage of a small sports plane and save the life of its youthful owner, Richard Mitchell. In a display of gratitude, Richard's father, a wealthy ranch owner, not only promises to keep Birkin on his ranch where the children can visit him, but also offers to subsidize Tony's education beyond high school.

During the year in which they have cared for Birkin, all three youngsters have gained self-assurance, and Tony has come a long way toward self acceptance.

Thematic Material

Rural life in Australia is vividly depicted in *Birkin*. In addition to its appeal as an animal story, it portrays wholesome family relationships and the warmth of close friendships. Courage, acceptance of responsibility and a child's need for understanding and love are secondary themes. The elements of suspense, adventure and humor are also present.

Book Talk Material

The naming of Birkin (pp. 33–35) is a humorous incident that would be excellent for retelling (he was named after two Australian explorers, Burke and Willis, who in the children's jargon become Birkin Wills). Other incidents that could be used are: Birkin's first taste of Mrs. Jackson's garden (pp. 39–43), the incident with the plane (pp. 46–48) and Francis and Tony ride Birkin into town (pp. 76–81).

Additional Suggestions

Similar books that are suitable for this age group are described elsewhere in this chapter. If you wish books for an older group (grades 8 and up), several adult titles that could be used are: Louise Baker's *Out on a Limb* (McGraw, $4.95), Alan Marshall's *I Can Jump Puddles* (World, $3.50), Peter Putnam's *Keep Your Head Up, Mr. Putnam!* (Harper, $3.50; lib. bdg. $3.27 net) and Henry Viscardi, Jr.'s *Laughter in the Lonely Night* (Hill & Wang, $5.00).

Helen Marie Pundt, *Spring Comes First to the Willows,*
Crowell, 1963, $3.75

Mrs. Pundt has written a sympathetic story about a girl's gradual transformation from an uncomfortable "foreigner" to a poised young woman. There is charm in the author's portrait of a Swiss-Austrian family whose wholesome spirit serves as a foil for some of the more shallow and superficial values in our society. Girls of junior high school age and older like this story.

Anna Maria Reichert, a new member of the senior class in a suburban community near New York City, is pleasantly surprised when Alan Newbury, the basketball star, invites her to join his school clique for lunch in the cafeteria. She has daydreamed about the handsome boy and his attractive crowd, but because of her old-fashioned appearance and quaint family, she never thought that she could be part of them.

Anna Maria knows how difficult it has been for her parents, leaving Europe one step ahead of the Nazis and raising a family in New York City. Still, she wishes she looked more like the other girls in her class instead of having long braids which her stern father likes, handmade dresses, and extra pounds (because of her mother's famous cooking).

The clique—beautiful Cecily Brewster, musical Gay Weatherill, and the Sanderson twins, Jill and Geoff—welcomes her. Because she wants to be accepted, she promises Alan that she will write to Basil Lons (a famous pop singer who is an old school friend of her older brother, Fritz) and ask him to be the attraction at their next school assembly. When Anna Maria tells her parents about the episode, Mr. Reichert is very upset and insists that she write a letter of apology to Mr. Lons immediately. She writes the letter, but is heartbroken to think that she has failed Alan and her new friends.

The basketball game and dance come, but Anna Maria, dateless, goes to a movie with her mother. She continues to see Gay and the twins, but she is sure that she will never be popular, especially when her mother decides to start a catering business to help the family finances.

The unexpected arrival of Mr. Lons, however, changes her opinion. Basil Lons urges her to accompany him at the piano on the day of the school assembly and she becomes the school heroine. This event, along with a new hairdo, some new dresses, and the loss of a few pounds gives Anna Maria new confidence. She begins to go steady with Alan, even though she knows her father doesn't like him.

In spite of her new assurance, Anna Maria panics when she wonders what Alan will say when he finds out about her mother's catering business. These fears abate after a distressing evening with the Newburys when Anna Maria learns that Alan and his father don't get along well. When Mr. Newbury promises Alan to return his car if he stays home every night after school, Anna Maria is dropped in favor of the car. Geoff comes to the rescue and takes her out several times. She likes this quiet, yet humorous boy who wants to be a veterinarian. But her infatuation for Alan is still strong.

Two days before the Senior Tea, Alan arrives at her home in his car. As they ride together, Anna Maria becomes irritated with his plans for her in the Dairy Beauty Queen Contest. But, when he parks off the road and kisses her, she responds. As a car pulls alongside flashing its lights, Anna Maria hears snickers. Humiliated, she leaves Alan, and starts to walk, but Alan picks her up and drives her home. He is furious.

The following morning, Anna Maria learns that Alan and Cecily are in the hospital after an automobile accident. Barely recovered from this shock, she is told that her older sister is ill and that her mother must leave for Switzerland to help her. Anna Maria, now alone, must fill in for her mother and cater the Senior Tea. She wrestles briefly with her conscience. Finally, with her father's help and encouragement, she puts the finishing touches on her mother's talented work.

The tea is a great success and all of her friends admire her spirit. She visits Cecily and Alan in the hospital and realizes that the beautiful Cecily and the glamorous Alan are really the unfortunate ones because they lack traditions like those of her family. She find a letter at home from Fritz telling her to expect both he and Basil Lons to escort her to the Senior Dance. She is proud to be surrounded by her loyal and affectionate family.

Anna Maria realizes that the graceful willows bending to the winter winds are the first to bloom. She is reminded that Mama says, "Spring comes first to the willows." (p. 112).

Thematic Material

Mrs. Pundt's characterization of the heroine shows feelings of inadequacy that many adolescent girls experience about their physical appearance. In addition, a young adult's relationship with her family and friends is well portrayed.

Book Talk Material

A simple plot resume will entice most readers. The scene in which Anna Maria talks to Alan for the first time will set the theme of the story (pp. 11–20). A brief introduction to the arrival of Basil Lons, followed by a reading of his plan for the school assembly, will also intrigue the Junior High School audience (pp. 99–105).

Additional Suggestions

Kristen Thorvall's provincial heroine in the novel *Girl in April* (Harcourt, $3.00) has similar problems to solve. Nan Gilbert's *The Unchosen* (Harper, $3.50; lib. bdg. $3.27 net) about three unpopular senior high school girls, would be a good follow-up title. *Whispering Willows* (Doubleday, $3.50) by Elisabeth Friermood is also recommended. *New Girl at Winston High* (Reilly & Lee, $3.75) by Arlene Swanson gives a convincing picture of a girl's struggle for acceptance. Younger girls will sympathize with Kathleen in *Don't Call Me Katie Rose* (Crowell $3.95) by Lenora Weber.

Veronica Robinson, *David in Silence,*
Lippincott, 1966, $3.25

Although such expressions as 'lorry' and 'petrol' might be strange to young American readers, the central conflict in this English juvenile novel is sufficiently universal to guarantee a receptive audience. The author, a children's librarian, carefully researched the problems of the deaf child by visiting several schools for the deaf in England. The result is a warm, sympathetic book that will appeal to boys and girls in grades five through seven.

The Williams family—Father, Mother, 13-year-old David, and older brother Eric—have moved from their rural home in Llandudno, Wales, to a suburban workingman's community on the outskirts of Birmingham. Unknown to David, who was born deaf, the family has moved so that he can attend a day school for the deaf. Up to this time, David has attended a special boarding school for the deaf and, apart from his immediate family, has had little contact with those who can hear.

The youngsters in the community first look upon David as subnormal. Some consider his garbled speech as a sign of stupidity. The Guest children live next door to David. They are 13-year-old Michael, his older sister Eileen, and young brother Tommy. Although they try to make friends with their naive, innocent neighbor, the difficulties in communication discourage easy give and take.

David has already learned the loneliness of his life of silence, and has developed solitary interests. His chief hobby is the construction of a model of a small town out of match sticks. One day while David is on his front steps working with his hobby, Michael accidentally hits a cricket ball so hard that it crashes into the model and destroys part of it. David is inconsolable, and feels that the incident is a deliberate act of cruelty. Only with the help of David's brother, Eric, is Michael able to explain that it was an accident. David and Michael work together to repair the damage.

One day while Michael is visiting Birmingham, David joins the neighborhood gang in a game of football. In an effort to gain the confidence of these children, he begins to show off. He hogs the ball and accidentally knocks down one of the younger children. Egged on by the town bully, the children turn on David and begin to chase him. Not knowing why he is being pursued, David, like a frightened animal, runs to the outskirts of town and hides in a deserted canal tunnel. In the dark, he loses his footing, falls in the water, and becomes confused in his sense of direction. Weak and frightened, he staggers to the wrong end of the mile and a half long tunnel, and discovers that he is lost. He tries to find a bus home, but is unable to make himself understood by passersby. Fortunately Michael finds him and brings him home.

David once more retreats into his solitary life. Michael persuades him to help a group of boys in a project to build rafts to float on the canal. Through David's sound advice the rafts are built and successfully launched. David has proven his worth and won the boys' respect. He no longer lives completely in silence.

Thematic Material

This is essentially the story of a boy's search for friends and self-esteem. The need for kindness and understanding in dealing with physical handicaps is stressed. Good family relationships, particularly in David's family, and the foreign setting also give additional dimensions to the story.

Book Talk Material

A short summary of the plot should serve as a good introduction. David's first encounter with the neighborhood children is told on pages 14–15. The incident with the cricket ball (pp. 32–37) and Michael's attempt to repair the damage (pp. 46–50) are other sections that will arouse interest.

Additional Suggestions

Alberta Armer's *Screwball* (World, $3.00; lib. bdg. $2.96 net) tells how a young boy overcomes shyness resulting from a physical handicap caused by a mild polio attack. In *Rebel in Right Field* (Morrow, $3.50) by Duane Decker, a young baseball player is so fearful of bodily injury that he risks losing an important game. The deaf and dumb hero of Edwin Teale's true story, *The Lost Dog* (Dodd, $3.25), conducts a seemingly hopeless search for his lost pet. Glendon and Kathryn Swarthout's excellent *Whichaway* (Random, $3.25; lib. bdg. $3.29 net) for an older audience, tells of a boy's struggle for survival after breaking both legs in a cattle ranch accident.

Kathryn Vinson, *Run with the Ring,*
Harcourt, 1965, $3.75

In *Run with the Ring*, Kathryn Vinson writes with understanding about an adolescent boy's sudden encounter with the formidable problems of blindness. Although this is the author's first junior novel, her ability to construct a fast-paced story and to develop her characters make it a worthwhile choice. In addition, the athletic and ham radio elements should appeal to most boys and some girls in grades 7 through 9.

Mark Mansfield, best sprinter and handsomest junior at Greenville High School, wants to study electronics and inwardly hopes one day to participate in the Olympics. Both ambitions become remote when a sudden fall on the cinder track blinds him. He refuses to believe, as the doctor does, that muscle fatigue caused his collapse. Bitter about his fate, Mark thinks that his competitor, Curt Trammel, has fouled him. He wants revenge. Mark begins to take heart, however, when he discovers that one of his radio pals has had to face blindness. He decides to enter Bayshore Academy for the Deaf and the Blind.

In addition to his regular class work at Bayshore, Mark learns a great deal about blindness and how to cope with it. His major problems are learning to "travel" by himself and conquering his fear of running again. He finds some comfort in his new friends: Scooter, an irrepressible youngster who looks up to him; Highpockets, his taciturn roommate; and Trish who becomes his steady girl. Although all the boys at Bayshore want Mark to represent them at the spring track meet, Mark's lack of confidence keeps him from trying.

One night he musters enough courage to try out on the track after hours. He is caught and punished. His spirits are even lower, but when he is able to save Scooter from being run over at a busy intersection, he again feels his own worth. With renewed confidence, he reports to Coach Gordon and begins an arduous period of training with the guide ring of the title.

The competition is too great at the spring meet and Mark comes in a close second. Disheartened, he refuses to join Trish and his friends at the dance that follows the meet. Instead, in a self-pitying mood, he returns to his room. Intent on his own problems, he smells smoke and hears the crackle of flames coming from the children's dormitory. With great heroism, he enters the old wooden building and leads the children to safety. On graduation day he learns that he will be awarded the Young American Medal for Bravery.

When he returns home for summer vacation, Mark is visited by his former track coach at Greenville High. The coach explains that unless Mark will vindicate Curt from blame for Mark's accident, Curt will be ineligible for a State scholarship. Searching his conscience, Mark tells the coach that Curt deserves the scholarship.

Thematic Material

In addition to sensitively interpreting how a young adult learns to accept his physical handicap, this story is an honest account of the problems of being blind. The hero is a vital, well-drawn character with whom boys and girls can identify. The book has greater depth and insight than the average sports story.

Book Talk Material

A brief retelling or reading of Mark's arrival at Bayshore Academy (pp. 53–59), prefaced by an account of his accident (pp. 9–19) will serve to introduce the book. A descriptive vignette of Mark's new friends will also be effective (pp. 63–78). Two exciting episodes are: Mark rescues Scooter from the terrifying intersection (pp. 188–195) and Mark saves the occupants of the children's dormitory from the fire (pp. 217–229).

Additional Suggestions

A Light in the Dark: The Life of Samuel Gridley Howe (Crowell, $3.50) by Milton Meltzer and *Journey into Light: The Story of Louis*

Braille (Hawthorne, $3.25) by Gary Webster are biographies that deal with the same theme. Most boys will also enjoy the following stories about courageous men: *Cancer, Cocaine and Courage, The Story of Dr. William Halstead* (Messner, $3.25; lib. bdg. $3.19 net) by Arthur J. Beckhard and William D. Crane; and *Young Olympic Champions* (Norton, $3.50; lib. bdg. $3.28) by Steve Gelman. Junior high age girls will like Marguerite Vance's *A Rainbow for Robin* (Dutton, $3.25; lib. bdg. $3.22 net), the diary of a young blind girl and her struggle to become a performing musician.

Herman Wouk, *The City Boy,*
            Doubleday, 1948, $4.50

This tragi-comic novel is as fresh and appealing as the day it appeared. A perceptive study of a young Jewish boy growing up in the Bronx in the late 20's, *The City Boy* has earned both author and hero a firm place in juvenile literature. The author's easy style and many humorous touches add distinction to an entertaining story. Readers of junior high school age and up will enjoy this story.

Herbie Bookbinder, age 11, is the smartest pupil in the seventh grade at P.S. 50. But he has a problem: he is fat. Herbie would like to be an athlete like Lenny Krieger but the only boy Herbie can beat at any game is so fat that winning is small consolation. He suffers silently the name Fatso and General Garbage—the latter because he is on the Social Service Squad at school. Lenny is on the Police Squad, an enviable position of power.

Herbie has another problem; he is smitten with love for Lucille Glass, a pretty little girl in the sixth grade. When she tells Herbie that she is going to Camp Manitou (the summer camp run by the principal, Mr. Gauss), Herbie concocts a scheme so that his father will send him too. He accomplishes this maneuver by telling Mr. Gauss that his father wants to send him to camp, and by telling his father that his partner's son, Lenny, and his lawyer's daughter, Lucille, are both being allowed to go. Mr. Gauss visits the Bookbinders and both Herbie and his older sister, Felicia, are signed up for Camp Manitou. As a result of Herbie's planning, Lenny is also signed up, as well as Herbie's cousin, Cliff.

Herbie has many adventures before summer finally arrives. He and

Cliff meet the feared "Creek Gang" during their explorations; they also manage, after much searching, to "meet" Lucille and her mother in the local museum. This latter adventure nearly ends badly, however, when Herbie gallantly pays for the ladies' ice cream with his return subway fare. However, a subway guard lets them ride home free after they promise to return the fare to the subway company.

His narrowest escape comes when he is caught passing an answer to the slow-witted Lenny during the promotion day tests. Herbie stands his ground and silently hopes that he will be deemed worthy to receive a "skip" to eighth grade. He "skips." As a reward, his proud father takes him to dinner with his business associates. Herbie, bored by the dull conversation, gorges himself: he becomes deathly ill and is disgraced.

Finally, the summer arrives; the eager campers and the overburdened counselors leave Grand Central Station. Because he is small as well as rotund, Herbie lands with the intermediates, but is rescued by his cousin, Cliff. Before the train ride is over he is compelled to sit next to Uncle Sandy, the head counselor, with a large sign, "Camp Goop # One" hung around his neck—all because he was caught talking to Lucille in the forbidden between-trains platform. It seems natural to Herbie that he is assigned to bunk 13.

Except for the food, camp is a bitter disappointment. There's only one old horse, Clever Sam, but he won't let anyone ride him except Cliff; there's the big annual basketball game with Camp Penobscot, but they lose that; even the big Gaussian victory dance ("Victory" is the principal's euphemism for defeat) is a disaster for Herbie because he can't dance. He loses Lucille to Lenny by default. Things get progressively worse until Herbie has a brilliant idea for the Manitou Mardi-Gras, which is held two days before the end of camp. If he can bring it off, he will win the "Skipper for a Day Contest."

With the help of Elmer the handyman, he devises a plan for a daring boat ride down the hill into the lake. The camp has a boat, but Herbie needs $50 to make rails for the ride.

Herbie and Cliff carry out an adventurous round trip, by horse and hitchhiking, to the Bronx where Herbie "borrows" $50 from his father's safe. During the "robbery," he overhears Mr. Krieger and the nefarious Mr. Powers, who holds the mortgage on the property, plot the theft of his father's proof of ownership. Although the boys get back to camp safely and the boat ride is a huge success, netting Herbie $200 and the contest, Herbie is miserable because Mr. Gauss forces him to turn over all the money to a camp-supported annual charity drive. Herbie is trapped; he can't repay the missing $50.

When Herbie learns that his father is forced to sell his business because of the missing proof of ownership, he confesses, and receives a well-deserved spanking. All is forgiven when Cliff and Herbie produce the proof of ownership that they have found in Mr. Krieger's apartment.

Herbie is still fat, but he has learned to respect himself.

Thematic Material

Mr. Wouk has delineated with uncanny ability the character of a young adult plagued by his ungainly appearance. All young people will respond to this boy who has so many good qualities but lacks the one thing he would most like, an athletic physique. This novel illustrates many of the problems in adolescence, for example, Herbie's friendships with his boy friends, and his tentative efforts to date a girl. The author's fond reminiscences of a city boy's life recreate a time that is gone, but should be remembered.

Book Talk Material

The book is full of wonderful vignettes. The scene in which Herbie (General Grant) triumphs over Lenny (General Lee) on the stage at P.S. 50 is hilarious (pp. 98–101). Herbie's drubbing in the lake after the first unsuccessful boat ride can be used (pp. 260–263). The boys' hair-raising escapade into the Bronx is very exciting (pp. 229–251). In addition, many chapters lend themselves to short readings, for example, the restaurant scene in which Herbie eats seven French pastries (pp. 118–127).

Additional Suggestions

I Bow to the Stones (Frisch, $3.75) by the late comedian Jimmy Savo also tells about a New York City boyhood. Younger girls will read *Hepatica Hawks* (Macmillan, $3.34) by Rachel Field, a story about an unhappy tall girl. Rumer Godden's book, *An Episode of Sparrows* (Viking, $4.50), the story of two London waifs, is a beautiful tale with special appeal to older girls. Older introspective readers will enjoy Laurie Lee's story of his boyhood, *The Edge of Day* (Morrow, $4.50).

5

Making Friends

A YOUNG CHILD's first social contacts are with his immediate family. As he grows and his sphere of activity broadens he observes other adult models and makes friends with young people his own age. Attitudes toward friends, toward strangers, toward people in general are formed during the middle childhood years.

Sexual maturation occurs at this time; the young person establishes relationships with the opposite sex. Girls become interested in home making and child care, boys in the role of the father. Because our society offers a rapidly changing set of values regarding family institutions and sexual behavior, young people find the process of social maturation a difficult and confusing one.

The books in this chapter explore some of the difficulties that confront young teens as they develop social relationships.

Esma Rideout Booth, *Kalena,*
McKay, 1958, lib. bdg. $3.29 net

Mrs. Booth has written a touching portrait of a young African girl's awaking love set against the tumultuous background of the rapidly changing Congo. The author's missionary experience in the Congo plus her sympathetic discernment of young love are both apparent in this provocative novel. This story is especially appealing to girls in the sixth through the ninth grades.

Kalena, first-born and only girl child, has been promised by her father to the son of a neighboring chief who pays a handsome dowry to seal the marriage bargain. However, the wedding has to be postponed so that Kalena can care for her ailing mother. Because of this delay, Mulela, the chief's son, moves to the city where he adopts the European name, Lucien. Meanwhile, Sana, a young medical student who works at the mission dispensary, persuades Kalena's father to bring his wife to the clinic for treatment. This permits Kalena to continue her precious education in the mission school. While there, Kalena enters the school story contest and receives honorable mention for her work. She joins Lucien and some mutual friends for an evening in the city. During the evening, Kalena realizes that she can never marry this impatient young man who has become an organizer of the many discontented young Congolese seeking opportunities in the city. As she compares Lucien to the serious, idealistic Sana, Kalena recognizes that she has already chosen Sana. However, she knows that if she cancels the bargain, the bride price will have to be repaid. When she approaches her father, Kalena learns that he is also somewhat skeptical about Lucien and his comrades, who have demanded their rights without assuming any of the responsibilities.

Kalena learns how much her father truly loves her when he agrees to repay the dowry. She, in turn, accepts an offer to teach in order to help him with the debt.

Thematic Material

This is a realistic presentation of young love under the changing cultural patterns of the Southern Congo. Social upheaval, tribal polygamy, and the violent differences in attitudes between adults and adolescents are vividly detailed through the author's artful portrayal of this African family. These social changes form an interesting secondary theme.

Book Talk Material

The plot could be told briefly up to the dance in the village when Kalena talks to Sana for the first time (pp. 29–37). This episode gives a good picture of a traditional tribal dance. For a glimpse of the changing patterns in African city life, the scene in which Kalena and Lucien join friends to go to a party will provide a good contrast (pp. 123–133).

Additional Suggestions

Young adults will want to read the sequel, *Kalena and Sana* (McKay, lib. bdg. $3.11 net). Older girls may be tempted to follow with Kamala Markandaya's *Nectar in a Sieve* (Day, $3.95), a tender sketch of an Indian girl's marriage. They will also enjoy Pearl Buck's *The Living Reed* (Day, $6.95), a compelling presentation of changing cultural patterns seen through the eyes of three generations of a Korean family. Recommended for more mature readers is Oliver La Farge's *Laughing Boy* (Houghton $4.00), the Pulitzer Prize novel about Navajo Indian life.

Betty Cavanna, *A Time for Tenderness,*
Morrow, 1962, $3.50

In spite of a rather contrived ending, Betty Cavanna has managed to combine effectively the color and excitement of Brazil with a poignant story of first love. The result is a superior novel which will appeal particularly to girls of junior high school age.

For business reasons, the Jamison family—mother, father, 16-year-old daughter Peggy and younger brother Tobey—has come from Charlotte, North Carolina, to spend a year in Rio de Janeiro. Peggy enrolls in the American School and soon makes friends with a young aristocratic Brazilian girl, Guida Almeida, and her handsome older brother Carlos. Peggy sees Carlos often and a mutual attraction develops. But, complications arise when Peggy first visits the Almeida household. It is Guida's 15th birthday and, by Brazilian tradition, a gala occasion. During the evening, an old, fragile Negress is introduced to the group. It is Carlos' grandmother. Peggy realizes that her mother, bred in the segregated South, will never approve of her friendship with Carlos. However, Peggy is too involved with Carlos to risk endangering their relationship. She clings guiltily to her secret even though she knows that one day her mother will find out.

Despite Brazilian mores, Peggy and Carlos manage to steal a few precious moments alone. Peggy visits the Almeida household as Guida's guest during the summer vacation; she helps Carlos at his uncle's medical clinic in the slums of Rio; and she and Carlos share a romantic evening during the Mardi Gras season. With each of these encounters, their feelings toward each other deepen. Two considerations tend to cloud the beauty of Peggy's idyllic happiness: Carlos' mysterious references to the fact that he is "not free as Americans are," and the presence of Cleo, the "other woman" who is very fond of Carlos as well as being a close member of the Almeida family group.

Events reach a swift and disturbing climax. The racial question comes into the open at last when Mrs. Jamison discovers Carlos' Negro background. Tobey openly defies his mother concerning his friendship with a Negro school friend. The explosive scene which follows is ended only upon Mr. Jamison's sudden announcement that the family must move again. He has been transferred to Salvador and is expected to leave Brazil within a week.

Peggy and Carlos meet. Before Peggy can tell him that she will be leaving, Carlos explains what he meant by not being free. His family has arranged for his marriage to Cleo and as a dutiful son he must obey their wishes. His family ties are stronger than his love for Peggy. Heartbroken, Peggy now welcomes the day when she will leave Rio. Though saddened by their experiences in Brazil, by the time they depart, each member of the Jamison family, feels a greater maturity.

Thematic Material

In addition to the boy-girl relationship, this novel humanizes the problem of racial prejudice. The differences between Brazilian traditions and customs and those of North America form a secondary theme.

Book Talk Material

The beginning of the plot could be briefly told. Incidents that could be used are: Carlos and Peggy meet in a restaurant (pp. 34–37), Mrs. Jamison and Peggy discuss racial prejudice (pp. 89–92), Peggy sees Carlos' grandmother (pp. 104–106) and Peggy helps in a clinic (pp. 115–119).

Additional Suggestions

Good junior romances abound. In addition to other titles by Betty Cavanna, the works of Zoa Sherburne, Ann Emery and other authors could be suggested. For better readers, try such titles as: Maureen Daly's

Seventeenth Summer (Dodd, $3.25), Mary Medearis' *Big Doc's Girl* (Lippincott, $3.95), Dorothy Smith's *The Blue Dress* (Dutton, $3.50), or Mary Stolz' *To Tell Your Love* (Harper, $3.95; lib. bdg. $3.79 net).

Richard Church, *Five Boys in a Cave*,
Day, 1957, $3.75

British born, Richard Church has written a superior junior novel with transcends the English idiom. Each of the five boys, perceptively characterized in this heroic suspense story, conclude their escapade one step closer to manhood. Boys and girls in grades six through eight enjoy this fine book. *Five Boys in a Cave* was originally published in Great Britain as *The Cave*.

When his family suffers financial reverses, John Walters has to forego his anticipated boat trip to the English Norfolk Broads. Instead, he and his brother are parceled out to relatives for the summer holidays. John lands at the home of his aunt and uncle.

The summer at the doctor's comfortable home has been quiet but somewhat boring when, one day, John finds the entrance to a gigantic cave. He alerts the four other members of the Tomahawk Club and together they plan secretly to explore the cave. Because the boys need equipment, John decides to confide in his uncle. A former mountaineer, the doctor is enthusiastic about the boys' project. With his uncle's blessing and equipment, John and the others—Alan, Meaty, Lightning, and George—gather early one morning to begin their adventure. Leadership of the small band is assumed preemptorily by Alan. Soon, through Alan's negligence, the rope that connects John and Lightning, who are investigating the river bed far below, falls, trapping the two boys at the river bed in the lower cave. Ignoring his responsibility for this frightening situation, Alan transfers his inner rage to Meaty. In his anger, Alan loses his father's flashlight which he had secretly borrowed. The thought of his parent's retribution incapacitates him.

At this climactic point, George calmly takes command of the situation. After individual acts of bravery, the boys rescue John and Lightning.

Finally, the explorers are united and emerge into the fading daylight. Triumphant yet chastened, they arrive home, as promised, before dark.

Thematic Material

Each boy's relationship with his friends portrays authentic adolescent reactions. The underlying secondary theme of personal courage is handled effectively. Each boy's growing maturity is presented as a third theme.

Book Talk Material

Give a brief resume of the story prior to the switch in command from Alan to George. The conflict among the three boys who are stranded could be shown by using pages 116–121 as the climax of the book talk.

Additional Suggestions

Other excellent adventure stories for boys are Paul Jacques Bonzon's *Pursuit in the French Alps* (Lothrop, $3.50) and Allan McLean's *Master of Morgana* (Harcourt, $3.00). Older boys will be interested in reading Eric Williams' *The Tunnel* (Abelard, $3.50), which shows the pressures of life in a prisoner-of-war camp. For those older boys who are interested in themes of personal courage, *Endurance* (McGraw, $6.50) by Alfred Lansing and *The Raft* (Noble, bd. with Daniel Defoe's *Robinson Crusoe*, $3.16) by Robert Trumbull are recommended.

Beverly Cleary, *Fifteen,*
Morrow, 1956, $3.50; lib. bdg. $3.32 net

Mrs. Cleary has produced a frank story about the difficult years of adolescence. The main characters, Jane and Stan, are likeable, sincere youngsters with whom young adults will identify. Although the character development is somewhat superficial, the growth in the heroine's insight makes this popular story worth reading. Girls in junior high school will adopt this book as their own.

Since Jane Purdy and her friend Julie share in a babysitting venture, they must take turns with their nemesis, "little" Sandra Norton. On one such assignment, Jane, disheveled from retrieving the Norton's dog from under the shrubbery, faces a major crisis when Sandra threatens to pour ink on the rug. Suddenly, a delivery boy appears. He takes one look, intones a few magic pig-Latin words to distract Sandra, and saves the situation. He says he will be a sophomore at Woodmont High. Jane figures that he must be about 16 and new in town.

Fifteen-year-old Jane is without boyfriends, unless one counts George, who talks only about his rock collection. So for the next few days she plots ways to meet this glamourous new boy. Her efforts pay off when the boy, Stan Crandell, calls to ask her to the movies. Overjoyed, she accepts. Then, she begins to worry about her hair, her clothes, her parents' appearance—everything. However, when the evening is over, Jane inadvertently sees Stan take his bicycle from its hiding place in the bushes. She feels very foolish for having wanted to put on such a big show.

Soon, Stan suggests that they go to the city with two other couples for a Chinese dinner. One of the boys, Buzz, dates Jane's friend, Julie. The three couples are forced to use the "Doggie Dinner" delivery truck because Stan's father unexpectedly needs his car. Jane is surprised, but assures Stan that the truck is just fine with her, even though the third girl, Marcy, pokes fun at it. The dinner in Chinatown goes badly for Jane who has never had such exotic food before. Stan understands her predicament and, away from the crowd, buys her a souvenir and a hamburger.

Everyone at Woodmont High now assumes that Jane is Stan's girl. Therefore she turns down George's invitation to the next school dance even though Stan has not yet invited her. When she finds out that Stan is taking someone else, Jane accepts a baby-sitting job for the evening.

The following day, Julie calls to say that Bitsy, Stan's date, was gorgeous. This blow is short-lived, for Stan arrives in his new car to take Jane to her job. Stan explains that he had promised to take Bitsy to the first dance at his new school before he moved to town. He also tells Jane that he wants her to be the first to ride in his car. Before the ride is over, they meet Buzz and Julie and on an impulse Jane kisses Buzz.

She doesn't hear from Stan until Julie calls to report that he has been hospitalized with an emergency appendectomy. Jane decides to bring him flowers, but by the time she gains the courage to buy them, Stan is already home. Now, with her huge bouquet, she has to walk from the florist past the drug store crowd to Stan's house.

Reconciled at last, she and Stan attend the next social event at Woodmont High. Here, Stan asks her to wear his bracelet.

The title comes from Jane's thoughts about being 16, "Will I still be so dumb about boys when I'm 16. Will I still be so dumb?"

Thematic Material

This is a story of a first romance. The growth of mutual self-confidence and insight that comes through this experience is competently shown. In addition, the warm attachment between Jane and Julie is shown in proper perspective.

Book Talk Material

A very brief introduction to the plot is sufficient to introduce this book to young girls.

Additional Suggestions

Young girls will want to follow this story with the author's *The Luckiest Girl* (Morrow, $3.50; lib. bdg. $3.32 net) and *Sister of the Bride* (Morrow, $3.50; lib. bdg. $3.32 net). Another title that lends itself well to this group is Margaret Craig's *Now That I'm Sixteen* (Crowell, $3.50). Junior high age girls will also enjoy Denise Brookman's *The Young in Love* (Macrae Smith, $3.50).

William Corbin, *High Road Home,*
Coward, 1954, $3.50

This novel deals with the wanderings of a 14-year-old French boy in America. William Corbin has accomplished for young people what John Steinbeck did for adults in *Travels with Charley* (Watts, $6.95). Both books contain a combination of keen perception and fine writing. This adventure story is enjoyed by junior high school boys.

Nico LaFlamme has been unwillingly scooped from his hand-to-mouth existence as an orphan on the streets of Paris, to a new life in America where he is to be adopted by a family he does not know—a Mr. and Mrs. Dennison of San Francisco. Nico has other plans for himself and they do not include the Dennisons. When the train taking him west stops in Cleveland, he escapes from his guardian. Although Nico is a bitter and lonely child who loathes Americans, believing them all overfed, over-rich, and arrogant, he is sure that America holds the key to his past. Nico has in his possession a clipping from an American newspaper that tells of a certain Achelle (the last name is missing) who has come from France to teach at a local university. Although the French authorities have told Nico that his father, Achelle LaFlamme, died during World War II, Nico believes (because the clipping was given to him by an American soldier whom he had asked about LaFlamme) that the item refers to his father. He has therefore set himself the impossible task of finding his father by trying to locate the paper in which the column appeared. His only clue is a picture of the columnist at the top of the clipping.

He tries the office of a Cleveland newspaper without success. Then, after a harrowing ride in a furniture van, he arrives in Columbus to try his luck there. In a coffee shop, Nico meets Dud Hamilton, a gangly, amusing redhead who is slightly older than Nico and also something of an escapee. Dud has left his small dull home town to try his hand at newspaper reporting in the big city. He has been entirely unsuccessful and so he too is ready to move on.

Together these boys experience a fantastic American odyssey—each searching for something that will bring fulfillment to his life. Their exciting adventures include a narrow escape from death at the hands of a robber on a freight train and a near-disasterous experience as pin-setters in a Chicago bowling alley.

Because of a misunderstanding, the boys separate in Chicago but, through Duds understanding they are reunited in St. Louis. As Nico's knowledge of America grows, his hatred and hostility lessen. Their travels, however, are cut short when the police catch Nico and turn him over to his foster parents.

Much to his surprise, Nico fits well into the lives of Cal and Sally Dennison. He grows to love them. This only produces more guilt because he knows that instead of gratitude for their kindness, he must hurt them by leaving to continue his search. When the opportunity comes, he again runs away and joins Dud in San Diego where Dud has traced Jack Dodge, the writer of the newspaper column. Here, Nico's search ends. The university professor is not Achelle LaFlamme but Achelle Chenier. Mr. Chenier, however, did know Nico's father during the war. Achelle LaFlamme saved the lives of many Resistance fighters and had died a hero's death.

His mission complete, Nico is once more ready to move on when he is found by the Dennisons. This time he willingly goes to San Francisco to be their adopted son. Dud also journeys to San Francisco, where he takes a job as a newspaper copy boy.

Thematic Material

The values of friendship and the need for understanding between peoples is stressed throughout this novel.

Book Talk Material

This novel abounds in short episodes that can be read or told in a book talk. Some examples: Nico's adventure locked in a moving van (pp. 34–37); his first meeting with Dud (pp. 50–57); the fight on the freight train (pp. 104–108).

Additional Suggestions

Similar titles are Margot Benary-Isbert's *The Long Way Home* (Harcourt, $3.25), *Tree House Island* by Scott Corbett (Little, $3.75) and *Kep* by Zachary Ball (Holiday, $3.25). Older boys might enjoy Siegfried Lenz' *The Lightship* (Hill & Wang, $3.50) or Paul Annixter's *Swiftwater* (Hill & Wang, $2.75).

August Derleth, *The Moon Tenders,*
Meredith, 1958, $3.50

Mr. Derleth has probably created the closest counterpart of Tom Sawyer and Huck Finn that we have in contemporary juvenile fiction. His heroes, Sim Jones and Steve Grendon, possess those "all-boy" qualities that always produce lively and humorous situations. Boys in grades six through eight particularly enjoy this book.

The setting is the small town of Sac Prairie, Wisconsin in the early 1920's. Steve and Sim have decided to build a raft and pole down the Wisconsin River to Bogus Bluff where, according to legend, the lost Winnebago treasure is buried in a cave. After overcoming delays caused by parental hostility and launching difficulties, the boys maneuver the raft downstream to Bogus Bluff. Inside the cave, they discover a walled-off inner section containing an assortment of furnishings and some strange metal objects. They are about to leave when the occupants return and take the boys prisoner. Their captors are a rather unusual pair of culprits; the first, Mr. Tom, is thin, taciturn and nasty; the second, Ellis, is fat, loquacious and very personable. Ellis is a lover of Emerson's *Essays* and a man who takes great pride in his work which, he reveals, is counterfeiting. At the moment, he is producing rare 1913 Indian head nickels to sell to coin collectors. The boys now realize the danger of their situation and want to escape. Their plans, however, are foiled by their shrewd captors. On the third day of their confinement, they are unexpectedly set free after they promise not to reveal what they have seen.

Back in Sac Prairie, Steve becomes increasingly upset at keeping the promise. He finally blurts out the truth to his understanding grand-father. Grampa Adams makes Steve realize that "concealing what you know about something dishonest, makes you dishonest, too." Both boys finally realize that in certain situations compromises must be made. They decide to tell the authorities. Although the counterfeiters have made their escape by this time, the boys' consciences are clear.

The title comes from a reference to the boys made by Grampa Adams (p. 5) : "Moontenders—with nothing better to do but tend the moon and the stars. I guess that's what it is to be a boy."

Thematic Material

The friendship of the two boys is an important aspect of the book. The themes of personal courage and the moral conflict of breaking a promise could also be utilized.

Book Talk Material

To create interest, tell part of the story and read parts of the cave exploration episode which ends with the boys' capture (pp. 70–81). To give an indication of the humor and local color in the book read the incident concerning the inept Sac Prairie Fire Department (pp. 9–11), or the visit to the Electric Theater to see a William S. Hart epic (pp. 156–161).

Additional Suggestions

Boys who like this novel should also enjoy its sequels: *Mill Creek Irregulars, Special Detectives* (Meredith, $3.50), *Pinkertons Ride Again* (Meredith, $3.00) and others. *Three Stuffed Owls* by Keith Robertson (Viking, $3.00; lib. bdg. $2.96 net) also contains both humor and mystery. László Hámori's *Dangerous Journey* (Harcourt, $3.25), also recommended, is an adventure story of two Hungarian boys who flee to Vienna from behind the Iron Curtain.

Annabel and Edgar Johnson, *Pickpocket Run*,
Harper, 1961, $3.50; lib. bdg. $3.79 net

The Johnsons have written a great many juvenile titles with diverse settings and periods. Each bears the refreshing stamp of good character portrayal and realistic plot development. This novel helps to bridge the gap between juvenile and adult reading and is popular with boys in both junior and senior high schools.

Pickpocket Run is the name given by drivers to the truck route that includes the little town of Sylvanite. It is called that because of the mercenary and unfriendly attitude of its inhabitants.

Dix has little reason to dispute this appraisal of his home town. He has recently graduated from high school and now feels completely at loose ends. He is without close friends and almost entirely alienated from his family. Only this morning, his father's use of unfair business methods had precipitated an argument that left Dix longing for freedom in the neighboring big city. Here he is at the beginning of the gala Fourth of July rodeo weekend without money and feeling trapped.

Kino Farley, an acquaintance from high school, approaches him with a scheme to make some fast money. Dix is interested until he learns the details of the plan. On the Fourth, at the height of the festivities, Kino and two other boys plan to rob a local motel run by an elderly couple, the Judds. Dix wants no part of the robbery, but he does promise not to reveal the plans to anyone, including Scanlin, the town's much disliked police officer.

However, Kino and his gang are afraid that Dix will talk. To make sure this doesn't happen, they meet him, that evening, on a lonely street and beat him up. Luckily, Dix is found by a passer-by, Matt Burnham and taken to Matt's place where he spends the night.

Matt Burnham has been considered the village eccentric since he arrived in Sylvanite a year ago. He is 30 years old, lives alone, and is unemployed and friendless.

The next morning Dix reviews the situation. He now knows how dangerous Kino and his gang really are. The robbery must be prevented at all cost.

Dix tries to warn the police but finds that Kino has already lied so convincingly to Scanlin that no one will believe the truth. Dix's father tells him to mind his own business and stay out of trouble. Dix finally confides in his older sister, Ruth, the only member of his family with whom he has any closeness. Ruth, although concerned and sympathetic, can offer no real help. Dix in desperation blurts out the truth to his savior of the previous night, Matt Burnham. The three—Matt, Ruth and Dix—spend the evening planning a course of action. Dix will trick Kino into thinking he has left town; but actually he and Ruth will gain access to the motel and warn the Judds. Meanwhile Matt will get the police and wait for the robbers.

The following day Dix and Ruth manage to enter the motel unseen. Ruth and the Judds remain in the motel while Dix stands guard in the office. The phone rings. It's Matt—the police will be delayed. He tells Dix to lock the motel and forget the plan to catch the culprits. But Dix refuses. He feels that for once someone in his town must take a rightful stand.

In the tense scene which follows, Dix, though wounded by a robber's bullet, is able to hold them at bay until Matt and the police finally arrive.

The novel ends on a positive note. The secret of Matt's identity is revealed—he was a crime-fighting District Attorney who found that he couldn't fight the political machine in the city. He had come to Sylvanite to sort out his thoughts. Now, with the help of independent supporters, he intends to return to the political fight. However, he plans to visit Sylvanite often—if only to see Ruth. Dix, now freed from self doubt and lack of direction, takes over Matt's small house and decides to give his home town another try.

Thematic Material

Two main themes are apparent: Dix' need for the help of others in spite of his supposed independence, and a young boy's victory over two adversaries—the criminal forces of Kino and the power of compromise and indifference represented by Dix' father and the town of Sylvanite.

Book Talk Material

Interest can be aroused by telling part of the story. One might use part of Chapter Five where the robbery plans are divulged (pp. 37–44), or the scene where Dix is attacked by Kino and his gang (pp. 61–64). Dix' appeal to his father (pp. 99–102) is also a crucial scene.

Additional Suggestions

Other appropriate works by the Johnsons' are *The Black Symbol* (Harper, $3.95; lib. bdg. $3.79 net) and *The Grizzley* (Harper, $3.95; lib. bdg. $3.79 net) . Alberta Armer's *Troublemaker* (World, $3.75; lib. bdg. $3.61 net) is a suitable novel for a slightly younger audience. The rehabilitation of a young delinquent on a Montana ranch is explored in Jo Sykes' *Chip on His Shoulder* (Funk, $3.25) .

Elizabeth George Speare, *Calico Captive*,
Houghton, 1937, $3.50

Mrs. Speare's careful attention to historical detail and realistic portrayal of her heroine make this an outstanding junior novel. Filled with the romanticism of youth, Miriam is the embodiment of the adolescent struggling with adult problems. This exciting story will delight girls in grades six through eight.

Because of the Indian raids, Miriam Willard has spent the hot, grueling summer of 1754, in Fort Number Four with her older sister, Susanna Johnson, and the three Johnson children. But when Captain Johnson returns from his journey down the Connecticut River they move back to their cabin outside the fort. Here, during one last gay party, Phineas Whitney, a young divinity student, declares his love to the shy Miriam before leaving for Harvard College.

At dawn on the following day, Indians surround the cabin. Each Indian takes one person as his captive. When Susanna Johnson gives birth to a daughter on the trail, no one is more pleased than the dark savage who then has two prisoners to ransom to the French in Canada. Only the little children fare well on the brutal forced march. Miriam is continually tormented by Mehkoa, an Indian boy about her age. But when she rescues Susanna's baby from the swirling waters of a deep stream Mehkoa stops his mischief and returns Miriam's blue calico dress.

The Indians bring the captives to their village, whereupon Mehkoa asks the Chief to give him Miriam for his squaw. Repelled, Miriam runs from the scene, bringing dishonor to the young brave and trouble to her family who are then parceled out as slaves to the Indian families. In time, Susanna persuades the Chief to sell her husband, children and sister to the French in Quebec. She and her six-year-old son, Sylvanus remain with the Indians as prisoners.

Miriam begins a new life as a servant in a wealthy French home where she becomes fast friends with the young maid, Hortense, and a sometime playmate of the pretty young daughter of the house, Felicité. Here, too, she meets Pierre, a rich, worldly, young adventurer, who proposes marriage. But even this opportunity to end her hard circumstances cannot change Miriam's belief that she loves Phineas and his way of life far more than all the worldly things that Pierre can give her.

After many discouraging months, Susanna makes her way to Quebec. She and Miriam finally arrange passage to England through the influence of the Governor's wife. From England, these valiant colonists will then attempt to find passage to their home in Massachusetts.

The word calico in the title refers to the cherished blue dress in which Miriam first learned of Phineas' love and in which she sustained the horrors of Indian captivity.

Thematic Material

Wholesome boy-girl relationships, climaxed by Miriam's choice of Phineas, are well presented. The sustaining quality of Miriam's friendship with the young girl, Hortense, is another important element in the story. In addition, the underlying themes of self-reliance and perseverance are also stressed.

Book Talk Material

To captivate a young junior high audience, the story could be introduced by reading aloud the third paragraph on page nine, followed by a description of the Indian raid (pp. 15–19). The romantic vignette in which Pierre tricks Miriam into going to a fancy dress ball for which she has sewn many of the gowns will interest potential readers (pp. 244–253).

Additional Suggestions

Mrs. Speare's award-winning novel, *The Witch of Blackbird Pond* (Houghton, $3.25) could be suggested. Cornelia Meigs' *Fair Wind to Virginia* (Macmillan, lib. bdg. $3.84 net) may also be used. Worthy of note are two books by Annabel and Edgar Johnson: *Torrie* (Harper,

$3.95; lib. bdg. $3.79 net) a tender love story about a young girl who crosses the American continent in the 1840's and *The Bearcat* (Harper, $3.50; lib. bdg. $3.27 net) a sensitive, romantic tale about a boy who works in the Montana mines at the turn of the century. This latter title will appeal to both girls and boys.

Mary Stolz, *The Organdy Cupcakes,*
Harper, 1951, $3.50; lib. bdg. $3.27 net

Mary Stolz' sensitive stories for girls stand out for their brilliant creation of character. In her portrayal of the late adolescent, she shows an unusual sympathy and understanding for the introverted girl who is somewhat estranged from the world around her. Eighth or ninth grade girls who need something more mature than the standard "girls' story" should enjoy this novel.

Three girls—all friends but vastly different—dominate the action in *The Organdy Cupcakes.* They are student nurses who are now in the last few months of their senior year in a suburban New York hospital. Graduation is approaching, when each will receive her organdy cupcake, the graduate's cap.

Gretchen Bemis, or as one intern has named her, Bemis de Milo, is pretty, warm and outgoing. With endless amounts of self-confidence and social poise, she has no difficulty securing dates or attracting boy friends. However, her primary purpose in entering nursing school remains unfulfilled—she came to Silbert Memorial to find a husband, "a sort of a medicine-man hunt," and as yet none of the interns have managed to sweep her off her very capable feet.

Rosemary Joplin is much more introspective. She is somewhat set back emotionally by her irrational dislike for her step-mother and the lingering memories of her playmate-mother who died when she was 14. This preoccupation with her own problems has made it impossible for Rosemary to give completely and unselfishly of herself either to her profession or to her friends.

The third, Nelle Gibson, is the Plain Jane of the group. Growing up in the shadow of a scatterbrained, domineering mother has left Nelle somewhat withdrawn, shy and unsure of herself.

During the last few months of training, the experiences of these three girls produce changes that leaves each a different person on graduation day.

Nelle meets Wally Chase, a young man interested in archaeology. As their attachment deepens, Nelle learns much about archaeology but more about the pleasures of being wanted and loved.

Through a mutual interest in music, Rosemary becomes acquainted with a young intern, Kenneth Grafton, who is also interested in psychiatry. During a severe attack of influenza, Rosemary is often visited by Kenneth, who listens patiently as she talks about her past. Through these meetings, Rosemary gains insight into her problems and gradually loses her feelings of hostility and hatred. Now more confident and self-reliant, she makes plans to become an Army nurse after graduation.

Gretchen's story is the most romantic of the three. She has a secret crush on the young and handsome Dr. Orin Whitney who, according to Gretchen, scarcely knows that she exists. But his sudden realization that Gretchen's graduation will mean their parting brings the two of them together. Gretchen's medicine-man hunt ends with a proposal of marriage.

As graduation day arrives, each realizes that her training has given her something even more valuable than an organdy cupcake.

Thematic Material

Friendship and self-fulfillment are the book's two themes. The book also gives a more accurate picture of the nursing profession than many so-called "career" novels. This aspect of service and sacrifice might be utilized in introducing the book.

Book Talk Material

Briefly introducing the three heroines should be enough to interest readers. One could use their conversations together in Chapter Two (pp. 21–26). Chapter Three, a two page description of what the nursing profession is all about, makes for excellent reading aloud (pp. 28–29).

Additional Suggestions

Hospital Zone (Harper, $3.95; lib. bdg. $3.79 net) by the same author could be suggested. More adult titles, such as Clara Burke's and Adele Comandini's *Dr. Hap* (Coward, $4.95), the Freedmans' *Mrs. Mike*

(Coward, $5.95) or Kathryn Hulme's *The Nun's Story* (Little, $4.95) might also be utilized.

Laura Ingalls Wilder, *These Happy Golden Years,*
Harper, 1943, $3.50; lib. bdg. $3.27 net

Mrs. Wilder's autobiographical story of courtship in the late 1800's creates a sentimental portrait of a loving family in the tradition of *Little Women*. Although the characters, Laura Ingalls and Almanzo Wilder, belong to a bygone era, they personify the many conflicts that all young people face when they approach adulthood. Girls in grades five through eight who are familiar with the earlier titles in Mrs. Wilder's "Little House" series will want to read this book. If they have missed the earlier titles, this story is complete and rewarding in itself.

Eighteen-year-old Laura, nicknamed "Half-pint" by her father, begins teaching at Brewster School, where three of her five students turn out to be taller than she. For the next three months, Laura works diligently to be a good teacher, to keep abreast of her own forfeited studies and to dispel the terrible loneliness in the cold, frightening house where she boards.

One Friday, Almanzo Wilder, a young homesteader from Laura's town, arrives unexpectedly with his sleigh to take Laura home for the weekend. Thus begins a three year courtship during which Laura continues her schooling, passes two teaching certification exams, teaches at Perry School and works intermittently as a dressmaker and mother's helper out on the prairie. All of her earnings go toward her blind sister Mary's education.

Although frontier life is never easy, Almanzo Wilder and his spirited horses (Almanzo is always breaking in a new team to sell) bring gaiety and excitement to Laura's life. During one of their Sunday buggy rides, with one of Laura's girl friends along, Laura discovers that she is not willing to share Almanzo's attentions. She realizes that she is falling in love, even though her Ma and Pa teasingly suggest that she seems to like young Wilder's horses better than she likes him. During a summer buggy ride to see his prairie claim, Almanzo gently suggests that Laura might like an engagement ring. Laura accepts. So the two young people devote themselves to marriage preparations, Almanzo building a small house on his land and Laura sewing her trousseau. After a simple ceremony and one of Mrs. Ingalls' delicious dinners, the couple move into their new home confident of their resourcefulness and love.

Thematic Material

In addition to the romantic theme, the author's emphasis on a warm-hearted family relationship makes this book an excellent choice for young readers. The personal fortitude and courage required of pioneers is also well depicted.

Book Talk Material

Interest in the romance can be aroused by telling some of the story preceding the episode where Laura discovers that she cares deeply about being alone with Almanzo (pp. 175–177). With some preliminary discussion about Almanzo's new horses and an exciting buggy ride could be used to intrigue girls who are especially interested in horses (pp. 204–206). The episode that takes place on a snowy Christmas Eve when the Wilders are not able to attend the church party in town conveys the meaning of the book (pp. 223–231).

Additional Suggestions

Younger girls who like this novel will relish its predecessors, particularly *The Long Winter* (Harper, $3.50; lib. bdg. $3.27 net). Girls of junior high school age will also enjoy Loula Erdman's *Room to Grow* (Dodd, $3.50) about a French family who settle in Texas at the turn of the century. These will lead to historical romances such as Ellen Turngren's *Shadows into Mist* (McKay, $3.50), a realistic tale about a young Swedish couple in Minnesota before the turn of the century, and Alonzo Gibbs' *The Fields Breathe Sweet* (Lothrop, $3.50) a vivid portrait of a New York farm girl on Long Island in the late 1600's.

6

Achieving Self-Reliance

A CHILD is dependent on his parents and other adults. As he reaches middle childhood, he begins to make his own decisions and to assert his independence. He must learn to build his own set of values, to think as an individual. He must maintain respect and affection for his parents, without undue dependence upon them. He should understand that a happy home life is built on sharing and self-discipline.

The struggle for emancipation from adult control can result in conflict and rebellion. Still, some youths achieve a relatively smooth transition from dependence to independence. A great deal depends on the attitudes and maturity of the adults as well as the young people involved. The books in this chapter explore many aspects of the development of self-reliance in young people.

Margot Benary-Isbert, *The Ark,*
          Harcourt, 1953, $3.25

During the years immediately following World War II, civilian life in Germany was completely disrupted. Germany was a conquered nation, without adequate food and supplies, and still staggering under the wholesale destruction that accompanied the defeat. In Western Germany, the situation was further complicated by the influx of thousands of refugee families from the East fleeing from Russian occupation. This story of one such family is a favorite with girls from grades six through nine.

After nine months of traveling, the Lechows have at last reached the safety of a West German city. There are five of them: Mrs. Lechow and her four children—15-year-old Matthias, Margret who is almost 14, ten-year-old Andrea and, lastly, Joey, who is only six. To sustain their morale, the Lechows rarely speak of the two missing members of their family—Margret's twin brother, Christian, who was shot by the invaders, and their father, Dr. Lechow, who the family hopes is still alive in a Russian prisoner of war camp.

By a stroke of luck, the Housing Authority has assigned them two rooms in a house on Parsley Street. Their new landlady, Mrs. Verduz, is a widow who resents having her privacy disrupted by the guests that the Housing Authority has thrust upon her. However, the family helps her with her chores and runs errands for her and soon, she is grudgingly won over.

With the exception of Margret, the children adjust to their new situation. Matthias becomes a mason's helper and develops a friendship with a co-worker, Dieter, who has formed a dance band named the Cellar Rats. Andrea and Joey attend school. One of Joey's classmates, an orphan boy named Hans Ulrich, spends so much time at the Lechows that he becomes part of the family. But Margret, who stays at home and helps her mother, seems unable to erase the scars produced by years of war. Mrs. Lechow, an untiring and unselfish person, valiantly tries to make a new life for her family.

A few days before Christmas the children go caroling. One of their stops is at Rowan Farm, owned by Mrs. Almut. Margret is so impressed with the kindness of this friendly old lady, and the beauty of her many farm animals, that arrangements are made for both her and Matthias to move to the farm and become Mrs. Almut's helpers.

With the help of Dieter and the Cellar Rats, Matthias converts an abandoned railroad carriage into living quarters for himself and Margret. Because they are continually surrounded by farm animals, they name their new home Noah's Ark. Margret thrives in this atmosphere. She showers all her warmth and affection on the animals and soon regains her interest in life.

Quite accidentally, Joey and Hans Ulrich contribute to the family's renewed good fortune. While "treasure hunting" in a bombed-out building, they find a suitcase full of valuable papers. As a reward, its owner, Mrs. Hertrich, gives clothing and provisions to the family.

In the spring, Mrs. Verduz dies of a heart attack. In her will, she leaves her furniture and many of her possessions to the Lechows; however, her house is claimed by the Housing Authority. The Lechows are asked to move but Mrs. Almut shows her kindness by letting them move into the Ark with Margret and Matthias.

It is almost Christmas time again and the Lechows begin preparations for the holidays. While Joey is out playing in the yard, a stranger approaches. He is haggard and lame. Margret is the first to recognize him—Dr. Lechow has returned.

In remembering all of the family's past experiences, Margret is reminded of the Old Testament story about Noah. It is as though God Himself has been saying to her family, "Fear not! For behold, here is the Ark."

Thematic Material

The author describes, from her own experience, how helpless innocents must suffer the effects of war. The novel also conveys a hope for the future through the Lechows strong family ties.

Book Talk Material

A short plot description will usually be enough to interest readers. To illustrate the author's sensitive writing and the warmth of the Lechow family's relationships, one of the following passages could be used: the family's reception by Mrs. Verduz (pp. 8–13) ; the children bargain for a few potatoes (pp. 29–32) ; a birthday party for Margret and Andrea (pp. 46–49) ; the children sing carols at Rowan Farm (pp. 64–68) , Christmas with the Lechows (pp. 82-88) .

Additional Suggestions

In *Rowan Farm* (Harcourt, $3.25) , a sequel to *The Ark,* Margret must make the difficult decision of whether to remain on the farm or go to America. Other recommended novels by Margot Benary-Isbert are *The Wicked Enchantment* (Harcourt, $3.25) and *Castle on the Border* (Harcourt, $3.50) . For young readers suggest: Claire Bishop's *Twenty and Ten* (Viking, $3.00; lib. bdg. $2.96 net) , in which a group of French children save ten Jewish girls and boys from the Nazis, or Meindert De-Jong's *The House of Sixty Fathers* (Harper, $3.50; lib. bdg. $3.27 net) , the story of a Chinese boy's search for his family during World War II. Additional recommendations for older girls are: *The Diary of a Young Girl* by Anne Frank (Modern Lib., $1.95) , and Maria Trapp's *Story of the Trapp Family Singers* (Lippincott, $5.95) .

Henry Gregor Felsen, *Hot Rod,*
Dutton, 1950, $3.25

Gregor Felsen has written a variety of juvenile books. His most popular books are those, like *Hot Rod,* which deal with teen-age drivers and their problems. This novel is popular with boys in the junior high grades. It can be used effectively with older boys who have reading difficulties.

At 17, Bud Crayne is much more independent and self-reliant than other boys his age. His life has not been easy—he was orphaned at an early age, and raised by an uncle who pays little attention to him.

Bud loves hot rods more than anything else. While most kids were learning to ride bicycles, he was already tinkering with automobiles. Now, he owns his own rod, and it's the best in town. He keeps it at Jake Clymer's gas station, where he works after school.

Bud is the envy of the gang that hangs around Clymer's garage: Bud's girl friend, LaVerne Shuler, and her sidekick, Marge Anderson; Walt Thomas, who uses hot rodding to compensate for his feelings of inferiority; pampered and somewhat spoiled Ralph Osler; and quiet, level-headed Chuck Liddell.

Mr. Cole, one of Bud's teachers, tells him about a countrywide Safe Driving Roadeo. The winner will be sent to the state Teen Age Roadeo, where the first prize is a college scholarship. Mr. Cole is confident that Bud can win if he will enter the Program.

However, Walt has bet Bud ten dollars that Bud cannot drive from Avondale to Trenton, a distance of 40 miles, in 30 minutes. Bud tries to call off the bet, but Walt continues to taunt him; even LaVerne openly shows contempt for what she interprets as cowardice. Against his better judgment, Bud consents to drive.

The ride is a nightmare of near-accidents. Bud is caught by the police and his driver's license is suspended until the time of the county Roadeo.

The rest of the group continue their reckless driving activities.

The only member of the gang that joins the Driver Program is Chuck, who as a result gains the nickname "Chicken" Liddell.

Bud enters the county Roadeo, confident of victory, but, to his amazement, he places second. The winner is Chuck Liddell. Bud realizes that, although he knows a great deal about motors and driving skill, he still must learn a lot about sane and safe driving before he can become a real expert. Suddenly, speed racing loses its thrill and challenge.

One evening, while Bud is on duty at the garage, the gang decides to play hide-and-seek in their cars. LaVerne and Marge pile in with Ralph in his car. Reluctantly, Chuck joins them. Walt, the hunter, drives alone. In an effort to remain undetected, neither driver turns on his lights. On the dangerous Ninety-Mile-Curve, both cars meet in a head-on collision.

Officer O'Day and Bud are the first to arrive at the accident. In the twisted pile of wreckage, four bodies are found. Although in critical condition Chuck is the only one still alive. Bud is so shaken that he feels he can never drive again, but O'Day forces him behind the wheel of the police car to drive the unconscious Chuck to the hospital in Trenton. For once, Bud's driving skill serves a useful purpose.

Because of the accident, Chuck is unable to compete in the Roadeo. Mr. Cole persuades Bud to undergo a period of retraining and enter in Chuck's place. Bud wins first prize. When asked to tell the secret of his fine driving, Bud says, "I kept telling myself I was Chuck. When I did it that way, I automatically did the courteous and thoughtful thing and that was the right thing. It's easy. That's all there is to good driving."

Thematic Material

Hot Rod spells out in graphic terms that driving, like many other adult activities, requires adherence to a set of rules. Failure to obey them can mean tragedy. Boys will identify with Bud and his growing sense of responsibility.

Book Talk Material

The novel can be effectively presented by giving a brief introduction to the plot. One might also read some of the questions from the written test given at the Roadeo (the questions are on pp. 127–128, the answers are at the back of the book).

Additional Suggestions

Other novels by Felsen about driving are: *Street Rod* (Random, $3.50; lib. bdg. $3.59 net), *Crash Club* (Random, $3.50; lib. bdg. $3.59

net) and *Boy Gets Car* (Random, $3.50; lib. bdg. $3.59 net). Practical information and advice about driving are given in the author's *To My Son, the Teen-Age Driver* (Dodd, $3.00).

There are many sports novels about the racing world. Some examples are: Don Stanford's *The Red Car* (Funk, $3.25), William Gault's *The Checkered Flag* (Dutton, $3.50) and Patrick O'Conner's *The Black Tiger* (Washburn, $3.25; lib. bdg. $3.11 net). Phyllis Fenner's excellent collection of stories, *Behind the Wheel* (Morrow, $3.75), is also recommended.

Jean Fritz, *I, Adam*,
Coward, 1963, $3.75

Jean Fritz, who usually writes for a younger audience, has created an extremely fresh and well constructed portrait of a boy growing to manhood in *I, Adam*. Boys, and some girls, in grades six through nine enjoy this novel.

The year is 1850, and summer has come to the small seaport town of Coveport, Connecticut. The harbor is alive with ships and the wharves hum with activity.

For 15-year-old Adam Crane this beautiful June day has special significance—this is the last day of school, not just for this year, but forever. For too long Adam has suffered beatings and humiliations from his cruel teacher, Mr. Stone.

Even on this last day, Mr. Stone seizes an opportunity to thrash Adam unmercifully. After school, the "graduating" class—Adam and his friends, Mulie, Stump, and Enock—show their contempt for their former teacher by carrying him bodily out of the schoolhouse and throwing him into a pile of hay.

In a few days the boys will be going their various ways to seek their fortunes. Stump and Enock are heading for New York where they hope to earn passage to the gold fields of California. Mulie, Adam's best friend, wants to be a sailor. Adam already has his future cut out for him. His father, Captain Crane, has bought a farm in upstate Connecticut where he hopes to retire with his family after his next voyage. Adam will precede his family to the farm in Fieldsdale and make sure that the former owner, Mr. Sharkey, lives up to his contract to remain on the farm and help with the harvest before he receives his last payment.

Adam is extremely disappointed when he reaches the farm. Nothing has been cared for properly, the spring planting hasn't been done, and some of the furniture and livestock are missing. Mr. Starkey claims that he has been severely ill with rheumatism and therefore unable to work. Adam gets a little help from Mr. Sharkey's nine-year-old son, Tyler, who is wild as a weed and twice as unmanageable.

Adam learns from the townspeople that Mr. Sharkey has been lying to him. Since his wife died, Sharkey has been systematically selling the farm's assets to purchase gold claims in California where he plans to settle after receiving the final payment.

Lacking positive proof of Sharkey's villainy, Adam decides to wait until after the harvest before confronting him with the facts. Adam hires Edward Hallam, a neighbor's son, to help on the farm. Secretly he pays him out of what will eventually be the final payment for the farm.

Adam becomes friendly with his neighbors, Mr. and Mrs. Newlands, their daughter, 15-year-old Sarah, and the Newlands' star boarder, Pen Jackson, the local schoolmaster. Unlike Mr. Stone, Pen is able to arouse in Adam an interest in learning.

As harvest time approaches, Adam notices that Sharkey is becoming more secretive. A young man, Noble Hanson, visits the farm and has a long conversation with Sharkey. Although Sharkey seems pleased with the visit, he gives no explanation.

A few nights later, Adam returns home from a country fair to find Sharkey and an unwilling Tyler making hasty preparations to leave. Adam is bound and gagged, and robbed of all of his possessions—including the deed to the land and the last payment. Sharkey and Tyler make their escape.

The following morning, Adam is found by the Newlands and Pen Jackson. As plans are made for pursuit, Noble Hanson arrives and announces that Sharkey has sold the farm to him. When Hanson learns the truth, both he and Adam leave to find Sharkey. They decide to try New York City first, a logical place to find a man seeking passage to the California gold fields.

Their hunch is correct. They find Sharkey and force him to return Noble's money and the Cranes' deed of property.

Before going back to the farm, Adam stops off at Coveport to see his mother. He brings Tyler, who wishes to be adopted by the Crane family.

Adam has done a great deal of thinking about his future. He now knows that he will never be happy as a farmer. Instead, he wishes to go back to school and eventually attend college. However, he feels that he can't disappoint his family who are relying on his help.

When Captain Crane's ship, the "Good Nellie," returns, Adam learns that his father has had a leg amputated as the result of a whaling accident. The boy feels even more obligated to stay with his family on the farm.

Finally, Adam summons the courage to tell his father how he really feels. Realizing that a boy's future is more important than any piece of land, Captain Crane decides to sell the farm to Noble Hanson and remain at home on the seacoast. Even Mrs. Crane, who wanted the farm more than anyone, says, "I'd live anywhere in the world if there was a scholar in the family who needed feeding." Adam's course is at last set in the right direction.

Thematic Material

Adam displays many positive characteristics: devotion, ability to accept responsibility, courage, and perseverance. He also displays a quality of self-reliance that allows him to live up to the maxim taught him by Pen Jackson, "This above all, to thine own self be true."

I, Adam presents a fascinating cross-section of life in the East during the 1850's. There are descriptions of a New England whaling village, an inland farming community and, finally, the busy seaport of New York.

Book Talk Material

Here are some passages that could be used in a book talk: Adam's last day in class (pp. 14–16) ; Adam has his fortune told (pp. 21–26) ; (the prediction comes true on p. 235) ; Adam apologizes to Mr. Stone (pp. 44–47) ; Mulie gets a tattoo (pp. 55–60) ; Adam sees the farm and meets Tyler and Mr. Sharkey (pp. 87–93) , he learns about conditions on the farm (pp. 101–105) .

Additional Suggestions

Both the author and the illustrator of *I, Adam* have written fine boys' stories about the American Civil War. The first is Jean Fritz's *Brady*

(Coward, $3.50) and the second, Peter Burchard's *Jed: The Story of a Yankee Soldier and Southern Boy* (Coward, $3.00). Two other novels with New England settings are Elspeth Bragdon's *That Jud!* (Viking, $3.00; lib. bdg. $3.04 net) and Jean George's *My Side of the Mountain* (Dutton, $3.50).

Fred Gipson, *Old Yeller,*
Harper, 1956, $3.50; lib. bdg. $3.27 net

Stories concerning a boy and his dog are common in both adult and juvenile fiction; but rarely do we find one of the quality of *Old Yeller*. All of the elements of good story-telling are here—suspense, heartbreak, humor and excitement. The plot is handled with unusual insight and without sentimentality. Its appeal is increased by making the boy the narrator and by using a natural, conversational style. Although this novel was originally written for adults, it has become a favorite of boys and girls from the upper elementary grades into high school. Its simple vocabulary and wide popularity make it an idea choice for older boys with reading problems.

In the years immediately following the Civil War, one commodity was in short supply for the farmers along Birdsong Creek in the Texas hill country. This was "cash money." To get money, the settlers decide to combine their herds and conduct a massive cattle drive to the new market in Abilene, Kansas, some six hundred miles away.

When his father leaves with the rest of the menfolk, 14-year-old Travis Coates suddenly becomes the man of the house. Travis has little trouble convincing Mama and his pesky five-year-old brother, Arliss, of his new role.

One day, an ugly stray yellow dog moves in on the family. The dog does nothing to endear himself to Travis—he eats a side of hanging pork, takes baths in the family spring water, and hides when the homestead is threatened by the anger of two fighting bulls. Only little Arliss' devotion and valiant protests save the dog from being driven away. The family names him Old Yeller, partly because of his color and partly because of his strange voice—halfway between a bark and a yell.

Little Arliss has a passion for collecting things. One day, while sitting in the spring, he succeeds in catching a bear cub. The whimpering of the cub attracts its mother but Old Yeller saves the boy's life by keeping the bear at bay while Arliss makes his escape. The dog, at last, has proven his worth.

As Old Yeller becomes more and more a member of the family, he also becomes more and more Travis' dog. Together, the two hunt wild turkey, protect the corn fields from marauding raccoons and subdue a wild heifer. Their most dangerous assignment is the catching and marking of the new pigs. The older bar hogs are murderous and fiercely protective of their young. On one of these expeditions, a near tragedy occurs. Old Yeller herds a group of wild pigs into a ravine while Travis, on the bank above, lowers a lasso to catch the young ones. Suddenly the bank gives way and the boy tumbles into the midst of the savage herd. Travis is badly gashed on one leg, but Old Yeller, though wounded himself, drives off the hogs.

A new danger threatens the homesteaders. A plague of hydrophobia breaks out among the animals. One of the cows becomes infected and Travis is forced to shoot it. To prevent further infection, Mama attempts to burn the body. She and a neighbor girl, Lisbeth, are attacked by a rabid wolf. Old Yeller drives the animal off, but is bitten during the fight. This means certain death for the dog and perhaps danger to the rest of the family. Travis must shoot him.

Travis is inconsolable at the death of his friend. Even the return of his father and the horse he brings him do little to comfort him. But one day, Travis sees their new puppy, sired by Old Yeller, steal a chunk of cornbread in the same way Old Yeller once did. He decides to take the pup out on his first squirrel hunt, for "if he was big enough to act like Old Yeller, he was big enough to start learning to earn his keep."

Thematic Material

Incidents of courage and devotion abound in this book. Graphic details of frontier life make it a valuable historic document. The basic theme, however, is a boy's growth toward maturity as a result of accepting the responsibilities of manhood.

Book Talk Material

Old Yeller contains many isolated episodes. A few that are excellent for use are: Travis hunts for deer (pp. 18–25) ; the fight between the bulls (Chapter IV, pp. 19–41—or excerpts) ; Arliss is saved from the bear by Old Yeller (pp. 45–53) ; Travis and Old Yeller are wounded by the hogs (pp. 100–106). For a wonderful description of a frontier feast, Texas style, see page 84.

Additional Suggestions

Savage Sam (Harper, $3.95; lib. bdg. $3.79 net), the sequel to *Old Yeller,* is popular as is the author's earlier *Recollection Creek* (Harper, $3.95; lib. bdg. $3.79 net). Zachary Ball's *Bristle Face* (Holiday, $3.50) and its sequel *Sputters* (Holiday, $3.50) are also recommended. Older readers might try Robert Murphy's *The Pond* (Dutton, $4.95), or MacKinlay Kantor's *Voice of Bugle Ann* (Coward, $3.95).

Jim Kjelgaard, *Big Red,*
Holiday, 1945, $3.50

The continued popularity of Mr. Kjelgaard's novel about a trapper's son and a champion Irish setter proves his ability to write compelling animal stories for young adults. The strong line drawings by Bob Kuhn accentuate the vitality of the tale's action. Boys and girls in grades five through eight find this story very exciting.

Ross Pickett and his 17-year-old son Danny live in a rent-free cabin on the edge of the Blue Ridge Mountain estate of the wealthy sportsman, Mr. Haggin. The Picketts earn their meagre living by farming and trapping.

While Danny is reporting to Mr. Haggin that the bear, Old Majesty, has killed a prize farm bull, he sees Mr. Fraley, the estate manager, maltreat Mr. Haggin's red Irish setter named Champion Sylvester's Boy. Danny wishes that he could own this wonderful dog. At home, he tells Ross about the dog, but Ross advises him to forget about it.

Ross awakens Danny the following morning to tell him that the red dog is on their porch and that he must return him. Although Danny wants desperately to keep him, he compromises and takes the long way back through the woods. Danny marvels at the dog's natural point toward game birds. When they unexpectedly encounter Old Majesty at the dead bull's carcass, the courageous dog attacks him. Danny tries to shoot the bear, but, unwilling to risk injury to the dog, he loses his opportunity.

Mr. Haggin is so impressed by Danny's story and the dog's devotion to him that he asks Danny to board him and accompany him to the dog show in New York City. Danny goes back to the cabin triumphantly.

Ross is also pleased to have such a fine dog around. He tells Danny that Red, as Danny names the dog, will make a great varmint hunter. Danny, however, wants to train Red to be a bird hunter.

At the dog show, Red wins Best of Breed. Mr. Haggin explains that this makes Red valuable as a sire of future champions. Although Danny learns about dogs on the trip and enjoys seeing the big city, he is happy to go home with Red.

The homecoming sours a little when he and Ross argue about Red's training. Ross insists that Red be trained to hunt fur-bearing animals so he can help them run their trap lines. He also tells Danny that whipping Red is the only way to break him of his bad habit of chasing small animals. Although Danny refuses to punish the intelligent dog, he can't find an answer to the problem. One day, however, Red himself provides the solution when he chases a skunk. The results of this escapade effectively discourage Red. Nothing, however, seems to change Ross's attitude about making Red a varmint dog. To make matters worse, Ross wants to use Red to track a vicious lynx as well as Old Majesty. Danny refuses, and a rift develops between them.

As Danny continues to train Red to hunt partridge, he notices that Ross has begun to shoot birds without a hunting dog. He realizes that his father is trying to show him how useless a bird dog is.

But the young man and the dog finally win the argument. After a heavy snow, Red tracks Ross from the scent of the partridge in his pockets and rescues him from a deep snowdrift. While Ross is recuperating, Danny and Red take over the running of the trap lines. They are attacked by a fierce wolverine and fight for their lives. Together, they subdue and kill the marauding animal, but Red is badly ripped in the fight. Luckily, he is not permanently injured. Danny returns to the cabin with the skins from the trap lines. Both men now know that Red has the heart and courage to be both varmint and bird dog.

When spring arrives, Old Majesty reappears and kills their mule. Leaving Danny behind to take care of Red's pregnant mate, Ross sets out with his hounds to kill their old enemy. The bear kills the dogs and badly wounds Ross. After nursing his Pa, Danny decides to kill the bear with Red's help. They find their quarry and, while Red attacks the bear, Danny pumps bullets into the huge animal. He kills him with his last shot. He realizes that if it were not for Red's blazing attack, they would be dead.

Danny tends Red's wounds for seven days before returning to the cabin. Danny is heartbroken because Red is scarred and has a useless front leg. Ross and Mr. Haggin reassure him and tell him that he has done the right thing—"a man's life is still more valuable than an animal's." Danny watches the new pups as Red limps up to them and sniffs. One of them seems to be a miniature Red.

Thematic Material

Most youngsters rarely experience the necessity for the early self-reliance that the wilderness demands. This story provides a satisfying portrayal of what it would be like. The realistic father-son relationship in *Big Red* is a classic in adolescent literature.

Book Talk Material

Dog lovers will respond to a brief description of the plot. To interest readers use the following incidents: Danny meets Red (pp. 11–14) and add, Red meets Old Majesty (pp. 18–26); the dog show (pp. 40–62); the skunk wins (pp. 98–105); Red saves Ross (pp. 147–152); the wolverine (pp. 183–196). The chapter on the arrival of Red's mate will amuse a group of potential readers (pp. 197–216).

Additional Suggestions

Suggest the sequels: Mr. Kjelgaard's *Irish Red* (Holiday, $3.25) and *Outlaw Red* (Holiday, $3.50). Readers can continue with the author's popular *Snow Dog* (Holiday, $3.50) and *Wild Trek* (Holiday, $3.50). The quality of self-reliance stressed in this story can also be found in A. J. Dawson's story about an Irish wolfhound, *Finn the Wolfhound* (Harcourt, $3.50) and Lee McGiffin's tale of a boy's trek across country with his dog, *High Whistle Charley* (Dutton, $3.00). Older boys will enjoy the daring exploits in Robb White's *The Survivor* (Doubleday, $3.50).

Emily Neville, *It's Like This, Cat,*

Harper, 1963, $3.95; lib. bdg. $3.79 net

Mrs. Neville's first novel—a teen-ager's account of his daily adventures and his inner struggles—is the 1964 Newbery Award winner. The author's perceptive observations about a normally rebellious boy living in a large metropolis are skillfully recorded. Young people in grades six though eight enjoy this introspective story.

Dave Mitchell, an only child, has lived all of his 14 years in a New York City apartment with his quiet mother and argumentative father. Dave figures that all the roaring and bickering between his father and him causes his mother's repeated asthma attacks. One constant source of irritation to Dave is his father's insistence that a boy should have a dog (Mr. Mitchell and his dog, Jeff, used to chase rabbits). Finally, in exasperation, Dave points out that you can't chase rabbits on Third Avenue and his father explodes in anger.

The only person in whom Dave is able to confide is a neighbor, Crazy Kate (so named because she keeps many cats). Although she occasionally feeds and soothes Dave, she lets him know that he acts a great deal like his father.

After another fight with his father, this time over a phonograph record, Dave decides to take his father's advice and get a pet—one of Kate's tom cats. He names him, appropriately, Cat. Although Dave successfully keeps Cat out of his parents' way, the animal's nocturnal meanderings keep him busy. One day, while Dave is searching for Cat in the basement of a nearby building, he stumbles upon 19-year-old Tom Ransom. Dave thinks Tom is a burglar and reports him to the building superintendent. Later, he reads in the paper that Tom has been arrested. Feeling guilty about this fellow who helped him rescue Cat, he writes Tom and gives him his address and an offer of help.

Meanwhile, Dave and Nick, a school chum, spend most of their spare time biking to different parts of the City. They take a trip to Central Park with Cat, an unwilling captive in the bicycle basket. Their fun is ruined because Dave can't leave Cat unattended. They decide to go to Coney Island and, in spite of Nick's objection, Dave once more brings Cat along. They unexpectedly meet three girls at the beach, but Cat gets in the way and again spoils Nick's day. Although Nick is disgusted with Dave and Cat, Dave feels that the day was a success because Mary, one of the girls, petted Cat and told Dave to bring him again. Nick arranges a movie date with the two other girls. Dave joins them, but shows little interest in his date. Later, when Nick taunts him, they fight. The boys' friendship ends abruptly.

Tom, who is on parole from the Youth Board, pays a visit to the

Mitchells' apartment. Tom tells Dave that he is lucky to have a father who is interested in him, and that he thinks one of the reasons he got into trouble was his father's rejection of him. To Dave's surprise, Mr. Mitchell volunteers to help Tom.

Cat continues to give Dave plenty of trouble by running away and getting into fights. At Aunt Kate's suggestion, Dave has him altered. After a successful operation, Dave sheds a few tears of relief, but Cat remains unperturbed.

One day as Dave is listening to records in a music store, he meets Mary. At his suggestion, they go to a movie; this time he enjoys every minute of it. Before they part, he asks Mary to meet him at Coney Island on Columbus Day.

After a pleasant vacation with his family, Dave begins his first year in senior high school. He and Ben Alstein, a new school chum, explore the city and share many adventures together. Before Dave knows it, Columbus Day arrives and he meets Mary. They have such an enjoyable day that Dave forgets the time. Before he leaves, Dave tells Mary he'll meet her at Coney Island on the next school holiday.

Aunt Kate receives exciting news. She has inherited a large sum of money from her rich, eccentric brother. The family all help her out by dealing with her new legal entanglements, taking care of her cats and warding off reporters and sensation seekers. Time passes swiftly. Before the next school holiday, Dave catches the flu. By the time he has recovered, he is too embarrassed to call Mary, and by Christmas, he has almost forgotten about the fiasco.

However, Mary calls Dave and asks for his help. She is stranded in a department store without funds. At his father's suggestion, Dave rushes to the store and brings Mary home to dinner. Dave is flattered by Mary's interest and is impressed by the way she and his parents get along.

On a final visit to the Mitchells', Tom and Dave have a long talk. Tom says that Dave and his father quarrel so often because they are so alike. Dave remembers that Aunt Kate had expressed the same opinion and feels perhaps they are right. He realizes that his father's deep concern for him is an asset at that.

Tom also talks about his own plans to get married and join the Army. He thanks Mr. Mitchell for his help. In comraderie, the men toast Cat who brought them all together.

Thematic Material

A boy's growing awareness of his role in the father-son relationship is sensitively portrayed. The hero's acceptance of his part in the family and toward friends and members of the opposite sex are also well presented. The details of a boy's adventures in a big city add great interest.

Book Talk Material

Everyone will want to meet Aunt Kate (pp. 3–9) ; Mr. Mitchell (pp. 2–3) ; and Cat (pp. 10–11). A group will also enjoy hearing about: Dave's episode with the "burglar" (pp. 14–22) ; Dave's date (pp. 34–42) ; Dave's daring rescue (pp. 93–98) ; Dave's Italian lunch (pp. 105–111) ; Kate's good news (pp. 151–161).

Additional Suggestions

Younger readers will enjoy a boy's search for his father in *Yugoslav Mystery* (Lothrop, $3.00) by Arthur Catherall. Boys will also like reading about the lonely Greg, in Theodora Koob's *Surgeon's Apprentice* (Lippincott, $3.50) and fathers and sons in Albert B. Tibbits' collection, *A Boy and His Dad* (Little, $3.95). *The Rock and the Willow* (Lothrop, $3.50) by Mildred Lee, the story of a Southern boy's life during the Depression, will appeal to boys. Girls will enjoy *Eighth Moon* (Harper, $4.95; lib. bdg. $4.43 net) by Sansan and B. Lord which is a true account of a young girl's life in Communist China with her foster parents.

Lulita Crawford Pritchett, *Cabin at Medicine Springs,*
Watts, 1958, $2.95

The author's grandmother is the model for the young heroine in this story set against the background of an Indian uprising (the Meeker Rebellion of 1879). The loneliness and hardships of pioneer life are contrasted skillfully with warm family relationships. Anthony D'Adamo's line drawings reinforce the emotional tone of the story. Girls in grades four through seven find this book fascinating reading.

Lulie Crawford, 12 years old, and her two younger brothers, Logan and John, live in a four room cabin at Steamboat Springs, Colorado.

Their nearest neighbors live 25 miles down the Bear River in Hayden. Although they have no close playmates, they have a menagerie of pets, and are kept busy with their own games and farm chores.

In early summer, while Pa is in Denver to stake a claim for his land, Trader Shouse comes to their cabin to barter with them. However, they have sent all their produce to Denver with Pa and have nothing. Before he leaves, young John blurts out that Mr. Crawford has gone to Denver to claim their land. Trader Shouse announces that this is his land and he's going to claim it.

Chief Yarmonite's band of Utes have spent every summer at Medicine Springs (the Indian name for Steamboat Springs). The Utes are very restless this summer because Yarmonite's brother Tabby, is dying and the Indian Agent Meeker is demanding that they build settlements and change their nomadic ways. The Chief is also having trouble with several of the braves who gamble and drink at Trader Shouse's post.

When Tabby dies, the Utes leave Medicine Springs to bury him. According to custom, they will not return during the same season. Although the Crawfords feel sorry for the friendly Chief, Lulie is secretly glad that they have gone because one of the braves, in a drunken rage, had threatened her life.

However, Uncle Tow, a friend from the mining town of Hahn's Peak, has come to barter with the Utes and is disappointed to find them gone. He goes instead to the post where he loses everything including his prize horse, Podge, to the dishonest trader. The following day, Uncle Tow and Mr. Crawford return simultaneously to the cabin. That night, Mr. Crawford tells his family and guests—Uncle Tow and the two mail riders, Ellis and Dick—that he must pay $1,200 to the land office in Denver for a survey before the land can be his. He alerts the riders to watch for a letter from his uncle in Missouri containing the cash. Everyone is concerned about the arrival of the letter, when Chief Yarmonite comes to warn Mr. Crawford about a possible Indian uprising.

While riding the mails a few days later, Dave has an encounter with a hostile Indian. He arrives in Medicine Springs with a torn mail pouch. The Crawfords are despondent because their uncle's letter had been in that sack. They search everywhere, without success. On a hunch, Logan goes to the trading post to see if Shouse has found and hidden the money.

At the trading post, Shouse offers Logan a chance to make some money by racing on horseback against the Indians. He tries. Encouraged because he wins easily on Podge, he returns a second day to earn more money and collect his winnings. However, when his Indian adversary loses after Shouse had plied him with liquor, the Indian crowd becomes agitated. Mr. Crawford arrives in time to protect Logan who rides away sadly without his pay.

By the middle of summer the discontented Indians have started several fires in the forest. Everyone knows that it will take a winter's snow to put out the deep smouldering blazes.

The Crawfords welcome the Metcalfs to Steamboat Springs. Captain Metcalf is a convalescent Army officer who has come for the mineral water's curative benefits. Although his wife is afraid of both the Indians and the fires, she wants to stay for her husband's sake. More welcome company comes—the surveyors who proceed with the work even though the payment has not been made. Everyone helps them because the fires and approaching winter make it imperative to finish the survey quickly. Two Indian visitors come—a young brave warns the surveyors that they are on Indian land and Chief Yarmonite tells Mrs. Crawford that danger is imminent.

Captain Metcalf gives Mr. Crawford a letter of credit on a Denver bank and Pa leaves to make his payment. While he is gone, the group at Steamboat Springs learns that Agent Meeker's station is under attack. Displaced settlers continue to arrive and they prepare to take a stand at the cabin. Mr. Crawford returns.

Several weeks pass. They learn that Chief Yarmonite was seen at the massacre at the Indian station at White River. However, Mrs. Crawford believes that he is responsible for sparing them. Finally the winter snows come, ending the Indian hostility until spring. The settlers depart and the Metcalfs return home.

Alone once more, the Crawfords complete their neglected chores. During a final trip to her favorite spot by the cottonwood tree, Lulie discovers a chewed-up letter containing the $1,200. Now, Mr. Crawford goes to Denver with the money.

Thematic Material

In this story, the youngsters develop early social and economic self-reliance. Because the harsh demands of pioneer life are emphasized, this theme of independence is reinforced. There is also the children's realization that people can be good or bad, regardless of color.

Book Talk Material

A general introduction will interest many readers. They will also enjoy a description of the Utes' arrival at Medicine Springs (pp. 17–23) ; Lulie's scare (pp. 28–33) ; the loss of the money (pp. 68–76) ; Logan's horse racing (pp. 82–90). The episode that describes the anticipated Indian attack is exciting (pp. 147–157).

Additional Suggestions

Holling C. Holling's *Tree in the Trail* (Houghton, $4.50; lib. bdg. $3.90 net), an unusual story about the growth of a cottonwood tree (just like Lulie's) is a good additional suggestion. Another fine choice is *The Nickel-Plated Beauty* (Morrow, $3.50) by Patricia Beatty. Boys will like Steve Frazee's *Year of the Big Snow* (Holt, $3.50; lib. bdg. $3.27 net), which is an account of John C. Fremont's fourth expedition. For older boys, recommend *The Arm of the Starfish* (Farrar, Straus, $3.50) by Madeleine L'Engle, the story of a young man who finds himself surrounded by international intrigue while on a summer research job in Lisbon.

Anna Rutgers van der Loeff-Basenau, *Avalanche*
Morrow, 1958, $3.50

Although the translation is awkward, this novel—the 1955 winner of the Best Children's Book Award in Holland—is popular with intermediate grade youngsters and reluctant readers of junior high school age. The author's familiarity with the locale enhances the exciting adventure story.

Although the Swiss Alpine villagers of Urteli have endured many avalanches over the span of years, 13-year-old Werner Altschwank, son of the schoolmaster, has never experienced one. This January, the radio is forecasting acute slide danger for Urteli due to the heavy snows and that soldiers are coming to evacuate the villagers. As he listens to the newscasts, Mr. Altschwank suddenly remembers that before the great storm, a group of school boys from the Pestalozzi Village had climbed to a ski hut far above Urteli. He knows that he must warn them.

Mr. Altschwank and Werner are the best skiers in the village. They borrow some bright-colored avalanche cord from old Aunt Augusta and start out. Although it is a dangerous trip, they reach the hut safely. Mr.

Hutamaki, the leader, is grateful for their concern. He introduces them to the boys, who are World War II orphans—Hans Peter, who is Werner's age, and the younger boys, Annti, Jean Pierre, Holdert, and the ebullient Paolo. They prepare to descend, but not before Werner discovers that Paolo, who had been buried for a week in some bombed-out rubble, is deathly afraid of the avalanches. To reassure him, Werner ties himself directly behind Paolo with the avalanche cord. They encounter some difficulty on the return trip when Paolo is trapped in a small slide. However, Werner reaches him and clasps his hand before a second slide covers him. They are dug out rapidly and are soon in warm houses in the village.

That night an enormous avalanche covers the center of Urteli. The boys, bedded in a barn at the edge of the village, are safe, but several people in the village are injured and the Altschwanks are completely buried.

Werner remains conscious even after the house collapses around him. With fierce determination, he manages to crawl out through a hole in the roof. By the time Werner is removed to a makeshift first-aid station, the soldiers arrive and start to dig for his missing parents. Werner lies speechless and despondent and is finally evacuated with the other villagers.

As the villagers descend, they hear a loud reverberation, signalling that another avalanche has inundated the village. Werner realizes that this new slide will impede the rescue effort and he is even more distraught.

After a long trip, the group of villagers reach Glarmätt, only to discover that it, too, has been hit by the record avalanches. The largest hotel has been leveled, the trains have stopped running and the town is swollen with refugees from the other stricken Alpine villages. In this tragic atmosphere, little Paolo goes around trying to be cheerful by singing, and telling exaggerated stories. However, as they wait for relief trains to take them further down the mountain, Werner becomes irritated by the younger boy's actions and blurts out, "I've no use for boasting. . . ." Stung by the older boy's denunciation, Paolo shouts back that he, too, has lost everything in life and calls Werner a bully. By the time the train arrives the next morning, the boys have resolved their differences and are friends. Paolo suggests that Werner come live in his village at Trogen with all the other boys.

As the train descends to Bracken, the engineer receives a message that a large avalanche is approaching them. He quickly backs the train into a tunnel, where the passengers spend the night. To pass the time, the boys start playing the game, "What I want most" but Werner cannot answer. Paolo blurts out for him that what he wants most is to have his mother and father alive again. Werner bursts into sobs.

Bracken is crowded, too. There are first-aid stations and stricken people everywhere. However, Werner hears on the radio that after a 57 hour search, his parents have been rescued and taken to a hospital. He rejoices. Werner begins to realize that the others around him are faced with tragic problems, too. He is especially sympathetic toward nine-year-old Klaus Watsig who has lost his parents and little sister Marie in a slide at Valgretto. Although the search at Valgretto has been postponed because of the danger of further slides, Werner persuades the boys from the Pestalozzi Village to accompany Klaus to the village to search for the pathetic youngster's family.

After an arduous journey and difficult work, the boys uncover a corner of the Watsig barn. Soldiers arrive to continue the boys' work and Marie Watsig is saved, though not the parents. The boys return to Bracken and Klaus becomes ill from shock and exposure.

Paolo and Werner visit the boy and his sister in the hospital and Paolo urges the youngsters to come to the Pestalozzi village where they will be welcome. Paolo still hopes that Werner will come, too. But now that the avalanche danger is over, he and Werner say goodbye. Each returns to his village.

Werner learns the electrician's trade while his parents recuperate. After he and his father have rebuilt their house, Werner asks for permission to go to the Pestalozzi village to find work. His parents consent and he leaves.

The boys meet him at the Trogen depot. Paolo invites him to dinner and tells him that Klaus and Marie are also coming to live in the village. The boys are happy to be together again.

Thematic Material

Personal courage and the interdependence of human beings are primary themes in this moving story. Self-reliance and innate strength of spirit are the qualities portrayed by the valiant boys, Paolo and Werner.

Book Talk Material

A brief introduction telling about the winter of the terrible avalanches and its effect upon the lives of the villagers will stimulate many
readers. Specific episodes which show the horror of the slides are: the
slide in which Paolo and Werner are buried (pp. 39–49) ; the avalanche
that buried Urteli (pp. 59–64) ; the train in the tunnel (pp. 122–131) .

Additional Suggestions

Boys will go on to read *Back to Anchorage* (Lothrop, $3.50) by Tom
E. Clarke, which also stresses self-reliance. Girls will find Maria Kirch-
gessner's *High Challenge* (Harcourt, $3.50) an interesting account of
four girls who are determined to refurbish a lodge in the Alps. Two
other good titles for girls are *Megan* (Messner, $2.95) by Iris Noble, the
story of homesteading in Canada around the turn of the century and
World of Their Own (Little, $3.75) by Laura Cooper Rendina, the
story of some teen-agers who undertake a working summer on a tobacco
farm in Connecticut.

Virginia Sorensen, *Miracles on Maple Hill,*
Harcourt, 1956, $2.95

Miracles on Maple Hill is the story of one year in a young girl's life.
In this book the author's extraordinary gift for characterization and
excellent sense of local color are used to produce a superior novel. This
is the Newbery Award winner for 1957. Girls in upper elementary and
seventh grades enjoy this story.

The old house on Maple Hill in rural Pennsylvania has been deserted
for almost 20 years. At one time, it had belonged to Marly's grandmother, and it was here that Mother had lived when she was Marly's
age—just ten. Now the entire family—Marly, her 12-year-old brother
Joe, Mother, and Daddy are moving from Pittsburgh to Maple Hill,
hoping for a miracle to take place. Dale, the father, has returned from
war shattered, both physically and mentally, by years spent in a prison
camp. The family hopes that the quiet and solitude of country life will
help restore his health and peace of mind.

Until summer vacation, Mother and the children will be able to visit only on weekends and holidays; but all four are looking forward to spending a whole uninterrupted summer together.

The family becomes very friendly with their next-door neighbors, Mr. and Mrs. Chris (Chris and Chrissie), and their hired hand, Fritz. Mr. Chris, a wise but simple and good-natured man, shows a particular fondness for Marly. He explains to her that Maple Hill produces all sorts of miracles. The first that he shows her is the miracle of collecting and processing sap to produce maple syrup. The second is the series of tiny miracles that turn winter into spring.

Marly develops a great love for nature, and a kinship with the plants and animals found on Maple Hill. She also has many small adventures. She almost sets the house on fire one morning while trying to bake pancakes for the family. On another occasion, she searches for meadow boots (marsh marigolds) and narrowly escapes injury from Mr. Chris' herd of cattle.

Marly shares many exploits with her brother. Together, they save a family of red foxes by driving them out of their lair before the hunters can shoot them. They explore the property of the village recluse, Harry the Hermit and, after conquering their initial fear, they grow to admire this gentle, knowledgeable man.

Soon the summer is over and a great decision must be made—whether to go back to Pittsburg or remain with Daddy at Maple Hill. After weighing pros and cons, the family votes unanimously to stay. As they are now year-round farmers, Harry gives each of the children a present —Joe receives two goats and Marly eight grown chickens.

Another series of nature's miracles takes place and autumn turns to winter. But Marly notices that gradually a more important miracle is happening—Daddy is becoming more relaxed, and more loving and understanding with the family.

Over the Christmas vacation, Joe becomes the hero of the family when he rescues Harry from possible death by freezing: the old man had fallen and injured his leg on the ice outside his home and Joe remained with him until help arrived.

Maple syrup time comes again, but Mr. Chris suffers a severe heart attack and is unable to tend his maple trees. Marly's family decides to help. Daddy assumes leadership and organizes the family. They work night and day to produce the syrup.

The truant officer, Miss Annie Nelson (nicknamed Annie-Get-Your-

Gun) arrives to inquire about the children's absence from school. She is so impressed with their project that she sends some boys from Joe's class to help.

At last, the processing is completed. When Mr. Chris returns home from the hospital, he is told the details of the miracle that has saved his maple syrup harvest. Marly realizes that this is just part of the much greater miracle that has reunited her family.

Thematic Material

This novel deals with the elements that produce happy family relationships—kindness, understanding, as well as mutual love and respect. It also contains a feeling for the wonders of nature. Marly's recurring questions regarding death and cruelty to animals form important secondary themes. The spirit of friendly neighborliness that is part of this book presents a wonderful argument for country life as opposed to city life.

Book Talk Material

Miracles on Maple Hill contains many incidents that lend themselves to use in a book talk. Some examples: Marly inspects her new home (pp. 24–29); Marly tries to save a family of mice (pp. 29–32); the first miracle (pp. 39–45); Marly tries to make pancakes (pp. 51–55); she is trapped by Mr. Chris' cattle (pp. 62–69); Joe and Marly save the foxes (pp. 81–86); the children's first encounter with Harry the Hermit (pp. 93–99).

Additional Suggestions

Two other recommended novels by Virginia Sorensen are *Curious Missie* (Harcourt, $3.00), about a girl's efforts to get a bookmobile for her county in Alabama and *Plain Girl* (Harcourt, $2.95), the story of Esther, a young Amish girl. Other family stories suitable for this age group are: Carol Brink's *Family Grandstand* (Viking, lib. bdg. $2.96 net) and Elizabeth Enright's Melendy family stories, such as *The Saturdays* (Holt, $3.50; lib. bdg. $3.27 net). Older students might enjoy Rebecca Caudill's *The House of the Fifers* (Longmans, lib. bdg. $3.11 net) or Mildred Pace's *Home Is Where the Heart Is* (McGraw, $3.00).

Kathryn Worth, *They Loved to Laugh,*
Doubleday, 1942, $3.75

Using genealogical records as historical sources, Mrs. Worth has
written a charming story about an orphan who is adopted by a North
Carolina Quaker family in the 1830's. The genial family and the
courageous heroine are vividly characterized. The charming black and
white illustrations by Margaret De Angeli are a noteworthy addition.
Girls from sixth grade through junior high school like this sentimental
family story.

When 16-year-old Martitia Howland's parents die of typhoid fever,
their physician, Dr. David Gardner, brings her to his farm in Guilford
County. Martitia is welcomed warmly into this large family. An only
child, she is overwhelmed by the good-natured teasing of the gregarious
Gardner boys: Jonathan, 21; Milton, 20; Clarkson, 18; Barzillai, 17;
and Addison, 15. She is also reassured by the presence of the patient
mother, Eunice, the industrious daughter, Ruth, and the kind grandfather.

Eunice teaches Martitia how to cook and weave. Although not
meaning to be unkind, Ruth keeps telling Martitia that, "a tub must
stand on its own bottom." This discourages the younger girl. The
grandfather befriends Martitia and explains that he and his granddaughter are very sobersided, but they love her, too. Martitia learns to
love the family and enjoys being part of it.

However, she feels that she must write to her Aunt and Uncle
Randolph in Virginia to tell them that she is now an orphan. Martitia
becomes attracted to Jonathan. Although he continues to be the ring-
leader in the tricks the boys play on her, Martitia senses that he likes
her, too. When she learns that he and Milton are going away in the fall
to pursue their studies, Martitia is heartbroken.

She receives a curt note from her aunt telling her to come to
Richmond immediately and get away from the influence of those
common Quakers. Martitia is incensed by this unfair appraisal of her
generous friends. She decides that she cannot bear to leave her new
home and friends to go to so callous a relative. When Dr. David says
that the family would welcome her as a daughter, she writes to tell her

aunt of her decision. Meanwhile, Jonathan, who is studying law, will institute a legal action to make her Dr. Gardner's ward. The case will be heard the following summer.

Martitia realizes that Clarkson is falling in love with her and although she doesn't love him, she responds to his kindness. The winter brings two tragedies. Vigilante, their brave sheep dog, is killed protecting Martitia from a hunger-crazed wolf. A much greater loss is the death of their beloved grandfather.

In the spring, Mr. Randolph journeys to the farm to demand Martitia's return. He claims to be her legal guardian, but Dr. David advises him to let the court decide the matter. Already upset by her uncle's visit, Martitia is further distressed when Clarkson and Barzillai announce that they are leaving for Wilmington to work as business apprentices. Before he leaves, Clarkson declares his love for Martitia. Although she does not reply, he takes her silence for assent and leaves contented.

When Jonathan returns in the summer, and talks about his cousin, Sarah Mendenhall of Jamestown, Martitia is jealous. The family visits the Mendenhalls' and Martitia is relieved to find that Sarah is very plain. She is not comforted, however, by Sarah's many skills: cooking, weaving, Latin and clever political conversation. Martitia, whose own skills are improving and whose knowledge of French endears her to Sarah's French seamstress, decides on their return to the farm that she will listen daily to Jonathan's declamation exercises in the Gardner's mulberry grove.

After a favorable court decision, Martitia learns that Dr. David is in financial difficulty because of the court costs. He is worried about raising the money to send Jonathan back to finish his two years of study. On top of this, the news that Clarkson has died in a yellow fever epidemic crushes Dr. Gardner. Martitia determines to repay some of her debt to this family.

Remembering that the seamstress in Jamestown buys silk cocoons, Martitia sends to Jamestown for instructions and materials to start a silk culture farm. She uses the mulberry trees on the property. With Ruth's help, Martitia raises the silk worms and sells the silk to pay for Jonathan's education.

When Jonathan comes home again the following June, he almost tells Martitia he loves her, but he is prevented from doing so by a bad fall

Martitia takes in the ice house. She recovers slowly; another school year passes.

Having completed his law studies, Jonathan returns and declares his love. Martitia tells him that she has always loved him and that she is very proud of him. She feels sure that one day Jonathan will make her the mistress of the Governor's mansion.

Thematic Material

The author recaptures the spirit of 19th century North Carolina. The heroine's resolve to become proficient and self-reliant in her work sets an excellent example for young girls. The emphasis on fine family relationships and an exposition of the precepts of the Society of Friends are of additional value. Older girls will enjoy the romantic triangle.

Book Talk Material

There are many vividly presented scenes that are good for reading. Representative ones are: the boys tease Martitia at the "Festival of the Dog" (pp. 26–33) ; Martitia resolves to be useful (pp. 34–43) ; Martitia learns to weave (pp. 75–80) ; Vigilante saves Martitia (pp. 116–128) ; Sarah Mendenhall meets Martitia (pp. 182–196) ; the silk worm project (pp. 227–238) .

Additional Suggestions

Suggest *Applesauce Needs Sugar* (Doubleday $3.95) by Victoria Case and *Never No More* (Templegate $3.95) by Maura Laverty as follow-up reading. Young people will also enjoy *Meggy Macintosh* (Viking, lib. bdg. $3.37 net) by Elizabeth Janet Gray, the story of plain Meggy who becomes beautiful Meg after her arrival in the Carolina Colony. Also use *A Traveler in Time* (Viking, $4.00; lib. bdg. $3.77 net) by Allison Uttley, the tale of a modern girl who goes back in time to the reign of Elizabeth the First. A more contemporary family story, with much humor, is Sara Sandberg's *Mama Made Minks* (Doubleday $3.95) . Boys may be encouraged to try the play, *Life With Father* (Knopf $5.95; bd. with *Life With Mother*) by Russel Crouse and Howard Lindsay.

7

Evaluating Life

CHILDREN develop a conscience early in life. Its codification into a moral and ethical value system is a continuing process, and with adolescence the individual's search for values is intensified. The development of this personal code, while stemming from basic drives, is shaped by the influence of others. The adolescent measures his behavior against the reactions of teachers, parents, other adults, and his peers. The paradoxes of this comparison leave unanswered questions and often result in confusion. The young teen makes moral judgments about the behavior of his family and friends. He is easily disillusioned, quick to apply ethical standards. Widening contact with the world brings constant reevalution of these standards and constant examination of his own behavior.

Each of the titles in this chapter provides another set of experiences, another index, against which the growing young person can evaluate his developing ethical values.

Thelma Harrington Bell, *The Two Worlds of Davy Blount,* Viking, 1962, $3.00

This convincing story about a young boy who finds that truth is not always a simple matter is a distinctive addition to the author's list of young adult titles. The different modes of life in North Carolina are beautifully portrayed in this well-written novel. Boys and girls in grades five through eight find this story absorbing.

Ten-year-old Davy Blount lives contentedly with his grandparents in Hatteras Village on the Outer Banks Islands off the coast of North

Carolina. Davy only dimly remembers his parents, who had disappeared in one of the furious storms off the Shoals. Grandmother has never forgiven the sea for their deaths and she doesn't want her husband, Grandy, to take Davy out on his trawler. She also talks incessantly about the mountains to the West where she lived until she came to Hatteras as Grandy's bride. Although she insists that Davy would love the mountains, he pays little attention. Davy loves his sea-shore home and enjoys crabbing, digging for treasure, listening to stories about shipwrecks and watching the fishermen.

Intrigued by stories of hidden treasure chests, Davy and his school chums, Chad Poyner and Sue O'Neal, go searching for one. After a day of digging, they are invited in for cocoa by Mr. MacTavish, a writer and local historian, who lives in a nearby cottage. He spins stories about what they have discovered: a broken rusty sword handle becomes a vital part of an old pirate battle, a tarnished button becomes the marker of a Civil War grave, and a corroded piping whistle becomes a piece of equipment from the famous ship, the Monitor, that had been sunk off the Shoals. Meanwhile, unknown to Davy, Grandmother is planning to send him to visit her nephew Tolvin for the summer. Tolvin has a farm in the Blue Ridge Mountains.

When Grandy brings Davy home wet and cold from an unfortunate encounter with a sudden squall, Grandmother decides that Davy must go away. Although Grandy wants Davy to stay, he explains to Davy that he has learned to handle Grandmother the way he treats the sea, "Respect her power and learn her ways." Davy isn't keen about missing all the fun he and his friends have planned, but he is curious to see the mountains, when Grandmother declares that on his return he will be able to tell them which is better, the mountains or the sea.

As soon as school is out, Davy leaves on the five hundred mile trip to Soco. After a long ride and a night's stopover with friends, he resumes his journey. When he sees his first mountain, he can scarcely believe that land can be so high. By late afternoon, he arrives at his destination in the pine and hardwood forest his grandmother loves.

Tolvin's wife, Sally, meets Davy at the bus stop at the foot of their steeply sloping land. The rest of the family—Kim, 11; Holly, nine; Mary, six; and Teddy, four—are away overnight. The following day, they return and he and Kim become friends immediately. Although everything goes smoothly, Davy feels uncomfortable because Kim deliberately leaves Holly out of their games. He tells Kim that she wouldn't plague them with her mischief-making, if they would include her in their fun. But Kim tells Davy to ignore her. However, after the boys return home from a visit to Uncle Tolvin's logging job and find their wash water filled with grit, Davy realizes that they must do something about Holly. He tells Kim that they should "learn her ways and respect her power." Aunt Sally agrees and together they prevail upon Kim to include her. Davy, an only child cared for by doting grandparents, begins to understand that living in a large family means a great deal of sharing.

Although there are many chores for the boys on the farm, they manage one weekend to go on a scouting expedition in the woods. Kim refuses to allow Holly to join them and Davy is so worried about keeping up with Kim that he doesn't protest. Davy gets lost trying to follow Kim's blue shirt. When the blue shirt reappears, Davy is relieved until he realizes that the shirt belongs to a stranger, who with another man, is taking samples from a rock outcrop. While retracing his steps, he is caught in a thunderstorm and forced to take cover in a small cave. Holly appears suddenly and Davy is pleased that she has been following him; he is reassured by her quiet presence. Finally, they are rescued by Kim and Uncle Tolvin.

When Davy tells his story about the men, Uncle Tolvin investigates and recognizes the outcrop as a small asbestos vein. He tells the boys that the two men want to buy some of the property, but that he will not sell it to them because their mining venture would deface the land.

As the days shorten, Davy recalls with desperation, his grandmother's unanswered question, "Which shall it be, mountains or sea?" Before he leaves, he asks Uncle Tolvin for advice on how to answer the question. His answer pleases Davy. Laden with mountain treasures for his grandparents and friends, he says goodbye to Kim and Holly and boards the bus.

The morning after his return, Davy tells his grandmother that he and Uncle Tolvin feel that it doesn't matter where you live as long as you truly appreciate each part of your wonderful country. Grandy smiles knowingly; Grandmother shakes her head thoughtfully.

Thematic Material

This story illustrates that life's demanding questions are not simply answered. The author also shows that sharing, kindness and understanding are important factors in family relationships. Mrs. Bell's facility in describing the diverse modes of living and geography of North Carolina contributes to the young reader's appreciaton of the many differences within America.

Book Talk Material

Three exciting episodes are especially good for dramatic presentation: the search for buried treasure (pp. 24–40) ; the Nancy Lee flounders in the fury of a squall (pp. 57–61) ; Kim and Davy go scouting and Davy gets lost (condense p. 148 and add pp. 168–183) . After a short introduction, ask the question, "Which would you choose, mountains or sea?"

Additional Suggestions

Young adults will also like William Mayne's adventurous story about some English boys' discovery of a dinosaur skeleton, *Sand* (Dutton, $3.75; lib. bdg. $3.71 net) and Paul Berna's suspenseful tale about the physical and emotional crisis of a schoolboy trapped in a bell tower, *Flood Warning* (Pantheon lib. bdg. $3.09 net) . Girls will appreciate the story of a girl in Medieval times who finds happiness with her father after a cloistered life with a strict aunt, *The White Twilight* (Holt $3.50; lib. bdg. $3.27 net) by Madeleine Polland. More mature girls will enjoy Dorothy Pitkin's sensitive novel *Sea Change* (Pantheon $3.50; lib. bdg. $3.39 net) about 16-year-old Vicky and her summer job in a marine biology lab.

Shelia Burnford, *The Incredible Journey,*
Little, 1961, $3.95

The author writes so convincingly about animal habits and of life in the Canadian north country that readers might feel that this is a true story rather than a work of fiction. When *The Incredible Journey* was first published, it rose immediately to the top of the adult best seller lists. Since that time, it has also become popular with younger readers. It can be enjoyed by better readers in the upper elementary grades, but its greatest audience is junior and senior high school students.

Jim Hunter, an English professor at a small Northern Ontario college, accepts an offer to teach in England for a year. As a result, he is forced to leave behind the family pets, in spite of the protests of his son, Peter, and daughter, Elizabeth. The children have grown extremely attached to their small menagerie: Bodger, an aging English bull terrier, Luath, a Labrador retriever and Tao, a beautiful wheat-colored Siamese cat.

The animals are placed in the safekeeping of John Lockridge, a writer, who lives in an isolated community over 250 miles to the west. Although they stay with Lockridge for several months, the animals fail to make a complete adjustment to their new home.

Three weeks before the Hunters are scheduled to return, Lockridge leaves on a hunting trip and asks a neighbor, Mrs. Oakes, to care for the animals. Before she is able to collect her charges, the three set out on a journey of their own—a journey back to their former home. Their trip is through a vast northern wilderness filled with great dangers, especially for three domestic animals not accustomed to foraging for themselves.

Bodger is the first to suffer ill effects. The old dog is easily exhausted, and soon falls behind the others. He is attacked and viciously slashed by a bear cub. Tao is able to drive the intruder away, but Bodger is so badly wounded that the party must halt for a few days until he recovers. During this time, Tao hunts for two and brings food to the ailing dog.

When they resume their journey, Bodger happens on an Ojibway encampment. The Indians, who regard the appearance of the animals as a sign of good fortune, feed them. But in the morning the three start off again.

While trying to cross a swollen river, Tao is swept downstream, many miles from her two companions. She is rescued from drowning by a young girl, Reino Nurmi, who takes care of Tao until she has recovered. After three days, the cat leaves to find her friends. On the way, she narrowly escapes death when she is treed by a vicious lynx. Eventually, the three are reunited.

During the journey, Luath has maintained leadership. But he, too, suffers misfortunes. He has been trained from birth to retrieve, but never to kill. Only when he is near starvation, is he able to break this habit. During one hunting expedition, he attacks a porcupine, and emerges with several quills painfully embedded in his face. His cheeks become so swollen and infected that he is scarcely able to open his mouth.

Once more, the animals are saved. They are found and given shelter by Mr. and Mrs. McKenzie, who farm a tract of land just fifty miles from the animals' destination. After Luath's wounds are healed, the three begin the last part of their journey.

Meanwhile, Mr. Hunter and his family return from England. The children are inconsolable at the news of their pets' disappearance. However, they hear from several of the people who have encountered the animals en route. One day, Tao, Bodger, and Luath appear at Mr. Hunter's home. Though battle-scarred and near starvation, they have completed their incredible journey.

Thematic Material

Through this story of three remarkable animals, the author has illustrated many admirable qualities: devotion to a cause, courage to face great difficulties, and the bonds of fidelity which can exist between animal and man.

Book Talk Material

To introduce the three animals, read their descriptions (pp. 5–7), and use Carl Burger's excellent black and white illustrations found at the beginning of each chapter. Incidents suitable for reading aloud are: the first day of the journey (pp. 24–27); the struggle with the bear cub (pp. 33–37); meeting the Ojibways (pp. 44–48); crossing the river (pp. 61–65); Tao is rescued by the Nurmis (pp. 70–78) and an encounter with the unfriendly farmer (pp. 83–86).

Additional Suggestions

Two other animal stories with the same theme are: Eric Knight's *Lassie Come Home* (Holt, $3.95; lib. bdg. $3.79 net) and Hetty Burlingame Beatty's *Bryn* (Houghton, $3.25). Robert Murphy's *Wild Geese Calling* (Dutton, $3.50; lib. bdg. $3.46 net) is the story of the northward migration of two wild Canadian geese. Older readers might enjoy Robert Froman's *The Nerve of Some Animals* (Lippincott, $4.95), a non-fiction title about some individualistic animals that outwit man, or the Mildred and Gordon Gordon's delightful novel *Undercover Cat* (Doubleday, $3.95—Film title: *That Darn Cat*).

Molly Cone, *Reeney*,
Houghton, 1963, $3.00

Miss Cone's story about a young girl whose mother's death forces her to assume many domestic obligations prematurely, has the same ingredients—easy style, interesting plot, credible characters—that make her titles, *The Trouble with Toby* (Houghton, $2.75) and *Only Jane* (Nelson, $2.95; lib. bdg. $2.92 net) popular. Girls in upper elementary grades and junior high school enjoy this novel.

After her mother's funeral, 16-year-old Reeney Johnson declares that she is going to take care of her father and older brother, Matt, without the help of Aunt Ada who has been staying with them temporarily. Although Reeney is only a sophomore, she believes that she is old enough to manage on her own. She has been going steady with Scot Montgomery, a senior, and feels more mature than her years. Her father comments vaguely that keeping house is a large job, but Reeney assures him that she can do it. Aunt Ada leaves after telling Reeney that she'll be back to check on things in a month.

All try to go back to their normal ways. Mr. Johnson goes to work; Matt and his friends, Lopey and Hank, resume their habitual tinkering with Matt's car; Reeney attacks the housework. Her first meal is miserable, the potatoes are lumpy, the peas cold and Aunt Ada's meat loaf remains frozen because Reeney forgot to turn on the oven. Matt leaves the table in disgust. When Mr. Johnson says absently that Matt needs more discipline, Reeney remembers longingly how her mother used to intercede at moments like this and she feels very inadequate.

Reeney decides to allow more time for her new home chores. Because she doesn't want to spoil her after school meetings with Scot, she eliminates her orchestra practice and reduces her homework time. Her housekeeping improves, but she finds herself wishing that Matt would help her. She starts to nag him. Matt responds by staying away from the house. Reeney knows that if she complains about Matt to her father there will be a bitter argument. Instead, she resolves to make the coming holidays pleasant for her family.

Her Christmas dinner is delicious, but the occasion is ruined by the men's argument over Matt's car. Reeney feels that her efforts are wasted.

Meanwhile Miss Lowe, her school counselor, tells her that she should join some sophomore activities, instead of spending all of her spare time with one boy. As Reeney mulls over this advice, she realizes that Scot is more interested in his own problems as the star of the senior play than he is in her present difficulties. She accepts his invitation to the Senior Prom, but she is not as elated as she would have been several months ago.

About this time, Mr. Johnson finds out that Matt is having serious difficulty at school because he has been cutting classes and not doing his homework. Unknowingly, Mr. Johnson precipitates a crisis when he forbids Matt to use his car until his schoolwork is finished. While Mr. Johnson is away, Matt disappears. Reeney discovers from his friends that Matt has left home for two reasons: he has lost his girl friend, Mary Ann, who won't go to the Prom with him because he no longer has a car, and he can't stand Reeney's constant nagging. Reeney realizes that she has made her brother's life miserable. She finally admits to herself that while she has improved her housekeeping, she has failed to provide the warmth and tenderness a family needs. Just when she is about to admit defeat, Mr. Johnson calls home. He consoles Reeney and admits that the situation is his fault, too.

Fortunately, Matt soon returns home and explains that he can't leave them because he knows how difficult it has been for them, too. He feels that he has not done his share, either. Reeney and Matt discuss their problems and decide to help each other. Matt admits that he has been using his car as a crutch; Reeney confesses that she has been doing the same thing by pretending interest in Scot. Reeney easily arranges to get out of her date with Scot and she and Matt spend that evening working on his overdue school assignments.

When Aunt Ada arrives, Matt has received a make-up grade and everything in the house is in good order. The Johnsons are delighted with their victory. Reeney knows that they will remain a loving family, just as their mother would have wished.

Thematic Material

The heroine's gradual realization that being a helpful family member means consideration for other people is a worthy theme. Readers can identify easily with this eager, but overly confident heroine. The story also points up a mature attitude toward dating.

Book Talk Material

Reeney's many disastrous encounters with housekeeping will make good introductory material: Reeney's first meal (pp. 17–25) ; the girls clean house (pp. 35–43) ; the laundry fiasco (pp. 44–48) ; the first pie (pp. 51–57). An interesting topic for group discussion is given in the advisor's talk about steady dating (pp. 69–72) .

Additional Suggestions

For young boys, recommend Kenichi Horie's *Ko-Do-Ku: Alone Across the Pacific* (Tuttle, $5.00), about a young man who sailed the Pacific Ocean alone. For girls, suggest the following high school stories: *Love, Bid Me Welcome* (Harper, $3.50; lib. bdg. $3.27 net) by Janette Sebring Lowrey; *The Dark Rosaleen* (Morrow $3.50) by Carole Bolton; and *If a Heart Rings, Answer* (Dutton, $3.50) by Russell Mead. The latter title is about a senior high school boy and his reaction to romance; it may appeal to some boys.

Robert A. Heinlein, *Citizen of the Galaxy,*
Scribner, 1957, lib. bdg. $3.31 net.

Mr. Heinlein's science fiction is far removed from the standard "space operas" inhabited by bug-eyed monsters. Instead, his novels explore contemporary problems in a setting far in the future. *Citizen of the Galaxy* deals with one boy's quest for justice and personal identity. This book is read and enjoyed by boys in both junior and senior high school.

Thorby—too young to remember anything about his past—is auctioned off in the slave market of Jubbulpore, capital of a group of outer planets known as the Nine Worlds. He becomes the property of Baslim, a crippled beggar. "Pop" Baslim and Thorby become close friends. They remain together for several years, during which Thorby helps Pop in many ways, and Pop in turn educates Thorby.

It soon becomes apparent that Pop's activities are not confined to begging—he appears to be part of an underground spy network that is plotting against the cruel dictatorship of the Sargon, hated ruler of the Nine Worlds.

These activities are discovered, and Baslim commits suicide rather than face the horrors of interrogation by the Sargon's police. Thorby

escapes and is smuggled aboard a space ship (a Free Trader) named
Sisu. The inhabitants of the *Sisu* had once been saved from destruction
by Baslim and, to show their gratitude, Thorby is adopted by the chief's
family, the Krausas.

Social structure aboard the *Sisu* is unlike anything Thorby has ever
encountered before. "The People," as they call themselves, have developed a tightly-knit, highly structured matriarchy, ruled by "Mother,"
the mother of Captain Krausa, and therefore Thorby's "grandmother."

The People live isolated, nomadic lives; their space ship is home and
their only contact with the planets is for trading purposes. Occasionally
celebrations, known as Gatherings, are held with other Free Traders.
During these festivals, the young girls from the space ships are swapped
as future brides.

Thorby is trained by his "nephew," Jeri, and Jeri's sister Mata, to
become a firecontrolman—the person responsible for tracking and
shooting down raiders, the pirates of outer space. Although the work is
exciting, and the visits to various planets interesting, Thorby finds that
he is unable to adjust to the social structure of the *Sisu*. With their
binding rules of tradition and family ties, the People seem to have as
little personal freedom as the inhabitants of the Nine Worlds.

Captain Krausa understands his son's problem, and manages to have
him transferred to the Guard Cruiser, Hydra, a space ship that is part of
the interplanetary police force. Here, Thorby learns that Baslim was
really Captain Richard Baslim, a member of this corps' X Division
(X for Exotic and Espionage). His mission at Jubbulpore had been to
collect information to help end the slave trade in the Nine Worlds.

By using Thorby's footprints as clues, the captain of the Hydra begins
an interplanetary identity search to determine Thorby's real parentage.
It is discovered that he is really Thor Rudbek, a member of the
fantastically wealthy Rudbek family, leading manufacturers of space
ships on the planet Earth. Thor's real parents were killed by space
raiders who had attacked their space craft and later sold Thor into
slavery.

When Thor reaches Earth, he discovers that his father's business has
been taken over by his uncle-by-marriage, Jack Weemsby, and his legal
advisor, Judge Bruder. Thor's suspicions are aroused when Uncle Jack
immediately suggests that Thor sign over to his care the entire control
of the Rudbek business. On investigation, Thor becomes convinced that

it is his uncle who is illegally selling space ships to the slave traders in outer space. With the help of a corporation lawyer, James Garsch, Thor is eventually able to assume control of the business.

By using the research facilities of his factories, Thor hopes to develop a superweapon to drive the raiders from the skies. His eventual goal is to join the X Corps and help complete the fight for freedom that Pop had left unfinished.

Thematic Material

Citizen of the Galaxy traces Thorby's life from boyhood to his late teens—it also recounts his search for values and ideals, and his growing sense of justice and the rights of others. Though its setting is far in the future, this book deals with universal conflicts that are with us today.

Book Talk Material

An introduction to the plot would be the most satisfactory method of presenting this novel. If specific passages are needed try: Thorby's first night at Baslim's home (pp. 10–14) ; his narrow escape (pp. 43–48) ; Thorby learns of Pop's death (pp. 57–61), and he hides from the Sargon's police (pp. 64–69) .

Additional Suggestions

Other excellent novels by the same author are: *Have Space Suit— Will Travel* (Scribner, $3.50; lib. bdg. $3.31 net) , *Rocket Ship Galileo* (Scribner, lib. bdg. $3.31 net) and *Time for the Stars* (Scribner, lib. bdg. $3.31 net) . Readers who like Heinlein's type of science fiction will also enjoy: *When Worlds Collide* by Edwin Balmer and Philip Wylie (Lippincott, $5.95, bd. with *After Worlds Collide*) , Ray Bradbury's *The Martian Chronicles* (Doubleday, $3.95) and Isaac Asimov's *I, Robot* (Doubleday, $3.50) .

Annabel and Edgar Johnson, *Wilderness Bride,*
Harper, 1962, $3.95; lib. bdg. $3.27 net.

Mr. and Mrs. Johnson, known for their well-written young adult titles, have produced an adventurous story of a young Mormon heroine unwillingly affianced to a stranger during the Latter Day Saints Westward Drive. Girls in grades seven through nine enjoy this fast-moving, romantic tale.

The history of the Mormons reflects the closely-knit structure and communal economy of their settlements (called Stakes of Zion) . History also indicates that because of these characteristics (particularly the economic success of the industrious Mormons) , the surrounding "Gentile" settlers often were afraid of the Mormons and directed their distrust primarily against the Mormon practice of polygamy. In their move West, the Mormons were often victims of persecution. They finally settled in Nauvoo, Illinois and became prosperous and politically influential. However, in 1846, some neighboring settlers, in an hysterical protest, arrested and killed the Mormon leaders. Under their new leader, Brigham Young, the Mormons planned to head West and establish a new Stake of Zion—Salt Lake City, Utah.

Motherless fifteen-year-old Corey (Corinne) Tremaine is apprehensive as she and her father go to meet her fiancé, 21 year old Ethan, at the encampment outside Nauvoo. Her father thinks that this is the best way to protect her while he goes to serve in the Mexican War, but Corey worries more about her unknown fiancé than she does about the coming journey West.

Her father introduces her to Dan Tanner's family: the first wife, Sister Trude, and her two daughters, Lucy and Meg; the second wife, Sister Millie, and her brood, including rugged Shad; and the third wife, Sister Elizabeth, and her English-born son, Ethan, Dan Tanner's stepson and Corey's betrothed. Mr. Tanner conducts the service pledging the two young people in the promise of marriage. Corey doesn't cry when her father leaves, but finally bursts into tears at the bedside of the invalid Sister Elizabeth, who tells her that "we all must cry when our carefree days slip away."

Everyone prepares for the coming trip. Corey works cheerfully trying to make up for the Tanners' displeasure with Ethan's clumsy efforts at manual work. They think he is a shirker and Shad warns Corey that she is losing a better man when she refuses his offer of matrimony. Corey becomes very fond of gentle Sister Elizabeth and her kind son, Ethan.

When the wagons move out, Ethan temporarily stays behind in Nauvoo to help evacuate the old and sick. At Ethan's bidding, Corey drives their ox team, and administers sleeping powders to his seriously ill mother. Mr. Tanner discovers Sister Elizabeth in her drug-induced state of drowsiness and forbids Ethan to give his mother any further medication because it is against the Mormon beliefs. Ethan tells Corey that he is not a Mormon (his father was an English physician) and does not believe in their teachings, but that Mr. Tanner insists that he be baptized if he is to remain with his mother. Corey realizes how difficult it must be for Ethan; she appreciates his kindness even more.

While on the trail, Ethan rescues Corey from the cruel taunts of two Missouri cowhands who have stolen one of their cows. Ethan saves the lives of some of the Mormons who permit him to treat them with natural remedies when a serious illness spreads through their winter camp west of the Missouri River. Finally, when Mr. Tanner and the Church Council demand that Ethan decide about his conversion, he consents.

Exhausted from his labors among the sick, and weakened by his baptismal immersion in the icy river, Ethan becomes gravely ill. Following the steps that she has watched him take with his patients, Corey nurses him diligently and saves his life. When he recovers, he tells her how much he has come to love her. He also explains sorrowfully that his mother has a fatal ailment and has only a brief time to live. Corey realizes how brave Ethan has been and determines to help him make Sister Elizabeth as comfortable as possible.

Because the food supply is exhausted, Ethan catches some trout in a swollen stream, while Corey picks berries for Sister Elizabeth. As they return to camp, they hear the good news that Brigham Young has located Zion just over the next hill. Before they start out, Corey receives a letter from her father releasing her from her betrothal vows.

By the time they get to Zion, Ethan is forced to operate on Corey's hand, which is dangerously swollen from an imbedded piece of fishhook. Even though he has saved Corey's life, Ethan is expelled from the group for this action. Ethan promises Corey that he will follow closely in the next "Gentile" wagon train.

In fulfillment of his promise to her father, Mr. Tanner asks the Council to permit Shad to take Corey as his second wife (he and Meg were married during the winter). Although Corey has no intention of marrying Shad, she remains with the wagon train to nurse Ethan's mother. When Sister Elizabeth dies quietly in her sleep, Corey joins Ethan's wagon train. Corey no longer has any doubts: she knows that they will have a good life together in California.

Thematic Material

In addition to the worthwhile historical background, the authors explore the quality of tolerance with a depth rarely attempted in young adult novels. The fact that maturity and independence is gained through responsible action is forcefully presented.

Book Talk Material

This novel has many exciting episodes. A few are: Corey meets the Tanners (pp. 19–25) ; Corey and Meg (pp. 34–41) ; Corey meets danger rounding up a stray cow (pp. 89–96) ; Corey meets Brigham Young (pp. 165–173) ; Ethan operates on Corey's hand (pp. 204–210) .

Additional Suggestions

Girls will find the following titles excellent follow-up reading: *Katherine Leslie* (Knopf, lib. bdg. $3.29 net) by Audrey White Beyer, *Our Year Began in April* (Lothrop, $3.75) by Meredith Reed, *Friendly Persuasion* (Harcourt, $2.95) by Jessamyn West, *Greenwillow* (Dutton, $3.95) by Beatrice Joy Chute, and *A Man's Calling* (Lothrop, $3.50) by Alonzo Gibbs. Mature boys will find the Indian youth, Tom Black Bull, an interesting hero in *When the Legends Die* (Lippincott, $4.75) by Hal Borland.

Frances Palmer, *And Four to Grow On,*
Holt, 1959, $3.50

Parts of this true story originally appeared in *McCalls* and *Reader's Digest* magazines. The expansion of these articles has been popular since it first appeared in book form in 1959 and is enjoyed by both junior and senior high school students.

Frances and Bill Palmer have remained childless throughout their years of marriage. They apply to the Department of Welfare to adopt two children, and after much waiting, are given a brother and sister— eight-year-old Joe and five-year-old Ruth. The past history of these children is a pathetic story of cruelty, neglect and separation in several foster homes.

When the children arrive, the Palmers feel that perhaps the challenge is too great for them. Ruth is sullen and suspicious. Joe alternates between periods of rebellious destruction and silent withdrawal. For the first weeks, only the Palmers' faith in God sustains them.

They shower love and affection on the two youngsters but find that this is not enough. The children must be taught to respect other people's feelings and property. To accomplish this, the parents establish codes of behavior and try to apply them fairly and judiciously. One by one, crises are met and overcome. Ruth, through work and play with the farm animals, regains her ability to love. Joe, too, shows great improvement. However, in spite of many reassurances, the children fear that one day they will be sent to another home. Only when the final adoption papers are signed, do the two children begin to believe that they have a permanent home.

The Palmers adopt two more children; Tom, aged seven, and his five-year-old sister, Beth. These two also have a background of neglect and unhappiness, but their adjustment to normal family life is rapid because of the Palmers' previous experience and the help of Ruth and Joe.

Remnants of Joe's past emotional problems remain with him. He continues to show fear and hostility toward strangers, and he finds it impossible to make friends at school. Frances constructs a chart, titled "Joe's Treasure Hunt," on which he records all of the good deeds that he has seen other people do. Gradually his attitude toward people changes, and he is eventually accepted into the group.

In the months that follow, the Palmers face other family problems: Tom's bouts of selfishness, Joe's broken arm, and Ruth's temporary amnesia after a fall from a horse.

At the end of the book, four years have elapsed since the arrival of Joe and Ruth. During this time, the Palmers, through faith and love, have become a strong family unit.

Thematic Material

The central theme of this book is the maxim that Frances' mother often repeated to her as a child, "It is never giving that empties the purse, nor loving that empties the heart." This moving story is filled with tenderness and pathos, as well as many charming touches of whimsy and humor.

Book Talk Material

There are scores of wonderful incidents that would be ideal for reading aloud. Here are a few: the arrival of the children (pp. 13–16) ; Frances buys new clothes for Ruth (pp. 26–28) ; Joe's school bus ride (pp. 39–42) ; Joe and the pineapple upside down cake (pp. 53–57) ; Beth and her one-way conversations (pp. 106–108) ; Beth learns about discipline (pp. 123–127) ; Joe's treasure hunt (pp. 131–134) ; Beth learns to ride a bike (pp. 156–158) .

Additional Suggestions

Either of Anna Perrott Rose's nonfiction titles, *Room for One More* (Houghton, $4.50) or *The Gentle House* (Houghton $3.95) would make excellent alternate choices. Also suggest Frances Ames' *That Callahan Spunk!* (Doubleday $4.50) or Vii Putnam's *Hard Hearts Are for Cabbages* (Crown $3.95) . For younger readers, use E. C. Spykman's *A Lemon and a Star* (Harcourt, $3.50) or Madeleine L'Engle's *Meet the Austins* (Vanguard $3.95) .

Carl Sandburg, *Prairie-Town Boy,*
Harcourt, 1952, $3.25

Although this autobiography is abstracted from the adult title, *Always the Young Strangers* (Harcourt $5.95) , Mr. Sandburg's lyrical style remains undiminished. The book contains many of the author's germinal ideas which are fully developed in his poetry and works on Lincoln. Joe Krush's illustrations successfully capture the action in the author's lively boyhood escapades. Junior high school youngsters enjoy this book and it is also useful with the reluctant reader.

In 1880, young Carl Sandberg (later changed to Sandburg) —the oldest boy in a Swedish immigrant family of nine—lives in Galesburg, Ohio. He is intrigued by the town's oldtimers and their recollections of historic events—the first train, the Lincoln-Douglas debates, the founding of the early machine factories, and the growth of the three colleges in town. Carl begins to use his town as a learning laboratory. His hard-working father doesn't understand the sensitive "Sholly," as he calls him. The unsettled longings of this perceptive boy are appreciated more by his patient mother.

The Panic of 1893 shapes Carl's life. The meals in their house are lean; lard is the only spread for their bread. The kitchen is the community room where eleven people huddle around a coal stove. Luckily, his Seventh Ward school has a library so he is able to indulge his love of reading. His eagerness to learn is encouraged by both his teachers and parents. Mrs. Sandburg is easily persuaded to purchase a set of encyclopedias, even though they can ill afford them. While Carl is still in school, he participates in a declamation contest, but loses to his older sister, Mary. During this period, he responds eagerly to his eighth grade teacher's inspiring love of American History. This is reinforced in the practical laboratory of the town when he attends numerous political rallies and witnesses the funeral parade for President Grant.

Carl and his young friends form an active sandlot baseball team. He pursues the game seriously and decides to become a professional ball player. When he crashes into a pole while diving for a ball, he changes his mind about his baseball career.

He is also fascinated with the annual arrival of the circus and gets up at four A.M. to meet the incoming trains. He becomes expert at spending an entire day at the circus for 15 cents. When the circus is not in town, errands to the grocery and butcher store provide entertainment, as well as licorice and baloney. Eventually, as he grows older, the backroom of the cigar store becomes the headquarters for a quartet he and his friends form. By the time Carl is 16, the group has expanded to 12 earnest male singers (the "Dirty Dozen"). One summer day when the group has a forbidden "skinny dip" in the Old Brick Yard close to town, everyone lands in jail overnight for the indiscretion. Through the group, Carl meets the first radical he has ever known, the father of one of his friends.

Carl attends school sporadically. Most of the time, however, he works to help implement the family's income. Some of his jobs are: collecting junk, cleaning offices, delivering papers and milk. It is during his milk-route days that diptheria claims the lives of Carl's two smallest brothers.

Carl runs through another series of jobs, always searching for something he really wants to do: drug-store helper, tinsmith's helper, factory bottle-washer, road worker, refreshment stand helper, ice-harvester, and race-track hand. Times are bad and Carl drifts from job to job. He likes only one job—working in the new Galesburg auditorium as a stage hand. He sees all the shows and speakers and learns a great deal, yet he leaves because he feels that he must learn a trade.

He becomes an apprentice to Mr. Humphrey, a local barber. He shines the shoes of all the "big bugs on the North Side." However, he doesn't get a chance to learn the barbering trade as promised, so he quits. He looks for a better opportunity and finds a promising job with Mr. Sam Barlow who is starting a new milk route. On his new route, Carl meets his first love. He discovers to his horror that he is tongue-tied in the face of love—"a young stranger."

At the age of 19, Carl feels that he is a bashful young man without a future. He goes on the road as a "hobo". He learns how to survive, riding the rails, doing odd jobs and panhandling. Finally, he returns home when he realizes that he wants to be more in life than a drifter.

After a brief time as a farmhand and a painter's apprentice, Carl joins the Army. He goes to San Juan to fight in "McKinley's War" and makes a startling discovery—the newspaper accounts of the War do not always accurately report what really happens. While he is on his way home, a fellow private tells Carl that Lombard College in Galesburg will give him free tuition because he is a veteran. This boon and a Fire Department job enable Carl to enroll. He has decided what he wants to do—he wants to learn.

Thematic Material

The boy's struggle for security, love and affection, and his need to express himself are forcefully presented. An adolescent boy's long and difficult search to determine a constructive attitude toward life and a worthwhile goal are problems that are shared by many boys.

Book Talk Material

Because the book is episodic, it lends itself to many interesting book talk vignettes. One could start with the Prologue (pp. 3–9) and continue with a description of "Prairie-Town" (pp. 27–30). Other parts are: kitchen reading (pp. 40–44); the old swimming hole (pp. 79–83); ice-harvesting (pp. 112–115); painful puppy-love (pp. 137–139); Chicago sights and sounds (pp. 143–145) ; on the road (pp. 146–147) ; in the Army (pp. 165–169) .

Additional Suggestions

Readers will also enjoy Elspeth Bragdon's *There Is a Tide* (Viking, $3.00; lib. bdg. $2.96 net) and Rosemary Manning's *Arripay* (Farrar, Straus, $2.95). Also use Margot Benary-Isbert's *Under a Changing Moon* (Harcourt, $3.75). Older boys and girls enjoy *A Song of Sixpence* (Little, $4.95) by A. J. Cronin, the story of a Catholic boy in a Protestant Scottish community at the turn of the century.

Elizabeth Borton de Treviño, *I, Juan de Pareja*,
Farrar, Straus, 1965, $3.25

Since moving from California to Mexico, Mrs. Treviño has written principally about her new home. Her knowledge of Mexico's heritage and culture is revealed once more in this biographical novel. The book was awarded the Newbery Medal in 1966 and will appeal to youngsters from grades six through nine.

"I, Juan de Pareja, was born into slavery early in the seventeenth century." So begins the story of a young Negro boy who eventually becomes the assistant to the great Spanish painter, Velázquez.

By the age of five, Juan is an orphan and the personal slave of Doña Rodriguez, the wife of a wealthy merchant in Seville. He is taught how to read and write, and soon answers all of his mistress's correspondence. But the plague strikes Seville and his quiet, sheltered existence comes to an abrupt end when both his master and mistress die. For a time he is placed in the care of kindly Brother Isidro, a Franciscan friar, who tells Juan that he has been inherited, along with the Rodriguez' other property, by their nephew, Don Diego Velázquez.

He is taken to Madrid by a cruel gypsy named Carmelo. Juan is beaten savagely by Carmelo, and forced to beg for his food. More dead than alive, he reaches the home of Velázquez.

Juan fits well into this new household. Both the mistress of the house, Doña Juana, and her daughter Paquita are fond of the young boy. Juan is now the personal servant of Velázquez—he helps him mix his colors, arrange his palette, and frame the canvases. A strong attachment develops between the taciturn but gentle painter and his eager and devoted slave. Juan longs to learn how to paint, but Spanish law forbids slaves to engage in the arts.

As Velázquez' fame grows, he becomes the official court painter of the Spanish king, Philip IV. He paints many portraits of the King, his family and advisors, and helps welcome the famed Flemish painter Rubens, to the Spanish court. Juan falls in love with Miri, a pretty slave girl who is part of Rubens' retinue, and his heart breaks when they must part.

Later, Velázquez and Juan are sent to Italy by Philip IV to buy and copy art works for the court gallery. While on the trip, Juan secretly tries his hand at painting. When they return, Juan helps promote a romance between Paquita and one of Velázquez' apprentices, Juan Bautista. The two are eventually united in a happy marriage.

Juan continues to paint secretly but feels increasingly guilty. He confesses all to his master's new apprentice, Bartolomé Murillo, who assures Juan that he has talent and should not stifle it.

On a second visit to Italy, Velázquez' right hand becomes seriously infected. Juan is able to nurse the painter back to health and restore his confidence. Velázquez resumes painting by creating a magnificent portrait of Juan. When the art patrons of Rome see this masterpiece, commissions pour in. Before he leaves Rome, Velázquez completes several portraits including one of Pope Innocent X.

Back in Madrid, Juan feels that he can no longer keep his secret from his master. Velázquez reacts by declaring Juan a free man and offering him a post as his assistant. He also gives freedom to a maidservant, Lolis, so that she and Juan may marry and have a family free from slavery.

Juan continues to work at the studio until Velázquez' death. Posthumously, King Philip confers knighthood on the painter. Juan de Pareja guides the King's hand as he paints the red cross of Santiago on Velázquez' only self-portrait.

Thematic Material

The principal theme is stated by the author in an Afterword, ". . . the story of Juan de Pareja and Velázquez foreshadows, in the lifetime of the two men, what we hope to achieve a millionfold today. Those two, who began in youth as master and slave, continued as companions in their maturity and ended as equals and as friends."

Book Talk Material

If possible, display some of the paintings of Velázquez; well-known "Las Meninas" includes the famous self-portrait with the Cross of Santiago as well as a study, in the distance, of the painter's royal patron.

Incidents for reading aloud are: Juan learns of his change of ownership (pp. 13–16); his journey with Carmelo (pp. 29–32); he leaves Carmelo and works in a bakery (pp. 33–36); Juan learns his duties (pp. 40–45); the apprentices (pp. 47–51); Rubens visits the Madrid Woodcutters (pp. 62–66); the first trip to Italy (pp. 84–90); Juan paints a Virgin, and confesses to Murillo (pp. 122–127).

Additional Suggestions

Elizabeth Ripley's biographies of *Velázquez* (Lippincott, $3.75; lib. bdg. $3.39 net) and *Rubens* (Walck, $4.00) could be used. A suitable fiction title for younger readers is Ann Nolan Clark's *Santiago* (Viking, $3.25; lib. bdg. $3.19 net). *Victory at Valmy* (Vanguard, $3.50) by Geoffrey Trease tells of a young French boy's love of painting and his adventures before the French Revolution. Also use Rafaello Busoni's biography of Cervantes, *The Man Who Was Don Quixote* (Prentice-Hall, $3.95) and Dorothy Loder's *The Land and People of Spain* (Lippincott, lib. bdg. $2.93 net). The latter gives excellent background material on Spanish history and culture. More mature readers will enjoy Mrs. de Treviño's stories of Mexican life, *My Heart Lies South* (Crowell, $4.95) and *Where the Heart Is* (Doubleday, $4.50).

John R. Tunis, *Silence Over Dunkerque,*
Morrow, 1962, $3.50; lib. bdg. $3.32 net

To young adult readers, the name John R. Tunis is associated with fast-action sports stories. In *Silence over Dunkerque,* the author has shifted to the difficult, early days of World War II. This novel deals with a short time in May, 1940, when France was overrun by the Nazis and Allied troops were evacuated from Dunkerque. Boys (and some girls) from grades six through nine find it enjoyable.

The war has separated the Williams family. The father, Sergeant George Williams of the Wilshire Regiment is fighting on the Continent, while the rest of the family—Mrs. Williams, the 15-year-old twins, Richard and Ronald, and younger sister, Penelope—remain at their home on Folkestone Road in the English coastal city of Dover.

On May 10, 1940, the German forces begin their push through the Low Countries. During the Allied retreat, Sergeant Williams and his six-man patrol are separated from the rest of the battalion and captured by the Germans. Although they make a daring escape from their captors, they are unable to find and rejoin their regiment. As the Nazis move in, George and his men head for Dunkerque and, they hope, evacuation to England. On the way, the patrol is adopted by a war orphan, an Airedale, whom Sergeant Williams names Candy, after his dog at home.

At Dunkerque, George cannot find an evacuation ship. He refuses an offer to take the last place aboard a small boat, because this would mean abandoning his men. Eventually all of them, including Candy, find places on a British warship, H. M. S. Wakeful.

In the meantime Richard and Ronald join the rescue operation in an attempt to find their father. They cross the Channel aboard a small boat owned and operated by a neighbor, Bill Bennett. As they return to Dover with a boatload of soldiers, the twins see in the distance a British destroyer that is following a different course from theirs. It is the Wakeful.

The destroyer hits a mine and sinks. In the ensuing confusion, Sergeant Williams is able to save one of his squad, an East Londoner named "Three-Fingers" Brown. The two manage to swim back to the shores of France.

While they lie exhausted on the beach, they are found by a teenage French girl, Gisele Bonnet, who hides them in the loft of the barn that adjoins her family's farm. They are now in enemy occupied territory, and the Germans have warned the townspeople that death is the penalty for harboring Allied soldiers. When George and Fingers narrowly escape detection by a band of Germans, Gisele's mother makes them leave.

Dressed in fishermen's clothes, they leave with Gisele for Calais where relatives of the Bonnets will try to arrange their escape to England. On the way, they are joined by Candy, who has miraculously returned from the sinking of the destroyer.

After several brushes with German patrols, the group reaches Calais and the home of Gisele's grandfather. Here plans are made for their escape. Aboard a fishing trawler, skippered by Gisele's uncle, the two are transported out of Calais. When they are safely out of the harbor, a dory is lowered with the two men and Candy aboard. In the middle of the English Channel, they rescue a German airman whose plane has been shot down and he reluctantly helps them with the rowing. Finally, exhausted and half-starved, they reach Dover, and home.

Thematic Material

This is a starkly realistic picture of warfare and its impact on both soldiers and civilians. It is filled with incidents that portray both valor and sacrifice. As such, it is a tribute to the unconquerable spirit of man.

Book Talk Material

Here are a few incidents that would be suitable for use in introducing this work: the Belgian civilians flee from the invaders (pp. 13–17); the patrol is captured and escapes (pp. 22–27); a brush with German officers (pp. 36–40); Sergeant Williams tries to find a boat for his men (pp. 63–67); the men board the Wakeful (pp. 68–74); the Germans search the barn (pp. 114–116). An excellent picture of the debarking of Allied soldiers at Dover is given on pages 135–141.

Additional Suggestions

In addition to John R. Tunis' other novels, suggest his autobiography *Measure of Independence* (Atheneum, $5.00). Books on John F. Kennedy's World War II experiences would also be suitable: Robert J. Donovan's *PT-109* (McGraw, $5.95) or the more juvenile *John F. Kennedy and PT-109* (Random, $1.95; lib. bdg. $2.28 net) by Richard Tregaskis. Robin McKown's *Patriot of the Underground* (Putnam, $3.75) is a story about teenage boys and the French Resistance during World War II. A non-fiction account of the evacuation at Dunkirk is given in Richard Collier's *The Sands of Dunkirk* (Dutton, $5.25). More mature readers will enjoy Irving Werstein's *The Long Escape* (Scribner, lib. bdg. $3.31 net) which tells of the flight of Madame Raymond and 50 youngsters from Belgium to England. Also suggest Willard A. Heaps' true account of escapes through the Berlin Wall, *The Wall of Shame* (Meredith, $3.95).

Phyllis A. Whitney, *Willow Hill,*
McKay, 1947, lib. bdg. $3.89 net

Mrs. Whitney's reputation as a writer of fine young adult stories was founded on this early title about a young girl's struggle against community prejudice. Although the novel predates most stories on this theme, it retains an enviable freshness of presentation. Girls in junior and senior high school find this vital and satisfying reading.

Before their senior year begins, Valerie Coleman and Judy Piper discuss the summer's news; Valerie's first prize in a Chicago newspaper essay contest, and the controversial Willow Hill Negro housing project. The girls also talk about Stephen Reid, the Colemans' young friend and boarder, who is also a senior, and Tony Millard, class president and star athlete, who has been dating Judy during the summer.

After a tennis match with the boys, the four argue about the merits of the new housing project. Tony repeats his father's comment that it will be bad for the town, and Val admits that her mother's club is also against having more Negro families move to Willow Hill. They finally walk down to investigate the project's model house.

Here they meet Mary Evans, one of the few Negro students at the high school. Mary introduces them to her younger brother, Jeff, who has been living in Chicago, but will also be attending high school in the fall. Stephen mentions to the group that Jeff would make a natural basketball player.

When Val and Steve arrive home, discussion of the project begins again. Mrs. Coleman raises the same misgivings as Mrs. Manning, her club president. She adds that her husband, the high school basketball coach, will never put a Negro on the team, but Mr. Coleman declares that he'll use anyone who can play well.

On the first day of school, Mary is decidedly cool toward Val and Steve, but Jeff remains friendly. Val introduces Steve to their principal and journalism teacher, Miss Kay. Val is certain that Miss Kay will soon announce that she has won the coveted editorship of the school paper, *The Willow Wand.* However, Miss Kay tells the class that Mary Evans, because of her skill and dependability, has been chosen editor. Val is crushed and refuses the associate editorship.

News spreads about the announcement. Mrs. Coleman reports that Mrs. Manning has summoned the entire town to a meeting to protest

Val's loss of the position. Val realizes that the situation has become dangerous and that she must stop feeling sorry for herself and reach a just decision.

Miss Kay calls a school assembly the following day and informs the students that they must *live* democracy, not just talk about it.

Everyone goes to the protest meeting. Mary's father, Dr. Evans, a minister, and Mr. Kincaid, the school board president, defend the project, but the opposition leaders, Mrs. Manning and Mr. Millard seem to be victorious. However, Val is so moved by Dr. Evans' plea for justice that she decides to take the associate editorship and try to help the project.

Her friends begin to help. Judy tries various schemes and Steve suggests a group of sponsoring senior "Angels" for the incoming Negro students. Val asks Mr. Kincaid to help and he assures her that he will not dismiss Miss Kay and Mr. Coleman as he has been asked to do by the opposition leaders. Meanwhile, Mary finds out that Tony is Jeff's "Angel"; she is furious because she feels that Tony will hurt her sensitive brother.

Val and Judy work after school in the editorial office trying to help Mary. But Mary remains distant. Finally, one afternoon, Val tells her that she is just as prejudiced as anyone because she has already prejudged Tony. Mary still does not soften her attitude until Val supports two new Negro girls who have had a lunchroom quarrel with Mrs. Manning's daughter, Dorothy. Then, Mary, in a display of friendship, offers to make Val a much-needed gown for the winter dance. Val accepts gladly.

Mary sews the gown in Val's house and the two girls and Mrs. Coleman become good friends. During this time, Mary sadly reports that her older brother has lost his job on the newspaper because of Mr. Millard's influence. Val calls an "Angel" meeting. Steve tells the group that if they all stick together, no one can take away their parents' jobs. At the end of the meeting, Mary thanks Tony for his kindness to Jeff. In confusion, Tony warns everyone that there might be an outbreak of prejudice at the coming basketball game.

Although the game starts well, the Willow Hill teamwork falls apart by the third quarter and the crowd begins to mutter "Negroes don't want to win." In the last quarter, Jeff fouls and the opposition wins by three points. Some of the crowd follows Jeff home intent on revenge.

Fearful for his safety, the two girls drive to Jeff's house with Tony and Steve, but find that Mr. Coleman and Jeff have already dispersed the group.

Tony admits to Jeff that his values have been distorted and that he was partly to blame for the ugly situation that developed.

Although the young people feel that there is still a great deal more to be done, they are pleased that there has been a significant change in attitude toward the project.

Thematic Material

The community strife that results from racial discrimination is skillfully drawn. The growing maturity on the part of the young people in this situation is forcefully explored and a constructive attitude toward life rewardingly developed.

Book Talk Material

Interest young adults by a simple description of the plot. Several exciting episodes that can be paraphrased or read are: the young adults investigate the project (pp. 31–38); the community protest meeting (pp. 76–87); Val and Steve visit Mary's home (pp. 91–100); the "Angels" gather (pp. 199–211); and the big basketball game (pp. 212–224).

Additional Suggestions

Younger girls will enjoy Mimi C. Levy's *Corrie and the Yankee* (Viking $3.00; lib. bdg. $3.04 net) about a Negro girl who hides a wounded soldier. Bob and Jan Young's *Across the Tracks* (Messner, $2.95), about prejudice against Mexicans in a California town, is also recommended. For more mature adolescents, suggest Calvin Trillin's account of Charlayne Hunter's career at the University of Georgia, *An Education in Georgia* (Viking $3.95); Harry Golden's collection of essays, *Only in America* (World $5.00); Alan Paton's moving stories about apartheid in *Tales from a Troubled Land* (Scribner $3.50); and Richard Llewellyn's poignant Welsh mining story, *How Green Was My Valley* (Macmillan $5.95).

8

Appreciating Books

I T IS difficult to find books for young teens that combine high interest, appropriate content, and excellent writing. During childhood, the youngster has been exposed to many types of reading material—good, bad and mediocre. Reading guidance for teenagers should attempt to help the reader learn to appreciate excellence in literature and to recognize fine writing. The young reader must develop his own standards for evaluating books.

The books selected for this chapter combine literary merit with an enjoyable reading experience. Each illustrates an author's creative use of language and writing skill; all will stretch the reader's imagination and expose him to fine literature.

Louise Fitzhugh, *Harriet the Spy*,
       Harper, 1964, $3.95; lib. bdg. $3.99 net

The vibrant Harriet—a memorable character—is the creation of Miss Fitzhugh, an author-illustrator whose bold portraits in both words and pictures are delightful and, at times, shocking. In this rollicking first novel, she presents an innocent's view of her small world. This book is for youngsters in grades four through seven to enjoy. Older adolescents will find that the story will stir memories of their childhood.

Eleven-year-old Harriet M. Welsch (the middle initial has been added at her insistence) and her beloved governess, Miss Catherine Golly, spend the last day of summer vacation with Mrs. Golly in Far Rockaway, a long subway ride from Harriet's fashionable Manhattan East Side brownstone. Although Ole Golly (a pet name) is trying to show Harriet that few people live as luxuriously as the Welschs, Harriet is more astounded by the difference between her intelligent governess and the stupidly childish Mrs. Golly. She observes everything carefully and notes that Ole Golly treats her foolish mother with great kindness. She jots this down in her current notebook.

Ole Golly has encouraged her to write down her observations in a notebook. Consequently, over the past three years, Harriet has filled fourteen composition books and developed a sharp eye for details. She has even set up a spy route, regularly investigating and noting the happenings of the De Santi family who own the corner grocery store, the Robinsons, an affluent childless couple, Harrison Withers, an artist who loves cats, and Mrs. Plumber, a wealthy widow. Although she has some narrow escapes from discovery, Harriet doggedly pursues her solemn rounds dressed in proper spy attire—blue jeans, sweat shirt, and a belt loaded with necessary equipment. Harriet carefully and truthfully writes up each adventure, sparing no one and following Ole Golly's maxim, "To thine own self be true."

Harriet returns to the Gregory School, a small private institution for young ladies and gentlemen, carrying her usual lunch, a tomato sandwich. She resumes her close friendship with her contemporaries, Sport (Simon Rocque), who wants to be a ball player, and Janie Gibbs, a budding scientist, who spends her afternoons in her home lab. The remainder of Miss Elson's sixth grade are classmates of long standing and unappealing to Harriet because they always support Harriet's nemesis, Marion Hawthorne, on important issues like class elections.

The loss of the class presidency to Marion is a minor tribulation compared to Mrs. Welsch's sudden announcement that Janie and Harriet must go to dancing school. Ole Golly manages to cajole Harriet into accepting her fate by suggesting that female spies must know how to dance. This crisis is followed by a more serious one. Because of a misunderstanding, Mrs. Welsch fires Ole Golly. Ole Golly, who is planning to marry her beau, Mr. Waldenstein, and move to Canada, decides to leave immediately after straightening out the situation with Mrs. Welsch. Harriet is dumbfounded at the thought of Ole Golly's departure. But, Ole Golly explains that Harriet is a big girl now and must carry on by herself.

Without Ole Golly, everything seems to go wrong. Her mother tries to help, but Harriet misses her governess. She tries unsuccessfully to become enthusiastic about her part as an onion in the school Christmas pageant.

One day, after a game of tag with her classmates, she drops her notebook in the park. When she goes back to reclaim it, she finds Janie reading selections from her notebook to the solemn-faced group. She sees Sport cry when Janie reads that he is "like a little old woman." Harriet, completely unnerved by their refusal to return her notebook, goes home and resolves to buy a new composition book.

The next day in school, her classmates start to write her nasty notes. Feigning illness, she stays home for three days until Dr. Andrews, a classmate's father, pronounces her well. He also tells her mother about the notebook. Back in school, Harriet silently plots revenge on everyone. Her resolve is strengthened when she discovers that her classmates are building a Spy Catcher's Club. Before she can act, however, her mother takes her to a psychiatrist, Dr. Wagner.

After an entertaining afternoon playing games with the doctor, Harriet makes a lame effort to make up with Janie and Sport, but finds them preoccupied with their own interests.

The following day, Dr. Wagner phones Mrs. Welsch and tells her to write and ask Ole Golly for help. Ole Golly writes a letter to Harriet giving her advice. She tells Harriet that she must apologize to the people she has hurt and that sometimes the truth must be softened to spare people's feelings. She also tells Harriet that she doesn't miss her because "gone is gone." Harriet is told to feel the same way.

To Harriet's amazement, Miss Elston announces that she will be the editor of the sixth grade page in the school paper. Harriet attacks her work with dedication and enlivens the page with many interesting tidbits of information. She also prints a general apology to her class. The desired effect is accomplished; Janie and Sport once again offer their friendship.

Thematic Material

The child's realization that people's feelings must not always be sacrificed to an individual's interpretation of truth is honestly explored. Too, the devotion that a youngster can feel for his current interest is forcefully stressed. The savagery of a child's innocent jottings about human behavior and the tenderness of the inward moments of childhood are effectively shown by the author's crisp, staccato style.

Book Talk Material

A brief introduction to Harriet and her friends, Sport and Janie, will arouse interest. A description of the spy route is also intriguing. Read the following passages: Janie's lab and dancing school (pp. 74–82) ; the Christmas pageant (pp. 149–155) ; the Spy Catcher Club (pp. 205–223) .

Additional Suggestions

Follow with the author's *The Long Secret* (Harper, $3.95; lib. bdg. $3.79 net) about Harriet and her summertime friend, Beth Ellen. Also suggest the following titles for younger readers: *The Noonday Friends* (Harper, $3.50; lib. bdg. $3.27 net) by Mary Stolz, about two 11-year-old New York City girl friends; *Laura's Luck* (Doubleday, $3.25) by Marilyn Sachs, about girls in summer camp; *Down to Earth* (Harcourt, $3.75) by Patricia Wrightson, about three youngsters, one a boy from outer space; and *D.J.'s Worst Enemy* (Viking, $3.00; lib. bdg. $2.96 net) by Robert Burch about D.J. who is his own nemesis. The two latter titles will also appeal to boys. The interesting account of life in a progressive boarding school, *Apples Every Day* (Harper, $3.50; lib. bdg. $3.27 net) by Grace Richardson is recommended for young adults.

Irene Hunt, *Across Five Aprils,*
Follett, 1964, $3.95

Mrs. Hunt's description of a young boy whose adolescence coincides with the period of American Civil War is both perceptive and moving. The intricate web of historical detail and the captivating picture of family life combine to make this book a worthy Charles W. Follett Award winner and Newbery Award runner-up for 1964. The appealing cover design and end-papers by Albert John Pucci are an attractive addition. Youngsters in sixth through ninth grades will appreciate this superior historical novel.

Nine-year-old Jethro and his mother, Ellen Creighton, are planting potatoes on their Southern Illinois farm on an April day in 1861. To keep his mother from worrying about the possibility of a civil war, Jethro tells her a story he has learned from Shadrach Yale, his 20-year-old schoolmaster. Jethro and the two next older boys, brother Tom and cousin Eb, think the talk of war is very exciting. But, Jethro knows that his Kentucky-born mother can't bear the thought of a struggle between the South and the North. He knows, too, that his father, Matt Creighton, disapproves of violence. Jethro saw his father disband a posse that was going to lynch young Travis Burdow whose drunken behavior had caused the death of Jethro's sister, Mary. His older brothers, the inseparable John and Bill, don't seem as exhilarated by the war talk as he.

Because he has helped with the planting work, when they celebrate the visit of his Kentucky cousin, Wilse Graham, Jethro is allowed to sit at the adult table while his 14-year-old sister, Jenny, serves. The dinner discussion on slavery becomes heated; Wilse Graham and, to everyone's surprise, Bill, defend the South. As Mrs. Creighton attempts to quell the argument, Shadrach Yale brings news of the firing on Fort Sumter. Jethro finally goes to bed, but he hears the adults' conversation long into the night.

By the time summer comes, the War is a full-scale conflict and there is a skirmish nearby at Wilson's Creek. Tom and Eb leave for the Union Army in August; John and Shadrach plan to go in February. John wants to help with the harvest and Shadrach wants to finish his teaching contract and get permission to marry Jenny. But, Mr. Creighton does not give his permission because of Jenny's young age.

Bill decides to enlist on the Confederate side. His decision causes a fight between himself and his brother, John. Soon after, Bill leaves for Kentucky and John joins the Union Army. The enmity between the two brothers distresses the family, but they respect Bill's right to make his own decision. They realize, however, that others will not be so open-minded and that the family will be labeled "Copperhead" and marked for retribution.

Jethro assumes many of the adult chores. One day, while he is in town getting supplies, he endures Guy Wortman's nasty remarks about Bill. The men in the general store rescue him. On the way home, Travis Burdow's father saves Jethro from the revengeful Wortman who is trying to ambush him. Jethro begins to think more kindly about peaceful ways as he realizes that this was Mr. Burdow's way of saying "Thank you" to his father.

Several tragic events occur during the early spring: Matt Creighton's heart attack, Mr. Wortman's repeated threats that lead to the burning of their barn, and the news of Tom's death. The War that the boys had thought about with anticipation has become a macabre reality.

As 1863 begins, great numbers of deserters from the Union Army begin to camp south of the Creighton's cabin. On an afternoon while he is plowing, Jethro discovers that Eb is among them. Jethro feeds and comforts him, but realizing that Eb will face a firing squad when he returns to his unit, Jethro writes President Lincoln pleading for mercy. Meanwhile, Jenny goes East to tend the wounded Shadrach. When he recovers, they marry before he returns to his unit.

Jethro receives a reply from the President which gives the deserters a general amnesty. Eb returns to his unit. From letters that the family receives, Jethro follows the conduct of the War. When John writes that Bill is a prisoner of war, the family is grateful to know that he is at least alive.

While everyone in the North awaits an imminent victory after President Lincoln's reelection in 1864, the War drags on with Sherman's Army apparently lost in its sweep through the South. Jethro thinks that peace will be wonderful, but Mr. Milton explains philosophically that Jethro is expecting too much from the peace, just as he had from the war.

As another April arrives and the War ends, Shad and Jenny come for a visit and to take Jethro East to school. War and time have changed the family. Across the five Aprils of Jethro's adolescence, he has done a man's work and learned a man's lesson.

Thematic Material

This story nobly emphasizes the futility of aggression. The American Civil War with its drama is expertly presented through the lives of an ordinary family. It will provide young adults with a clearer understanding of and compassion for this country's conflict. In addition, the worthy values of a devoted family relationship and the traditional American emphasis on education are stressed.

Book Talk Material

This story may be introduced by a brief resume of the plot. Several dramatic episodes, however, make excellent reading. Divided loyalties occur when Wilse Graham appears (pp. 32–42), and when Bill explains to Jethro why he must fight for the South (pp. 51–54). Jethro's overnight visit with the schoolmaster (pp. 58–76); Mr. Burdow's repayment of kindness (pp. 100–101); or Jethro's discovery of Eb (pp. 154–166) followed by Mr. Lincoln's letter to Jethro (pp. 174–175) will also elicit interest.

Additional Suggestions

Other books of superior merit that will interest the same readers are: *Odyssey of Courage* (Atheneum, $3.75; lib. bdg. $3.59 net) by Maia Wojciechowska, and *Talargain* (Holt, $3.75; lib. bdg. $3.45 net) by Joyce Gard. For younger readers, recommend William O. Steele's *The Perilous Road* (Harcourt, $2.95), about the American Civil War. Girls will enjoy Ruth Painter Randall's *I, Varina* (Little, $3.95) with its fine portrayal of a girl's life. For junior high school girls you could also suggest the 1967 Newbery Award winner *Up the Road Slowly* by Irene Hunt (Follett, $3.95; lib. bdg. $3.99 net).

Norman Juster, *The Phantom Tollbooth*,
Random, 1961, $3.95

This book is an hilarious tale about a small boy who escapes boredom through a series of fantastic adventures in a magic land, only to discover that his ennui is of his own making. It is also a brilliant satire on life in general, education in particular, and the separation of the humanities and the sciences, specifically. The author's skillful use of words strengthens the unmistakable quality of the work and the line drawings by Jules Feiffer reinforce its imaginative spirit. Readers of all ages will enjoy this allegorical story.

Milo, a cosmopolitan young lad, is bored by life, particularly school. Seeing little reason to study, he mopes about. Returning to his apartment one afternoon, he finds a large present in his living room. The attached note is unsigned. It reads ". . . for use by those who have never traveled in lands beyond." Milo dispiritedly assembles the strange gift which becomes a tollbooth, complete with map and coins. Curious, Milo gets in his red toy car, studies the map, drops a coin in the tollbooth, and sets off for the city of Dictionopolis (somewhere beyond Expectations).

He soon meets the "Whether Man" who tells him that he is on the right road because "there are no wrong roads to anywhere." Milo starts to daydream and takes the wrong turn. He finds himself in the Doldrums, a terrible place where nothing every happens or changes. The Lethargarians tell him that thinking is not allowed. Milo pauses drowsily until everyone starts to shake in fright at the approach of a large shaggy dog with a tremendous clock in the center of his body. The dog barks at everyone to stop killing time. Milo asks the dog to help him get out of the Doldrums, but the dog barks back, "Help yourself." As Milo starts to drive away, the dog climbs in the car explaining that he likes to ride in cars; he also tells Milo the sad story about his twin brother Tick (who was born tocking.)

At the gates of King Azaz the Unabridged's city of Dictionopolis, they are stopped by the guard who asks their reason for entering. Milo is nonplussed. The guard, however, pins a "Why Not" button on Milo and they enter. Since it happens to be market day, they are welcomed by the King's Cabinet, whose duty it is to see that all the words sold are proper ones. There is such confusion that Milo doesn't know whether to buy a crisp, crunchy C or a package of Happy H's. He finally decides to save his one coin for the return tollbooth fare.

Suddenly, a large bee appears and introduces himself as the Spelling Bee. An elegantly dressed large beetle also joins them. The spelling bee disdainfully introduces Milo to the Humbug. The two insects argue; their antics knock over all the stalls in the Word Market. A policeman, Short Shrift (two feet tall and twice as wide), arrives to arrest the group. As he leads them into a dungeon, Short Shrift warns them to beware of the witch.

Milo is appalled to think that mixing up words has caused all this trouble; he tells Tock that he is going to learn about words. Hearing this, the witch, Faintly Macabre, comes out of a dark corner. The little old witch explains that she has been incarcerated because she was in charge of choosing words for all occasions (the Official Which), but that power corrupted her. She eventually put up a sign, "Silence is Golden," and the whole economy floundered. She also tells them about the princesses, Rhyme and Reason, who are imprisoned in the Castle in the Air by their two stubborn, older step-brothers, King Azaz and the Mathemagician. When the two golden-haired girls had ruled that, "It is no more important to count the sands than it is to name the stars," they were banished by the jealous Kings. Since then there has been no peace in the Kingdom of Wisdom.

After Milo and his friends escape, they attend a very strange royal banquet where everyone eats his own words. When King Azaz sorrowfully confides that things are so confused nowadays with nothing but words around, Milo suggests that he be allowed to rescue Rhyme and Reason. Although Azaz outlines many difficulties, Milo pleads for permission to try. Azaz won't tell Milo what the most serious deterrent is until he returns, but he does give him a satchel full of words and the conscripted services of the Humbug.

The three heroes set out for the Mountains of Ignorance to get the Mathemagician's permission to rescue the princesses. On the way they meet a lad named Alec Bings who "stands" suspended in mid-air and sees through things; they pass through the beautiful, uninhabited city of Reality and the gloomy, populated city of Illusions; they enjoy a colorful, soundless symphony that causes the sun to rise and set; they stumble across the horrible, noisy Dr. Dischord and his genie, Dynne; they free the imprisoned sounds from the castle in the Silent Valley; they jump to the Island of Conclusions, but swim back through the dry sea of Knowledge; they solve the problem posed by the fellow, Dodecahedron, to find the correct road to Digitopolis, the Mathemagician's city.

Upon arriving, they are escorted into a mountain shaft where the Mathemagician in his equation-covered robe shows Milo the numbers they mine. They even polish and sell the broken numbers (fractions), but not the precious stones which are discarded. The Humbug is aghast. While there, Milo tastes subtraction stew (and is hungrier than ever) and meets five-eights of a boy (part of the average 2.58 family) who is sitting on the endless steps to infinity. When Milo descends after an impossible climb, the Mathemagician reassures him by explaining that anything worth doing is difficult. By using some logic, Milo tricks the Mathemagician into granting him permission to rescue the princesses.

Armed with his satchel of words and the Mathemagician's pencil, Milo and his two friends begin to climb to the Castle in the Air. They are confronted by various demons: A Very Dirty Bird (the ever-present word-snatcher); the faceless Terrible Trivium (a monster of habit); the Demon of Insincerity; the Gelatinous Giant (who hates to be conspicuous); and finally the Official Senses Taker. They are able to elude each demon, however, and finally emerge into the princesses' domain.

The princesses comfort Milo: Reason tells him to take heart over his past mistakes, while Rhyme explains that he is beginning to understand why he should make an attempt to learn. Together they return to the Mountains of Ignorance, dashing past all the demons until, at the bottom, they see the golden armies of the Kingdom of Wisdom awaiting their triumphant return. Everyone is there. King Azaz tells Milo that the most serious problem about the entire rescue is that it was impossible. They celebrate with a parade. Then the princesses tell Milo that it is time for him to leave. Tock and Humbug say goodbye tearfully as Milo drives away in his little red car.

The following day school passes quickly; Milo hurries home in anticipation of another trip, but to his dismay the tollbooth is gone. In its place is a note which reads, "For Milo, Who now knows the Way." Although Milo is disappointed, he understands that there are other boys and girls who may want the tollbooth. He now knows that if he wants to take other journeys, he can find his own way.

Thematic Material

Young readers will enjoy the fantastic adventures which combine the elements of both fairy tale and epic literature. Youngsters will also appreciate the humor and moral of the story. Older readers will find the sophisticated meaning inherent in the style very engaging. Milo, a juvenile Everyman, is a satisfying hero with whom to identify.

Book Talk Material

Each adventure in Milo's journey can be effectively paraphrased or read aloud. Young audiences find Tock's story humorous (pp. 32–34). Some students will recall the description of the Doldrums as a place they have visited (pp. 22–31). Faintly Macabre's story about the two princesses, Rhyme and Reason, is successful with young girls (pp. 71–77). The story is full of intriguing vignettes for retelling.

Additional Suggestions

It is difficult to suggest a title similar to this remarkable book. There are, however, many good stories of fantasy which please the young reader. *The Magician's Nephew* (Macmillan $3.95) about two children's adventures among magic talking beasts, is a fine title from C. S. Lewis's "Narnia Series." Elizabeth Enright's story about the only golden-haired, brown-eyed girl in the Kingdom, *Tatsinda* (Harcourt $3.50; lib. bdg. $3.60 net) is also a popular choice for younger readers. The 1960 Newbery runner-up, *The Gammage Cup* (Harcourt $3.25) by Carol Kendall, about the Minnipins and the Mushrooms and *Time at the Top* (Parnassus $3.50) by Edward Ormondroyd, about a girl who travels ahead in time in an apartment elevator are good additional selections.

Madeleine L'Engle, *A Wrinkle in Time,*
Farrar, Straus, 1962, $3.25

A Wrinkle in Time can be read at many levels. Regardless of its interpretation, this Newbery Award winner remains an unusual, thought-provoking book that continues to gain an enthusiastic audience. It is especially enjoyed by children from the sixth through ninth grades.

Twelve-year-old Meg Murry is hardly an ordinary child; nor is her family, by any means, conventional. Her father is a physicist who has disappeared mysteriously a year ago while on a secret space mission. Her mother, a research scientist, has tried to cultivate individuality in each of her children. Meg's ten-year-old twin brothers, Sandy and Dennys, appear to be average youngsters but her favorite brother, five-year-old Charles Wallace, is extremely precocious, highly intelligent, and gifted with certain powers of clairvoyance.

One dark, stormy night, Meg is so upset by her difficulties in adjusting to dull schoolwork and equally uninspiring classmates that she finds sleep impossible. She leaves her warm bed to think her problems through over a cup of hot chocolate in the kitchen. She finds that her brother Charles Wallace has already preceded her. They are soon joined by Mrs. Murry and, lastly, by an old lady who comes seeking shelter from the storm. It is Mrs. Whatsit, a strange creature, who has taken up residence in a "haunted" house close to the Murry's home.

Meg and Charles Wallace are so intrigued by this old lady that, on the following morning, they decide to pay her a visit. On the way, they are joined by Calvin O'Keefe, a 14-year-old friend from Meg's school. The three meet Mrs. Whasit's two companions, Mrs. Who, who speaks in aphorisms from several languages, and Mrs. Which, whose voice seems to emanate from an echo chamber. All three ladies appear to have supernatural powers, and they promise to help the three children find Mr. Murry. To accomplish the rescue, the children must travel in space by the fifth dimension, a tesseract, which reduces the distance between two points by creating a wrinkle in time.

Their first tesser takes the three children to a friendly planet where they learn from the three ladies that Mr. Murry is being held prisoner on the distant planet, Camazotz. They also spy their adversary, The Power of Darkness—a giant black cloud that represents all the evil and negative aspects in life. Camazotz has already surrendered to it, and the children see, by looking into the crystal ball of the Happy Medium, that the people on Earth are also threatened by its power.

Before leaving the children to accomplish the rest of their mission, the ladies issue warnings of the dangers that lie ahead. Mrs. Who gives Meg her magic eyeglasses, to be used, she says, only in an extreme emergency.

Another tesser, and the children, now alone, reach Camazotz. They find that here the people have given up their identity to live in mechanical, robot-like conformity. In the huge CENTRAL Central Intelligence Building, the three are confronted by the Prime Coordinator. In a duel of wits, he hypnotizes Charles Wallace and turns him into another dehumanized citizen of Camazotz.

Meg finds her father entrapped behind a transparent wall. By using Mrs. Who's glasses, she is able to pass through the wall and free him. However, when they encounter the chief power on the planet, a large pulsating brain named IT, Meg is so close to submitting that Mr. Murry tessers Meg, Calvin and himself to a nearby friendly planet. Charles Wallace, now a slave of IT's power, remains behind.

Meg slowly recovers from her ordeal. She is nursed by one of the planet's faceless inhabitants, whom she calls Aunt Beast. But the problem of how to rescue Charles Wallace remains. The three ladies return and tell Meg that she alone controls enough of the necessary power to save her brother. Meg does not understand what this power can be, but she consents to return to Camazotz.

When she confronts Charles Wallace once more, she suddenly knows what this power is—it is love. By repeating "I love you" to her brother, she is able to free him from the Power of Darkness. Together, they rejoin Mr. Murry and Calvin, and, with one more tesser, all return to Earth.

Thematic Material

Although this can be read superficially as an exciting science fiction adventure, the author has tried to explore such serious themes as: the need for individuality and respect for others' differences, the power of love and the nature of good and evil.

Book Talk Material

Interest can be created by using the following incidents: the children meet Mrs. Whatsit (pp. 16–21); their first tesser (pp. 56–62); they see the Power of Darkness (pp. 71–73); the Happy Medium's crystal ball (pp. 86–89); Camazotz (pp. 103–106); the CENTRAL Central Intelligence Building (pp. 115–120). An explanation of a tesseract is given on pages 75–78.

Additional Suggestions

For boys try Robert A. Heinlein's *Between Planets* or *Red Planet* (both Scribner lib. bdg. $3.31 net). Many of André Norton's titles are also suitable, for example *The X Factor* (Harcourt, $3.25) a science fiction novel of a boy who is unable to fit into his father's world, or *Night of Masks* (Harcourt, $3.25), the story of a young man who finds that actions rather than physical characteristics determine a man's worth. Younger girls will enjoy Pauline Clarke's *The Return of the Twelves* (Coward, $3.95), the story of twelve toy soldiers that once belonged to the Brontes. Older girls will wish to go on to Madeleine L'Engle's *Camilla* (Crowell, $4.50) and Nora Johnson's *The World of Henry Orient* (Little, $4.75).

Robert Nathan, *The Weans,*
Knopf, 1961, $2.95

This brilliant satire on American culture and mores was scarcely noticed when it was first published in 1961. In only 56 pages of text, Mr. Nathan has compressed a powerful supply of both wit and wisdom. Some of Mr. Nathan's more subtle references might be too obscure for the average reader. In general, this book is read and enjoyed by more discerning junior-senior high school students.

The book takes the form of a report on several archaeological expeditions from Kenya and Uganda in the years 7857–9. These expeditions have uncovered amazing facts about the former inhabitants of the Great West or Salt Continent. They were not sub-human as once thought, but did have some form of culture. The people are known as the Weans, because they called their land the WE, or sometimes the US. Interesting finds have been uncovered in some of their principal cities, such as: n'Yok, Bosstin, Cha'ago, Oleens, and their capital, Pound-Laundry.

Several recent discoveries prove that the Weans were an inhospitable group. For example, the reconstruction of a giant statue found near n'Yok shows a goddess—named Lib or Libby—in a threatening, war-like pose. Part of the inscription at the base of this statue reads, "Keep off the. . ."

The Weans were probably a religious people. There is evidence to show that they worshipped many queens, such as, Homecoming Queen, Memphis Queen, and even Queen for a Day. In the West, the natives revered a many-hatted goddess named Hedda; while in the South, there has been found an inscription praising "cocacola" an Aztec root-deity.

Little is known about the political organization of the Weans—we believe that they were divided into states ruled by Senators and Sheriffs. In the Cha'ago area, the ruler was known as a hofa, named after a famous leader who brought his people together in a great union. The inscription, "I Like Ike" found on a metal device near Pound-Laundry, attests to the popularity of at least one of their leaders.

Numerous other finds have supplied fascinating details about the science, domestic life and recreations of the Weans, but the cause of their destruction is still shrouded in mystery. Two theories are current: some believe that they were attacked by a hostile tribe from the East, the More We (or Usser) ; others maintain that they were invaded by mantis-like insects. Their contemporary sculpture depicts many such unusual animal forms. That they were destroyed by some such catastrophe seems likely from the inscription found in n'Yok, "nor rain nor heat nor gloom of night . . . their appointed rounds (pointed wounds?) ." Whatever the cause, they have perished, leaving many questions and only a few meager clues to the answers.

Thematic Material

Mr. Nathan has given us the opportunity to see ourselves as others might see us. Behind the humorous exterior is a serious comment on the validity of our present-day sense of values.

Book Talk Material

It is not difficult to interest young people in reading this book—usually a description of one or two "archaeological finds" is enough. Here are some samples: the Weans are shown to be inhospitable (pp. 19–21) ; the religion of the Weans (pp. 22–25) their political organization (pp. 28–30) .

Additional Suggestions

Richard Armour's satiric retelling of American history *It All Started with Columbus* (McGraw, $3.95) is equally as popular. Try Vern Sneider's *Teahouse of the August Moon* (Putnam, $3.95) or Leonard Wibberley's "Mouse" series (e.g. *The Mouse That Roared*, Little, $4.50) for a more gentle spoof on contemporary America. Politically-minded students will enjoy George Orwell's *Animal Farm* (Harcourt, $2.95) . Two recommended novels by Robert Nathan, that are well-liked by older girls, are: *Portrait of Jennie* and *One More Spring* (both Knopf, $4.50) .

Agnes Smith, *An Edge of the Forest,*
Viking, 1959, $3.00

A young shepherd, a small black lamb, a young black leopardess and the meaning of selfless love are the ingredients of this unusual story. Mrs. Smith's elegant style conveys an enchantment which adds to the allegorical aspects of the tale. Perceptive young readers in grades five through eight will enjoy this.

Many stories are told about strange occurrences in an ancient, impenetrable forest; one, about a little black lamb, takes place on an edge of this forest.

One day while a young shepherd boy is tending his father's sheep, a half-crazed dog separates a prize white ewe and her black lamb from the flock and herds them into the forest. The family—the chief shepherd, his wife, daughter and three sons, and the shepherd's mother—are upset by the loss of these sheep. Although the grandmother loves the young boy, she feels that he is not as capable as his elder brothers and should not have been entrusted with the care of the flock. His younger sister is sick with dread for she suspects that it was her former pet dog, now gone wild, who caused the trouble. But none is more concerned than the young shepherd boy himself. He feels that he has failed his father. To make amends, the young boy goes to the farm sheds at the forest edge to help care for their sick animals.

Meanwhile, from her hillside lair, a young black leopardess watches the dog kill the ewe. Then, she intervenes and rescues the lamb. Because of her lone struggle to survive, the leopardess is wise in the ways of the forest. She finds the lamb endearing, yet different and frightening. She remembers only that lambs belong to Man. Yet, she decides to help the little animal.

A nearby owl tells the leopardess that the bleating lamb must have milk. While she arranges an amnesty with a doe to receive the animal's milk, the leopardess is told by the doe that she must be very young not to know that "you will break your heart if you try to break the customs of your kind." Soon, all the animals are wondering about this strange and frightening new creature. The leopardess tells them that the little lamb is no more unusual than any other living thing and they accept her word. In an attempt to find its rightful place, the lamb accompanies the doe. However, the lamb cannot keep pace with the deer herd and so it returns to the leopardess's lair.

At first, the lamb is lonely with only the screeching owl for company. But soon, a little field mouse becomes her playmate and together they explore the woods. On one of her expeditions, the lamb comes upon a large spotted leopard with a thorn-inflamed eye. The lamb asks the owl and the leopardess to pull out the thorn, but they both fail. Unused to defeat, the leopardess strides away in anger. The lamb thinks that the leopardess is angry with her. Fortunately a hummingbird volunteers and succeeds in extracting the thorn.

When the leopardess finally returns to her lair, she is attacked by a defiant spotted leopard who claims her and her hillside as his own. She fights and kills him. Soon after this struggle, the leopard with the healed eye confronts the tired leopardess. He does not wish to fight her, but wishes only to offer his love. He tends her wounds and hunts for her. She succumbs to his gentle approach.

As soon as the leopardess recovers from her fatigue, the owl tells the pair that the little lamb has gone and is returning to the flock and Man. Thinking the leopardess's anger over her failure to pull the thorn from the leopard's eye is a sign of disapproval, the little lamb feels that she does not belong in the forest.

The leopardess gathers all the animals and together they follow the lamb to witness the reunion. They are curious to find out if Man, too, is afraid of the little lamb.

At the same time, the young shepherd boy, striding from the shed near the edge of the forest, approaches his grandmother who has come to visit him. As he comes closer, he sees that she is staring in astonishment at the circle of animals in the woods. He also sees the little black lamb standing on the edge of the forest. Thoroughly frightened, his grandmother orders him to pick up the lamb, slit its throat, and throw it to the animals. Instead the young shepherd lifts the lamb into his arms and walks toward the circle of animals in the woods. He hears his grandmother gasp, "They're afraid of us;" the young boy replies, "Not as much as we are of them." As he turns and walks back to his grandmother with the lamb in his arms, the animals disappear into the forest. The old woman and the young boy resolve to tell no one about the unbelievable scene.

Thematic Material

The theme of love, compassion, and understanding among all living things is the timeless thread of this fable.

Book Talk Material

For an introduction read the lyrical prologue (pp. 7–8). The story can also be told as a fairy tale with the details to be filled in by the reader. Some youngsters may be interested in the episode of the adoption of the lamb by the leopardess (pp. 30–35).

Additional Suggestions

For young readers suggest : *Rinkin of Dragon's Wood* (Dutton, $3.00; lib. bdg. $2.97 net) by Thora Colson, a story about forest life as seen by a fox; *Gentle Ben* (Dutton, $3.95; lib. bdg. $3.91 net) by Walt Morey, a tale about a boy and a brown Alaskan bear; and *The Bushbabies* (Houghton, $3.50) by William Stevenson, about an African chief who helps a game warden's daughter to return a pet to its native home. Reminiscent of the latter title is Joseph Kessel's *The Lion* (Knopf, $3.95; lib. bdg. $3.99 net), suitable for more mature young adults. Also appropriate are: A.T.W. Simeons' *Ramlal* (Atheneum, $3.95; lib. bdg. $3.81 net) and Norton Juster's *Alberic the Wise and Other Journeys* (Pantheon, $3.50; lib. bdg. $3.49 net) .

John Steinbeck, *The Red Pony*,
Viking, 1945, $2.75; lib. bdg. $2.73 net

The Red Pony is a collection of four short stories, each dealing with separate incidents in the boyhood of Jody Tiflin. The setting is the author's birthplace, Salinas County, California. This book has appeal for sensitive readers from grades eight through high school.

Ten-year-old Jody lives on a small farm outside of the town of Salinas, with his parents and a hired cow-hand, Billy Buck. In the longest and best-known story, "The Gift," Jody receives a red pony colt as a present from his father. The boy's life soon revolves about the care and training of this beautiful animal. He names the pony Gabilan, after the majestic mountain range that can be seen in the distance from the farm. Under Billy Buck's guidance, Jody begins to break Gabilan—first the training on the long halter, then work with the saddle and bridle. Each step is successfully accomplished with patience and love.

One day, while the boy is at school, Gabilan is left outside in the corral. In the afternoon, the countryside is soaked by a driving rain. The horse catches cold, and in spite of Billy Buck's reassurances, the animal's condition grows steadily more serious. During the agonizing period of waiting, Jody and Billy tend Gabilan night and day with massages, steam bags and other medications. Pneumonia sets in, and Billy is forced to cut an opening in the horse's throat to prevent strangulation. Jody realizes now that there is no hope of saving his pony.

During one of his all-night vigils, the boy falls asleep. In the morning, he awakens to find that the barn door has been blown open by the force of a strong wind. Gabilan is gone. The boy follows the pony's trail. In the distance, he sees a circle of buzzards. When he reaches the spot, Gabilan is already dead.

The second story, "The Great Mountains," is a moving vignette that deals with the arrival of a very old "paisano," Gitano, at the Tiflin farm. He has come back to spend his last days in the valley where he was born. Jody's father, Carl, explains that he may only stay the night because the Tiflins are too poor to house and feed a stranger who would be of limited help around the farm. In the morning, the family finds that both Gitano and their ancient mare, Easter, have disappeared. The old man has ridden into the mountains where he will die alone, but with dignity.

"The Promise" tells of a year in Jody's life during which he diligently tends the mare, Nellie, because he has been promised, by his father, the mare's next colt. When the time of delivery arrives, the birth becomes complicated. Billy Buck is forced to kill the mare, in order to bring a new life into the world.

"The Leader of the People" refers to Jody's grandfather who, in his youth, had led a wagon train across the prairies to California. The old man now lives entirely in the past and dwells continually on his past feats of valor when he fought off Indians, and safely conducted the settlers to their new home.

During a visit with the Tiflins, Grandfather again begins recounting these experiences. Carl Tiflin unintentionally expresses impatience at having to listen to the old man's oft-repeated reminiscences. Grandfather realizes his time of usefulness is over, but Jody tries to comfort him and help him relive, once more, his moments of greatness.

Thematic Material

With simplicity and tenderness, the author explores many themes: a boy's search to understand adult standards, the loneliness of the elderly, the tragedy of death and the beauty and savagery in nature. Although many of the details in these stories are grim, the author conveys a love and respect for humanity.

Book Talk Material

The author's simple and poetic prose style are well illustrated in the following passages from "The Gift": Carl gives his son the red pony (pp. 14–17); the training of Gabilan (pp. 20–23); the rainstorm and its effects (pp. 29–33); caring for the sick horse (pp. 35–38). The opening pages of "The Promise" (pp. 69–71) give a delightful picture of Jody's daydreams.

Additional Suggestions

John Steinbeck's *The Pearl* (Viking, $3.00) is also well-liked by the same age group. This short novel, in parable form, tells of the changes that occur to a simple Mexican family when they find a great pearl. *The White Falcon* by Charlton Ogburn, Jr. (Houghton, $3.25) is the story of a boy's growing attachment to a wounded bird that he has found. *The Small Miracle* (Doubleday, $2.00), by Paul Gallico, is a popular title. Also use Nicholas Kalashnikoff's *The Defender* (Scribner, $2.95) and Leonard Wibberley's story of a California fisherman who tries to save a young boy stricken with diphtheria. *The Island of the Angels* (Morrow, $3.50).

J. R. R. Tolkien, *The Hobbit or There and Back Again*, Houghton, 1938, $3.95

In structure and content, J. R. R. Tolkien's *The Lord of the Rings* resembles Richard Wagner's operatic cycle, *The Ring of the Nibelung*. Here, too, we have an introductory prelude (*The Hobbit*) followed by a trilogy which completes the saga.

In 1938, *The Hobbit* won the New York Herald Tribune prize for the best children's book of the year. Since that time, it has provided enchantment and delight for thousands of readers. Although this book was written for children in grades four through eight, like *Alice in Wonderland*, it can be enjoyed by a much older audience.

In *The Hobbit*, the author introduces the reader to a land peopled by gnomes, dwarves, goblins and elves (some friendly, others, as mean and avaricious as even humans can be!) The hero of the story is a hobbit named Mr. Bilbo Baggins of Bag-End, Underhill, Hobbiton. Hobbits are smaller than dwarves but larger than Lilliputians. They are gentle and peace loving, and enjoy frequent repasts (they are inclined to be fat), and giving and receiving presents.

Bilbo is persuaded by Gandalf, a wizard, to join 13 dwarves (because 13 is an unlucky number) on a dangerous mission to Lonely Mountain. Here the dwarves hope to recapture a vast treasure that had once belonged to their ancestors but is now guarded by a wicked dragon named Smaug.

Their journey across the Misty Mountains, through the dense forest, Mirkwood, to Lonely Mountain, is filled with adventure and narrow escapes. They are captured by trolls who wish to roast them over their open fire. Only Gandalf's intervention saves them from certain death. In the Misty Mountains, they are taken prisoner by a band of goblins.

Although the dwarves, with Gandalf's help, are able to kill the Great
Goblin and make their escape, poor Bilbo gets lost in the goblin cave
and encounters Gollum, a slimy reptile who lives in an underground
lake. Bilbo wins his freedom by playing a game of riddles with Gollum.
While in the cave, he finds a magic ring that will make its wearer
invisible.

He rejoins the dwarves, but soon the group is attacked by friends of
the goblins, a pack of evil wolves called Wargs. Bilbo and his companions are saved by a band of eagles who swoop down and carry them
to safety.

When they resume their jouney, they make some friends: Elrond and
his family who live in the Last Homely House, and Beorn, a woodsman
who can turn himself into the form of a bear.

In Mirkwood, the party is captured by giant spiders and held in
cocoon-like webs. Through the ue of his magic ring, Bilbo is able to free
his friends but soon after, they again encounter enemies. They are
taken prisoner by wood-elves, who take them to their castle, Elvenking's
Hall. Once more, Bilbo's ring comes to the rescue, and the dwarves
escape by floating down a river inside empty wine barrels.

Before proceeding to Lonely Mountain, the group stops at Lake
Town where the inhabitants welcome them warmly and supply them
with provisions for the remainder of their journey.

At last in the territory of Smaug, the group finds a secret entrance
into the mountain, but they are powerless to recapture the treasure
because the fire-breathing dragon keeps a constant vigil over it. Smaug
is aware that there are strangers in his cave, but he is unable to find
them.

One night, the dragon mysteriously disappears. He has accidentally
discovered that the people of Lake Town have aided these intruders
and has left to seek his revenge. During his attack on Lake Town,
Smaug is killed by an enchanted arrow shot from the bow of Bard, a
hero of the Lake People.

The treasure is now free but soon greed and avarice take over. The
Lake People, accompanied by the Wood-elves, arrive at Lonely Moun-
tain to demand their share. They are followed by the goblins and the
Wargs. A great struggle—the Battle of the Five Armies—takes place in
which the leader of the dwarves, Thorin, is killed. The goblins and
Wargs are driven off and, by Bilbo's sacrifice of his share of the treasure,

a truce is arranged between the other parties. Bilbo Baggins wants only to return to his quiet hobbit hole in Hobbiton, where he will live out the rest of his days in peace and quiet.

Thematic Material

The world of the hobbit bears a striking, and, at times, disturbing resemblance to the world of man. In this tale of wonder, fantasy, and quiet humor, are revealed human foibles and basic moral principles.

Book Talk Material

How this book is introduced will depend largely on the audience. Here are some exerpts from which to choose: what is a hobbit? (pp. 11–12) ; details of the quest for treasure (pp. 32–36) ; the incident with the trolls (pp. 44–52) ; imprisonment by the goblins (pp. 74–79) ; riddles with Gollum (pp. 85–94) ; capture by giant spiders (pp. 162–169) and the escape in barrels (pp. 183–190) .

Additional Suggestions

For younger children, try Edith Nesbit's stories of the Bastable family, such as *Five Children and It* (Random, $1.95; lib. bdg. $2.49 net) or Mary Norton's stories about *The Borrowers* (Harcourt, $3.25) or Margery Sharp's *The Rescuers* (Little, $4.50) . Also use Henry Winterfeld's *Castaways in Lilliput* (Harcourt, $3.00) ; and Lloyd Alexander's *The Book of Three* (Holt, $3.75; lib. bdg. $3.45 net) and *The Black Cauldron* (Holt, $3.95; lib. bdg. $3.59 net) . For older readers, suggest one of James Thurber's many fantasies, such as *The Thirteen Clocks* (S&S, $3.95) or *The White Deer* (Harcourt, $3.50) . Also use Rudyard Kipling's *Phantoms and Fantasies* (Doubleday, $3.95) , as well as the J.R.R. Tolkien trilogy *The Lord of the Rings,* which consists of *The Fellowship of the Ring* (Houghton, $5.95) , *The Two Towers* (Houghton, $5.95) and *The Return of the King* (Houghton, $5.95) .

E. B. White, *Charlotte's Web,*

Harper, 1952, $3.95; lib. bdg. $3.79 net.

Mr. White's wit and grace—the hallmarks of his style—are exemplified in his delightful fantasy about a young girl, a little pig, and a spider. Following the example of the author's earlier title, *Stuart Little* (Harper, $3.50; lib. bdg. $3.27 net) this story has become a treasured addition to the literature for children. Because of its philosophical overtones, it is also a favorite with discerning adults.

Although eight-year-old Fern Arable faithfully tends her runty piglet, Wilbur, she cannot dissuade her father from selling him. Mr. Arable, a busy farmer who cannot afford to raise hogs, suggests that Fern try to sell Wilbur to her Uncle, Homer Zuckerman. Uncle Homer not only agrees to buy Wilbur, but also allows Fern to visit her pet as often as she wishes.

Through the spring, Fern sits on a milk stool in the barnyard quietly observing Wilbur and the other animals. She enjoys watching them and spends much of her spare time listening to their interesting conversations. One day, however, Fern does not arrive and Wilbur misses her. He has made no friends and lives only to eat his wonderful slops and to await Fern's visit. After several days of her absence, Wilbur loses his usually hearty appetite. When he starts to cry, Templeton, the sly rat who lives under Wilbur's trough and eats his leftovers, tells him to stop his foolishness or he'll eat all his food. But Wilbur continues to weep.

Suddenly, a clear voice announces, "I'll be your friend." The voice turns out to be that of Charlotte A. Cavatica, a large, grey spider whose web is in the barn doorway. Although Wilbur is repelled by her habit of eating insects, he likes her gentle and wise manner. She helps to fill Fern's place by mothering him.

Once school is over, Fern comes to visit Wilbur again, and Wilbur now has two good friends. However, the happy mood is jarred by the sheep's announcement that Uncle Homer and Mr. Arable are going to kill the hogs at Christmas time. Wilbur is terrified by the news and begins wailing until Charlotte promises to save him.

Patient Charlotte tries to think of a plan to save Wilbur from his fate. When Lurky, the hired man, comes to the barn the following morning, the early morning dew has outlined the words, SOME PIG, which have been expertly woven into Charlotte's web. Everyone is confounded by this miracle, as Wilbur stands proudly under his web-banner. People come from miles around to see Wilbur and the message. Charlotte continues to change the sign. Templeton is pressed into service looking for words from the magazines in the rubbish heap. He contributes RADIANT. Wilbur, delighted with his notoriety, acts out each part faithfully. Mr. Zuckerman is so overcome that he enters him in the County Fair.

During all this excitement, Charlotte continues to care for Wilbur, telling him exciting stories about her relatives and singing him to sleep each night. However, as the summer wanes, Wilber notices that Charlotte is losing her strength. She explains that she is going to lay thousands of eggs soon and may not be able to go to the Fair. He pleads with her to come. Exerting every effort, Charlotte rallies herself and cajoles Templeton into accompanying them. Together they leave in the crate with a truly radiant Wilbur (Mrs. Zuckerman has given him a buttermilk bath).

Everyone attends the Fair. Fern and Avery head immediately for the amusements, the grownups for their favorite exhibits, and Lurky goes to visit some friends. The first night, Templeton has a gargantuan feast while Charlotte painstakingly spins the word HUMBLE in her web above Wilbur's crate. She also surveys Wilbur's competition, an enormous, arrogant hog named UNCLE. Knowing that Wilbur cannot compete with Uncle, Charlotte consoles her friend by explaining that they have accomplished what they set out to do. He is now safe from the Christmas hog slaughtering. Templeton, his stomach distended from feasting, returns the following morning with the news that there is a blue ribbon on Uncle's crate. Nevertheless, Wilbur is taken to the judge's stand for a special award.

When Wilbur returns to his stall, Charlotte tells him that she has laid her eggs and that her life is ebbing. In response to Wilbur's sorrowful question, Charlotte replies that she befriended him because it made her life a little richer. Wilbur quickly decides that he must take Charlotte's eggs back to the barn with him. Templeton retrieves the egg sac after much persuasion (Templeton is tired of being a rat, and told to do this, do that. . .) and Wilbur carries it gently on his tongue, back to the barn.

The following day as the Fair is being dismantled and Charlotte dies, there are few who know the part a common spider has played in saving Wilbur's life.

Thematic Material

The profound themes of selfless love and acceptance of death are found in this story, and are significantly although delicately explored.

On a superficial level, the scenes of barnyard life are explicit and yet charmingly drawn. A child's instinctive love of nature and animals is recreated through the eyes and ears of the heroine.

Book Talk Material

A few sentences to explain how Fern adopted Wilbur will suffice to interest most readers. For brief character sketches, try reading the description of: Wilbur (pp. 8–11); Templeton (pp. 29–30); Charlotte (pp. 36–40); Wilbur tries to spin a web (pp. 55–60); the children's swing (pp. 68–71); the trip to the Fair (pp. 118–129).

Additional Suggestions

Good titles for reading aloud are: William Cole's collection of poetry, *The Birds and the Beasts Were There* (World, $4.95) and James Thurber's whimsical story *The Wonderful O* (S&S, $3.95). Young readers will enjoy the beautiful Christmas allegory, *A Certain Small Shepherd* (Holt, $3.50; lib. bdg. $3.27 net) by Rebecca Caudill; the story of a hunter's family, *The Animal Family* (Pantheon, $3.50; lib. bdg. $3.39 net) by Randall Jarrell; and the story of two boy's unusual weapons in their journey in a magical world, *Steel Magic* (World, $3.50; lib. bdg. $3.41 net) by André Norton. Recommend the wistful story of *The Snow Goose* (Knopf, $2.45) by Paul Gallico for more mature young adults.

T. H. White, *The Sword in the Stone,*
Putnam, 1939, $4.95

Fable, adventure story, fantasy, or satire—it is impossible to classify the richness, beauty, and humor found in the pages of *The Sword in the Stone*. This novel, which tells of the boyhood of King Arthur, has already been hailed as one of the classics of English literature. Although this work is often found in elementary school collections, the complexity of backgrund and the subtlety of its humor make it more suitable for an older group. Astute junior and senior high school students should enjoy this story.

The young boy, Wart, (a corruption of the name Art) lives in the Castle of the Forest Sauvage with his guardian, Sir Ector and Ector's son, Kay. One day, while trying to recapture a trained falcon named Cully, Wart is lost in the woods. He meets a bumbling, gentle old knight named King Pellinore whose life has become an endless search for the elusive Questing Beast. Pellinore succeeds only in confusing Wart about directions but eventually the boy happens upon a cottage in a forest clearing. Here he meets the wise but extremely absentminded magician, Merlyn and his pet owl, Archimedes. Merlyn is living backward instead of forward in time, and therefore has a perfect knowledge of what will happen in the future. Wart is fascinated by Merlyn's wonderous magic and by Archimedes' ability to speak. When Merlyn promises to become Wart's tutor, the three set out, together, for Sir Ector's castle.

Through actual experience, Merlyn teaches Wart about life's mysteries. In the form of fish, he and Wart explore life in the moat surrounding the castle. Here, Wart hears the philosophy of power and tyranny expressed by a feared giant pike. On another adventure, Kay and Wart narrowly escape being a delightful dinner for a forest witch, Madame Mim and her gore-crow, Greediguts.

Wart is shown two aspects of the world of chivalry. He witnesses an hilarious jousting tournament between King Pellinore and the equally inept Sir Grummore Grummurson, and, as a result, thinks that chivalry is a pompous, meaningless set of conventions. Later, however, while transformed into a falcon, he learns the code of courage and honor that these birds live by, and realizes that humans, too, need ideals to pursue.

Merlyn continues to supply experiences to round out the boy's education. Wart learns from a snake of the origins of life; from a wise old badger, the story of how man was given power over other animals. In the company of Archimedes, he visits Athene, the goddess of wisdom, and learns many secrets of Nature.

The boy has other exciting adventures: he helps Robin Hood (the author maintains that his real name is Robin Wood) and Maid Marian rescue Friar Tuck from the castle of Morgan the Fay, an enchantress; and he accompanies William Twyti, the king's huntsman, on a wild boar hunt. On another occasion, he and Merlyn narrowly escape death at the hands of the giant, Galapas.

Merlyn stays at Sir Ector's castle for a total of seven years—during which time both Wart and Kay grow to young manhood. News reaches the castle that their king, Uther Pendragon, is dead, and that his successor will be the person who is able to free a sword embedded in a stone in a London churchyard.

The family travels to London to see the sword in the stone, and also to enter Kay (who is soon to be knighted) in his first tournament. In London, Wart utilizes the advice and truths that Merlyn has taught him, and he is able to exert the proper pressure necessary to draw out the sword. With Merlyn by his side, Wart is proclaimed King Arthur.

Thematic Material

Mr. White pokes fun at many human foibles, yet he reveals a reverence and respect for all forms of life. Merlyn teaches Wart to be a fine human being, not only by giving him knowledge, but also compassion and understanding. The author shows an outstanding knowledge of falconry and medieval customs.

Book Talk Material

In order to savor fully the book's style and content, it is suggested that a passage be read from the book. Here are a few suitable ones: Wart's first encounter with King Pellinore (pp. 21–26); he meets Merlyn and Archimedes (pp. 28–35); Wart as a fish (pp. 52–58); the duel between King Pellinore and Sir Grummore (pp. 96–106); the boar hunt (pp. 217–223), and stalking the giant Galapas (pp. 257–269).

Additional Suggestions

Many students who enjoy *The Sword in the Stone* might have difficulty with its three sequels that make up the tetralogy, *The Once and Future King* (Putnam, $6.95). However, they will enjoy the author's fantasy, *Mistress Masham's Repose* (Putnam, pap. $1.65). Mark Twain's *A Connecticut Yankee in King Arthur's Court* (Dodd, $3.95) and Rosemary Sutcliff's *Sword at Sunset* (Coward, $6.95) explore the Arthurian lgend from two other points of view. In *The Sword in the Stone,* Wart and Kay study a book of tales and legends from the Middle Ages called *Gesta Romanorum.* A modern selection from this work has been made for young people by Thomas B. Leekley in *The Riddle of the Black Knight and Other Stories and Fables from the Middle Ages Based on the Gesta Romanorum* (Vanguard, $3.00).

INDEX

SUBJECTS

The subject index is designed to suggest themes for book talks beyond the goals or chapter headings under which the titles in *Juniorplots* are arranged and discussed. This brief listing includes only those titles fully summarized and discussed in the book. Additional titles relating to these subjects can be found in the "Additional Suggestions" that accompany the discussion of the books listed below.

Adventure Stories

Allen, Merritt Parmelee, *Johnny Reb*, 7
Church, Richard, *Five Boys in a Cave*, 110
Clarke, Tom E., *The Big Road*, 67
Corbin, William, *High Road Home*, 113
Derleth, August, *The Moon Tenders*, 115
Farley, Walter, *The Black Stallion Mystery*, 37
Fritz, Jean, *I, Adam*, 130
Johnson, Annabel and Edgar, *Pickpocket Run*, 117
Kjelgaard, Jim, *Big Red*, 135
Meader, Stephen, *Who Rides in the Dark?*, 42
Peyton, K. M., Pseud., *The Maplin Bird*, 73
Steele, William O., *The Year of the Bloody Sevens*, 26
Van der Loeff-Basenau, Anna Rutgers, *Avalanche!*, 143
Wibberley, Leonard, *Kevin O'Connor and the Light Brigade*, 28

Africa—Fiction

Booth, Esma Rideout, *Kalena*, 106

Animal Stories

Bagnold, Enid, *National Velvet*, 32
Burnford, Sheila, *The Incredible Journey*, 155
Gipson, Fred, *Old Yeller*, 133
Kjelgaard, Jim, *Big Red*, 135
North, Sterling, *Rascal: A Memoir of a Better Era*, 45
Phipson, Joan, *Birkin*, 95
Steinbeck, John, *The Red Pony*, 195
Street, James, *Good-bye, My Lady*, 50

Australia—Fiction

Phipson, Joan, *Birkin*, 95

Biography

Dooley, Thomas A., *Doctor Tom Dooley, My Story*, 16
Killilea, Marie, *Karen*, 90
Latham, Jean Lee, *Carry on, Mr. Bowditch*, 19
Sandburg, Carl, *Prairie-Town Boy*, 167